SPECTRUM

Grade
4

ILLINOIS Test Prep

Align to Achieve
The Academic Standards e-Library

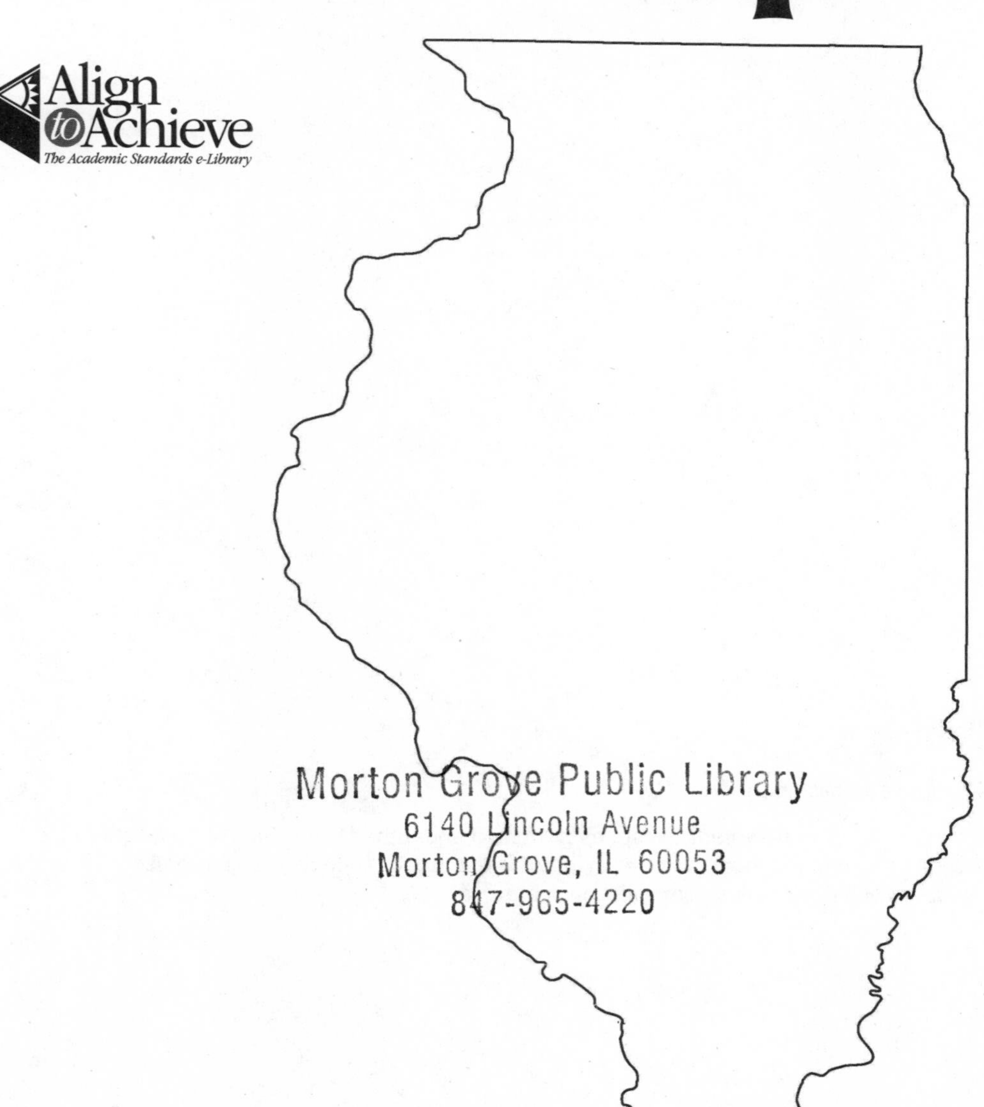

Children's Publishing
Columbus, Ohio

 **Children's Publishing**

Send all inquiries to:
McGraw-Hill Children's Publishing
8787 Orion Place
Columbus, Ohio 43240

ISBN 0-7696-3484-2

1 2 3 4 5 6 7 8 9 10 PHXBK 09 08 07 06 05 04

The McGraw-Hill Companies

Table of Contents

What's Inside?

This workbook is designed to help you and your fourth grader understand what he or she will be expected to know on the Illinois fourth grade state tests.

Practice Pages

The workbook is divided into a language arts section, mathematics section, science section, and social science section. Each section has practice activities that have questions similar to those that will appear on the state tests. Students should use a pencil to fill in the correct answers and to complete any writing on these activities.

Illinois State Standards

Before each practice section is a list of the state standards covered by that section. The shaded "What it means" sections will help to explain any information in the standards that might be unfamiliar.

Mini-Tests and Final Tests

Practice activities are grouped by state standard. When each group is completed, the student can move on to a mini-test that covers the material presented on those practice activities. After an entire set of standards and accompanying activities are completed, the student should take the final tests, which incorporate materials from all the practice activities in that section.

Final Test Answer Sheet

The final tests have a separate answer sheet that mimics the style of the answer sheet the students will use on the state tests. The answer sheet appears at the end of each final test.

How Am I Doing?

The "How Am I Doing?" pages are designed to help students identify areas where they are proficient and areas where they still need more practice. Students can keep track of each of their mini-test scores on these pages.

Answer Key

Answers to all the practice activities, mini-tests, and final tests are listed by page number and appear at the end of the book.

Frequently Asked Questions

What kinds of information does my child have to know to pass the test?

The Illinois State Board of Education provides a list of the knowledge and skills that students are expected to master at each grade level. The practice activities in this workbook provide students with practice in each of these areas.

Are there special strategies or tips that will help my child do well?

The workbook provides sample questions that have content similar to that on the state tests. Test-taking tips are offered throughout the book.

How do I know what areas my child needs help in?

A special "How Am I Doing?" section will help you and your fourth grader evaluate progress. It will pinpoint areas where more work is needed as well as areas where your student excels.

Illinois Language Arts Content Standards

The language arts section of the state test measures knowledge in reading.

Goal 1: Read with understanding and fluency.

Goal 2: Read and understand literature representative of various societies, eras, and ideas.

Illinois Language Arts Table of Contents

Reading Standards

Read with Understanding and Fluency

Goal 1: Read with understanding and fluency.

Learning Standard 1A—Students who meet the standard can apply word analysis and vocabulary skills to comprehend selections.

1. Use a combination of word analysis and vocabulary strategies (e.g., phonics, word patterns, structural analyses) to identify words. *(See page 8.)*

What it means:
- Students should be able to use several different strategies to help them determine the meanings of unfamiliar words.

2. Learn and use high frequency root words, prefixes, and suffixes to understand word meaning. *(See pages 9–10.)*

What it means:
- Students should be able to use their knowledge of base words or root words to help them define unfamiliar words. For example, knowing the meaning of the word *reflect* will help them determine the meaning of the words *reflection* and *reflective.*

3. Use synonyms and antonyms to define words. *(See page 11.)*

What it means:
- Students should be able to identify synonyms (words that mean the same) and antonyms (words with opposite meanings).

4. Use word origins to construct the meanings of new words. *(See page 12.)*
5. Apply word analysis and vocabulary strategies across the curriculum and in independent reading to self-correct miscues that interfere with meaning.
6. Recognize the difference between denotative and connotative meanings of words. *(See page 13.)*
7. Determine the meaning of a word in context when the word has multiple meanings. *(See page 14.)*

What it means:
- Students should be able to identify multiple-meaning words (words that are spelled the same but have different definitions).

8. Use additional resources (e.g., newspapers, interviews, technological resources) as applicable to clarify meanings of unfamiliar words.

Learning Standard 1B *(See page 16.)*

Learning Standard 1C *(See page 29.)*

Name ______________________________ Date ______________

Reading

1A.1

Defining Words

Read with Understanding and Fluency

DIRECTIONS: Choose the word that means the same or about the same as the underlined word.

Examples:

A. detect a clue

- (A) to find
- (B) to hide
- (C) to enjoy
- (D) to make up

Answer: (A)

B. She had to select the book for the next meeting. To select is to __________ .

- (F) find
- (G) review
- (H) read
- (J) choose

Answer: (J)

Make sure you look at the underlined word. Eliminate answer choices you know are wrong.

1. venomous snake

- (A) vicious
- (B) poisonous
- (C) sharp
- (D) huge

2. encourage friends

- (F) fascinate
- (G) worry
- (H) cheer up
- (J) disappoint

3. mature person

- (A) grown-up
- (B) dying
- (C) new
- (D) green

4. The teacher was irritated. Irritated means __________ .

- (F) excited
- (G) helpful
- (H) annoyed
- (J) boring

5. His pants were baggy. Baggy means __________ .

- (A) loose
- (B) brown
- (C) too small
- (D) made of cotton

6. He was the first conductor of the train. A conductor is a __________ .

- (F) driver
- (G) janitor
- (H) owner
- (J) rider

7. Sharon was elated when she won. Elated means __________ .

- (A) grim
- (B) joyful
- (C) outside
- (D) unpleasant

Name ______________________________ Date ______________

Reading

1A.2

Root Words and Prefixes

Read with Understanding and Fluency

DIRECTIONS: Choose the correct definition for the root in each word.

Example:

In the word *candle, cand* means ________ .

(A) erase
(B) dark
(C) glow
(D) invisible

Answer: (C)

1. **In the word *abbreviate, brev* means ________ .**
   (A) to lengthen
   (B) to shorten
   (C) to make a list
   (D) to learn how to spell

2. **In the word *autograph, graph* means ________ .**
   (F) to read
   (G) to draw a picture
   (H) to write
   (J) to measure something

3. **In the word *telescope, tele* means ________ .**
   (A) empty space
   (B) far away
   (C) close up
   (D) temperature

4. **In the word *geography, geo* means ________ .**
   (F) stars
   (G) earth
   (H) the human body
   (J) insects

5. **In the word *triangle, tri* means ________ .**
   (A) one
   (B) two
   (C) three
   (D) four

6. **In the word *bicycle, cycl* means ________ .**
   (F) wheel
   (G) handlebars
   (H) spokes
   (J) chain

7. **In the word *action, ac* means ________ .**
   (A) eat
   (B) fill
   (C) subtract
   (D) do

8. **In the word *autobiography, auto* means ________ .**
   (F) car
   (G) friendly
   (H) self
   (J) television

GO

Name ______________________________ Date ______________

DIRECTIONS: Choose a prefix from the Prefix Bank and add it to the root word to make a new word. Then, use the new word in a sentence.

Prefix Bank

Prefix	**Meaning**
anti-	against
be-	cause to be
co-	with or together
dis-	not or without
pre-	before
pro-	in place of
re-	again
un-	not

A prefix is a word part that when added to a root word changes the word's meaning.

9. ________ + *view* = **"to see before"**

10. ________ + *happy* = **"not happy"**

11. ________ + *little* = **"to cause to feel small"**

12. ________ + *workers* = **"people one works with"**

13. ________ + *trust* = **"without trust"**

14. ________ + *play* = **"to play again."**

STOP

Name ______________________________ Date ______________

Reading

1A.3

Synonyms and Antonyms

Read with Understanding and Fluency

DIRECTIONS: Read each item. Choose the word that means the same or about the same as the underlined word.

1. attend a conference

- (A) party
- (B) game
- (C) meeting
- (D) race

2. beautiful painting

- (F) pretty
- (G) interesting
- (H) colorful
- (J) light

3. repair the car

- (A) clean
- (B) drive
- (C) fix
- (D) sell

4. thin slice

- (F) short
- (G) skinny
- (H) long
- (J) wide

5. To rush through your homework is to _________ .

- (A) relax
- (B) slow
- (C) finish
- (D) hurry

DIRECTIONS: Read each item. Choose the word that means the opposite of the underlined word.

6. Banana slugs are moist to the touch.

- (F) dry
- (G) slimy
- (H) rough
- (J) rubbery

7. The dog's fur felt silky.

- (A) soft
- (B) smooth
- (C) rough
- (D) dirty

8. docile animal

- (F) vicious
- (G) gentle
- (H) shy
- (J) active

9. active child

- (A) immobile
- (B) exhausted
- (C) bored
- (D) thrilled

10. left promptly

- (F) late
- (G) recently
- (H) quietly
- (J) slowly

STOP

Name ______________________ Date ______________

Reading

1A.4

Word Origins

Read with Understanding and Fluency

DIRECTIONS: Read each question. Choose the English word that comes from the Latin or Greek word defined in the question.

1. **Which of these words probably comes from the Greek word *mikros,* meaning small?**
   - Ⓐ microscope
   - Ⓑ meter
   - Ⓒ macaroni
   - Ⓓ motor

2. **Which of these words probably comes from the Latin word *centum,* meaning hundred?**
   - Ⓕ recent
   - Ⓖ ocean
   - Ⓗ century
   - Ⓙ sent

3. **Which of these words probably comes from the Latin word *circuitus,* meaning going around?**
   - Ⓐ curious
   - Ⓑ circuit
   - Ⓒ cirrus
   - Ⓓ cut

4. **Which of these words probably comes from the Greek word *bios,* meaning life?**
   - Ⓕ biology
   - Ⓖ bicycle
   - Ⓗ bison
   - Ⓙ binocular

5. **Which of these words probably comes from the Latin word *lampein,* meaning to shine?**
   - Ⓐ lampoon
   - Ⓑ lament
   - Ⓒ lamp
   - Ⓓ lamprey

6. **Which of these words probably comes from the Latin word *magnus,* meaning great?**
   - Ⓕ magnet
   - Ⓖ mangle
   - Ⓗ major
   - Ⓙ minor

7. **Which of these words probably comes from the Latin word *bene,* meaning good?**
   - Ⓐ beneath
   - Ⓑ bendable
   - Ⓒ bentwood
   - Ⓓ benefit

8. **Which of these words probably comes from the Latin word *tactus,* meaning touch?**
   - Ⓕ tactic
   - Ⓖ contact
   - Ⓗ taco
   - Ⓙ retract

STOP

Name ______________________________ Date ______________

Reading

1A.6

Recognizing Denotative and Connotative Meanings

Read with Understanding and Fluency

DIRECTIONS: Choose the word that has the more connotative meaning.

Example:

Charlotte was being ________; she refused to change her mind.

- (A) stubborn
- (B) pig-headed

Answer: (B)

The denotative meaning of a word is the literal, dictionary definition of the word. The connotative meaning includes the emotional feelings or value judgments associated with the word.

1. It was ________ at the lake.
- (A) quiet
- (B) peaceful

2. Lili ________ the last of her chocolate bar.
- (F) savored
- (G) ate

3. Ted was Bill's ________ in the plan.
- (A) accomplice
- (B) partner

4. The football game against our ________ was set for Friday.
- (F) opponents
- (G) rivals

5. Sharon made a ________ chess move.
- (A) smart
- (B) brilliant

6. Sean ________ incoherently.
- (F) babbled
- (G) talked

7. Holly was 17 when I last saw her four years ago; she had ________ during that time.
- (A) grown
- (B) matured

8. Ashton ________ at the stars in the sky.
- (F) gazed
- (G) looked

STOP

Name ______________________ Date ______________

Reading

1A.7

Words With Multiple Meanings

Read with Understanding and Fluency

If you are not sure which answer is correct, eliminate answers you know are wrong and then take your best guess.

DIRECTIONS: Choose one word from the list that correctly completes both sentences.

1. **The player began to _________ .**
   Put the new _________ on the car.
   - (A) run
   - (B) fender
   - (C) weaken
   - (D) tire

2. **The sun _________ at 5:45.**
   A _________ grew beside the steps.
   - (F) appeared
   - (G) rose
   - (H) flower
   - (J) set

3. **My _________ is in the closet.**
   Add a new _________ of paint.
   - (A) hat
   - (B) color
   - (C) shirt
   - (D) coat

4. **Do you feel _________?**
   We get our water from a _________ .
   - (F) well
   - (G) good
   - (H) pipe
   - (J) sick

5. **Mrs. Johnson said Carrie was a _________ student.**
   The light from the headlights was _________ .
   - (A) noisy
   - (B) red
   - (C) bright
   - (D) hard working

DIRECTIONS: Choose the answer in which the underlined word is used in the same way.

6. **Please <u>file</u> these papers.**
   - (F) The counselor pulled out her file on the Jones family.
   - (G) Sally used a file to smooth her fingernails.
   - (H) I put the file cards in order.
   - (J) Jane asked her secretary to file the reports on water safety.

7. **I used a <u>lemon</u> to make lemonade.**
   - (A) The color of the baby's room is lemon.
   - (B) That car was a lemon.
   - (C) This cleaner has a lovely lemon scent.
   - (D) Rachel bought a lemon at the store.

Name ______________________________ Date ______________

Reading

1A

For pages 8–14

Mini-Test 1

Read with Understanding and Fluency

DIRECTIONS: Choose the word that means the opposite of the underlined word.

1. The tortoise took a <u>leisurely</u> walk.

Ⓐ lovely
Ⓑ swift
Ⓒ leathery
Ⓓ delicious

2. She couldn't <u>recall</u> her friend's number.

Ⓕ forget
Ⓖ remember
Ⓗ write
Ⓙ find

3. Brendan was <u>disappointed</u> when it rained.

Ⓐ saddened
Ⓑ pleased
Ⓒ relieved
Ⓓ entertained

4. The car was <u>swift</u>.

Ⓕ shallow
Ⓖ sluggish
Ⓗ speedy
Ⓙ rabbit

DIRECTIONS: Choose the word that best answers the question.

5. José __________ his report to include a section on bugs. Which word means he changed it by adding something?

Ⓐ wrote
Ⓑ amended
Ⓒ erased
Ⓓ corrected

6. __________, Mom had forgotten the can opener. Which of these words means that it was unlucky?

Ⓕ Fortunately
Ⓖ Mournfully
Ⓗ Excitedly
Ⓙ Unfortunately

7. Dave __________ around the room. Which of these words means that he walked in a bragging manner?

Ⓐ tiptoed
Ⓑ strutted
Ⓒ ran
Ⓓ skipped

DIRECTIONS: Read the paragraph. Choose the word that fits best in each numbered blank.

Leslie is becoming __________(8). People know about her art and her athletics. She's __________(9) in the music department for her skills.

8.
Ⓕ famous
Ⓖ released
Ⓗ exhausted
Ⓙ fragile

9.
Ⓐ disliked
Ⓑ prepared
Ⓒ respected
Ⓓ always

STOP

Reading Standards

Read with Understanding and Fluency

Goal 1: Read with understanding and fluency.

Learning Standard 1A *(See page 7.)*

Learning Standard 1B—Students who meet the standard can apply reading strategies to improve understanding and fluency.

1. Identify purposes for reading and adjust as necessary before and during reading. *(See page 17.)*
2. Use self-questioning and teacher questioning to promote active reading.
3. Infer before, during, and after reading. *(See page 18.)*
4. Select and use appropriate strategies according to textual complexities and reader purpose before and during reading. *(See page 19.)*
5. Make connections from text to text, text to self, and text to world. *(See page 20.)*
6. Demonstrate an accurate understanding of information in the text by focusing on the key ideas presented explicitly or implicitly and making connections text to text, text to self, and text to world. *(See page 21.)*
7. Identify explicit and implicit main ideas. *(See page 22.)*
8. Differentiate between fact and opinion. *(See page 23.)*
9. Infer cause/effect relationships in expository text. *(See page 24.)*
10. Paraphrase/summarize information in a text. *(See page 25.)*
11. Clarify understanding continuously (e.g., read ahead, use visual and context clues) during reading.
12. Critique text using personal reflections and responses. *(See page 26.)*
13. Generalize meanings from figurative language. *(See page 27.)*
14. Apply self-monitoring techniques to adjust rate and utilize various resources according to purposes and materials.
15. Read age-appropriate material aloud with fluency and accuracy.

Learning Standard 1C *(See page 29.)*

Name ______________________________ Date ______________

Reading
1B.1

Reading for Purpose

Read with Understanding and Fluency

DIRECTIONS: Choose the best answer for question 1.

1. **Why might you read an advertisement or announcement?**
   - (A) to learn about a product
   - (B) to learn details about an event
   - (C) to help you determine whether to buy an item or participate in an event
   - (D) All of the above

DIRECTIONS: Read the ads below and answer the questions.

2. **What is the ad trying to do?**
   - (F) announce a new cereal
   - (G) persuade people to buy Brainy Flakes With Muscle Nuggets
   - (H) show that Brainy Flakes With Muscle Nuggets costs less than other cereals
   - (J) offer a discount price

Brainy Flakes With Muscle Nuggets

The nutritous cereal that will make you smart, strong, and fast. You'll see results after eating just one box! Amaze your friends and family with high grades, great strength, and lightning speed.

3. **What is this announcement trying to do?**
   - (A) sell pizza
   - (B) buy stickers
   - (C) raise money for new books
   - (D) jump rope for books

4. **List the words or phrases that are used to persuade the reader.**

____

____

____

____

____

____

Join your classmates and read just 10 books each to raise money for new books for our library.

You can help get books for research and for fun while experiencing the joy of reading.

For every ten books you read, you will get your name on a special sticker inside one book.

AND

Each class that reaches its goal will get a pizza party!!!

Don't miss out on the fun—start today!

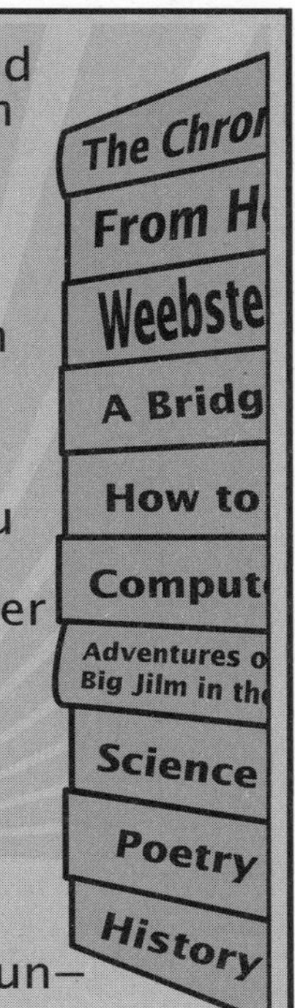

STOP

Name ______________________________ Date ______________

Reading **1B.3**

Making Inferences

Read with Understanding and Fluency

DIRECTIONS: Read the story, then answer the questions.

Cassie's mom has errands to run, so Cassie agrees to stay home to babysit for her little brother, who is asleep. Her mom also leaves Cassie a list of chores to do while she is gone. Cassie will be able to go to the mall with her friends when her chores are finished and her mom gets back. As soon as Cassie's mom leaves, Cassie starts calling her friends on the phone. She talks to Kim for 20 minutes and to Beth for 15 minutes. She is supposed to call Maria when she finishes talking to Jackie.

After talking on the phone, Cassie decides to do her nails while she watches a movie on TV. After the movie, Cassie listens to the radio and reads a magazine. Before Cassie realizes it, three and a half hours have passed and her mom is back home. Her mom walks in and finds the kitchen still a mess, crumbs all over the carpet, dusty furniture, and Cassie's little brother screaming in his room.

1. What is the setting for this story?

- Ⓐ the mall
- Ⓑ Cassie's house
- Ⓒ Jackie's house
- Ⓓ the kitchen

2. What do we know about the main character?

- Ⓕ She has errands to run.
- Ⓖ She has chores to do.
- Ⓗ He is asleep.
- Ⓙ He is screaming in his room.

3. What is the plot of this story?

- Ⓐ Cassie must do her chores if she wants to go to the mall. But she wastes the time instead.
- Ⓑ Cassie's mother has errands to run. She leaves Cassie in charge of the house.
- Ⓒ Cassie's brother is asleep in his room. He wakes up screaming.
- Ⓓ Cassie is grounded.

4. Which of the following is a chore Cassie probably wasn't supposed to do?

- Ⓕ dust
- Ⓖ listen for her brother
- Ⓗ do her nails
- Ⓙ clean the kitchen

5. What do you think the resolution to this problem will be?

- Ⓐ Cassie's little brother will have to do all the chores.
- Ⓑ Cassie will be punished and will not go to the mall.
- Ⓒ Cassie's mom will drive her to the mall.
- Ⓓ Cassie, her mom, and her brother will go to a movie.

Name ______________________________ Date ______________

Reading

1B.4

Using Reading Strategies

Read with Understanding and Fluency

DIRECTIONS: Read the passage and answer the questions that follow.

Clouds

Do you like to watch clouds float by? You may have noticed that there are many different shapes of clouds. Clouds are named for the way they look. Cirrus clouds are thin and high in the sky. Stratus clouds are low and thick. Cumulus clouds are white and puffy.

Do you know how clouds are formed? The air holds water that the warm sun has pulled, or evaporated, from the earth. When this water cools in the air, it forms clouds. When a cloud forms low along the ground, it is called *fog.* Clouds hold water until they become full. Warm clouds that are full of water produce rain; cold clouds that are full of water produce snow. When water falls to the earth as either rain or snow, it is called *precipitation*.

Skim the passage, then read the questions. Refer back to the passage to find the answers. You don't have to reread the passage for each question.

1. **What is the effect of water cooling in the air?**
   - (A) Evaporation occurs.
   - (B) The sun warms the earth.
   - (C) Fog forms.
   - (D) Clouds form.

2. **Which sentence explains what causes fog?**
   - (F) A cloud forms low to the ground.
   - (G) A cloud is white and puffy.
   - (H) A cloud is thin and high in the sky.
   - (J) A cloud is full.

3. **One effect of evaporation is ________ .**
   - (A) rain creates moisture in the soil
   - (B) the air holds water
   - (C) clouds float through the sky
   - (D) the sun pulls clouds higher

4. **Write three short sentences that explain how clouds are formed.**

____

____

____

____

____

____

____

____

____

____

Name ______________________________ Date ______________

Reading

1B.5

Connecting Texts

Read with Understanding and Fluency

DIRECTIONS: Read the passage, then answer the questions.

The Goldilocks Report

At 5:05 P.M., we were called to the home of a Mr. and Mrs. Bear. They had been out for the day. Upon returning, they found the lock on their door had been broken. Officer Paws and I went into the house. We found that food had been stolen and a chair had been broken. Paws searched the backyard while I went upstairs. I found a person asleep in a small bed. The subject is a female human being with curly blonde hair. She was unknown to the Bear family. The human being claimed her name was Goldilocks. She could not prove that fact. She will be questioned at the police station.

Officer Grizzly

1. This is another view of the fairy tale ________ .

- (A) Goldilocks and the Three Bears
- (B) Jack and the Beanstalk
- (C) Little Miss Muffet
- (D) Officer Grizzly and the Report

2. Which character tells the story "The Goldilocks Report"?

- (F) Goldilocks
- (G) Baby Bear
- (H) Papa Bear
- (J) Officer Grizzly

3. How is the ending of "The Goldilocks Report" different from the traditional fairy tale?

____

____

____

____

____

____

____

____

____

Name ______________________________ Date ______________

Reading

1B.6

Evaluating Information

Read with Understanding and Fluency

DIRECTIONS: Tomas keeps a journal for his All-Year Project in English. On the entry for this day, he wrote about an assignment. Read the journal entry, then answer the questions.

October 19

"Boy, does this sound like a goofy assignment," I said to Kendra, rolling my eyes. We were walking home after school talking about what Mr. Stewart had given us for homework this week. We were supposed to listen—just listen—for a total of two hours this week. We could do it any time we wanted, in short periods or long, and write down some of the things we heard. We also had to describe where we listened and the time of day.

As we walked by a small corner park, Kendra stopped for a moment and suggested, "Hey, I have an idea. Let's start right here. We should just sit down in the park and get part of the assignment done. It will be a breeze."

I told her it was a great idea, then spotted a bench beside the fountain. "Let's get started," I said.

We sat down and pulled out notebooks and pencils. After just a few seconds, Kendra began writing something down. For the next half hour, we did nothing but sit, listen, and take notes.

At about three o'clock, Kendra said, "That's enough for me now. Do you want to compare notes? I want to be sure I did this right."

"Sure," I answered. "I can't believe all the things I heard. Maybe this isn't such a goofy assignment after all."

1. Why did Mr. Stewart probably give the students this assignment?

- (A) It would be an easy way for them to get a good grade.
- (B) It would give them a chance to work together.
- (C) It would give them more free time for other assignments.
- (D) It would help them understand the world around them better.

2. Tomas and Kendra live in a city. Which of these sounds are they most likely to hear on the way home?

- (F) birds chirping
- (G) the wind in the trees
- (H) traffic sounds
- (J) planes landing

3. What lesson did Tomas probably learn?

- (A) Some assignments are better than they first seem.
- (B) Kendra is a better student than he first thought.
- (C) Mr. Stewart usually gives easy assignments.
- (D) There is no reason to go right home after school.

4. Briefly describe an assignment that you thought was "goofy" but ended up learning more than you expected. What did you learn?

____

____

____

____

____

STOP

Name ______________________ Date ______________________

Reading

1B.7

Identifying Explicit Main Ideas

Read with Understanding and Fluency

DIRECTIONS: Read the passage, then answer the questions.

Ice Cream

Almost everyone loves to eat ice cream. In fact, ice cream has been a favorite treat for thousands of years. Long ago, Roman rulers enjoyed eating mountain snow. In Europe, people flavored ice for a special dish. Later, cream was used to make ice cream much like we enjoy today.

Until 1851, ice cream was made most often at home. Today, most ice cream is produced in ice-cream plants. These plants use machines to mix milk, sugar, and water. The mixture is pumped into a cooler. After it is chilled, it is put into storage tanks. Special flavors and colors are added to make many different kinds of ice cream. The mixtures are then frozen at a temperature of -22°F. Then, fan-like blades slice through the frozen mixture and whip air into it. This fluffy ice cream is placed in a hardening room for 12 hours. Then, it is delivered to stores.

1. Which sentence best states the main idea of the first paragraph?

- Ⓐ Ice cream has been a favorite treat for thousands of years.
- Ⓑ In Europe, people flavored ice for a special dish.
- Ⓒ Later, cream was used to make ice cream.
- Ⓓ Roman rulers ate the mountain snow.

2. Which sentence best states the main idea of the second paragraph?

- Ⓕ Until 1851, ice cream was made most often at home.
- Ⓖ After it is chilled, the mixture is put into storage tanks.
- Ⓗ Today, most ice cream is made in ice-cream plants.
- Ⓙ After the hardening room, off to the stores it goes!

Name ______________________________ Date ______________

Reading

1B.8

Distinguishing Fact and Opinion

Read with Understanding and Fluency

DIRECTIONS: Read the passage and answer the questions that follow.

Stonehenge is an ancient monument made up of a group of huge stones. It is located in Wiltshire, England. No one knows who put the stones there or what they are for. Some scientists think that they were put there thousands of years ago by people who worshiped the sun.

Through the years, many of the original stones have fallen or have been carried away and used to build other things. But many stones still stand in place. From these stones and other markings, scientists think they know how the monument looked when it was first built. Some think that Stonehenge was built by ancient people to study the sun. These people may have used the monument to predict changes in the seasons—even eclipses of the sun. Today, Stonehenge is one of the most popular tourist stops in England.

1. Which of the following is a fact about Stonehenge?

Ⓐ Scientists know what Stonehenge looked like when it was first built.

Ⓑ Stonehenge is located in Wiltshire, England.

Ⓒ Scientists know why Stonehenge was built.

Ⓓ Stonehenge helped people study eclipses of the sun.

2. Which of the following is an opinion about Stonehenge?

Ⓕ Some of the stones were carried away.

Ⓖ Stonehenge is in England.

Ⓗ The stones are in a circle.

Ⓙ Stonehenge is the most popular tourist stop in England.

3. Write *F* if the statement is false and *T* if it is true.

_____ Over the years, many stones have fallen or were carried away.

_____ Only five stones remain as a monument.

_____ Ancient people may have used the monument to study the sun.

_____ Stonehenge was built hundreds of years ago.

Name ______________________ Date ______________

Reading

1B.9

Inferring Cause

Read with Understanding and Fluency

DIRECTIONS: Read the passage, then write **dry ice** or **regular ice** to show the cause of each of the effects that follow.

Dry Ice

Do you know what dry ice is or how it is used? Dry ice is the name for solid carbon dioxide. Carbon dioxide is a chemical.

You know that when regular ice melts, it changes from a solid piece of ice into a liquid. But dry ice does not melt into a liquid. It changes from a solid piece of ice into a gas. Dry ice can be as cold as −112°F. That is much colder than ordinary ice. Although it is safe to eat ordinary ice, dry ice can cause death if eaten. That is because it is extremely cold.

What is dry ice used for? It is used to refrigerate many things that need to be kept cold. Many foods are packed and sent from place to place in dry ice. Because dry ice does not melt into a liquid, it can keep food frozen for several days.

1. **An ice cube leaves a puddle of water on a table.**

   ____

2. **A cheesecake is kept frozen for several days.**

   ____

3. **Ice is eaten safely.**

   ____

4. **A solid melts into a gas.**

   ____

5. **Foods are packed in ice to be shipped.**

   ____

6. **The temperature of a solid piece of ice is −112°F.**

   ____

Name ______________________________ Date ______________

Reading

1B.10

Summarizing Information

Read with Understanding and Fluency

DIRECTIONS: Read the passage, then choose one sentence from **Group 1** and one sentence from **Group 2** to form a brief summary of the letter.

Breakfast of Winners

"Why Crunchy Munchy Bunches of Bananas and Bran Flakes Is My Favorite Cereal" Contest

Dear Cereal Maker,

I try to eat your delicious cereal every day. It is my first choice for breakfast (except for cold pepperoni pizza—but Mom says I can only eat that on my birthday). Why do I like your cereal so much? First of all, Mom always says that I act like a monkey when I climb all over the furniture, and we all know that monkeys love bananas. Second, my big brother constantly tells me not to act so flaky! And your cereal has lots of big flakes. Anyway, I guess liking your cereal is just in my genes!

Your friend,

Horace

Group 1

Ⓐ A child has entered a contest to determine which contestant eats the most of a particular type of cereal.

Ⓑ A child has entered a contest to determine which person has the best reasons for eating a particular brand of cereal.

Group 2

Ⓕ He feels that his behaving like a monkey and acting a bit flaky should make him the winner.

Ⓖ He feels that Crunchy Munchy Bunches of Bananas and Bran Flakes has the best combination of fruit and bran flakes.

Name ______________________________ Date ______________

Reading

1B.12

Critiquing Text Using Personal Reflections

Read with Understanding and Fluency

DIRECTIONS: Read the passage and answer the questions.

Waterland

"Hurray!" cried Meghan. "Today is the day we're going to Waterland!" It was a hot July day, and Meghan's mom was taking her and her new friend Jake.

Just then, Meghan's mom came out of her bedroom. She did not look very happy. "What's the matter, Mom? Are you afraid to get wet?" Meghan teased.

Mrs. Millett told the kids that she wasn't felling well. She was too tired to drive to the water park.

Meghan and Jake were disappointed. "My mom has chronic fatigue syndrome," Meghan explained. "Her illness makes her really tired. She's still a great mom."

"Thank you, dear," said Mrs. Millett. "I'm too tired to drive, but I have an idea. You can make your own Waterland, and I'll rest in the lawn chair."

Meghan and Jake set up three different sprinklers. They dragged the play slide over to the wading pool and aimed the sprinkler on the slide. Meghan and Jake got soaking wet and played all day.

"Thank you for being so understanding," Meghan's mom said. "Now I feel better, but I'm really hot! There's only one cure for that." She stood under the sprinkler with all her clothes on. She was drenched from head to toe.

Meghan laughed and said, "Now you have chronic wet syndrome." Mrs. Millett rewarded her daughter with a big, wet hug.

1. **Which sentence best tells the main idea of this story?**
   - Ⓐ Meghan's mom has chronic fatigue syndrome.
   - Ⓑ Jake and Meghan miss out on Waterland, but they make their own water park and have fun anyway.
   - Ⓒ Jake and Meghan cannot go to Waterland.
   - Ⓓ Sprinklers make a great backyard water park.

2. **Think of a time when something happened that caused you to be disappointed. Were you able to turn it around and have a good day like the characters in this story? Tell your story below.**

____

____

____

____

____

____

Name ______________________________ Date ______________

Reading

1B.13

Defining Figurative Language

Read with Understanding and Fluency

DIRECTIONS: Read the passage and then match each idiom with its meaning.

Food for Thought

A waiter was taking a break. He said to a brand new employee, "You just have to be the one to break the ice with the chef. Sometimes, it seems like he has a chip on his shoulder, but he's okay. This is a busy place. You've jumped out of the frying pan and into the fire, let me tell you. I hope you don't have any pie-in-the-sky ideas about taking things easy here. Some days, I feel like I'm going bananas. It might not be your cup of tea. I think we've got the cream of the crop here; everybody does a great job. It's hard sometimes not to fly off the handle when things are so hectic, though. I think you'll do all right if you don't mind hard work.

Figurative language is language that is used to help describe something. An *idiom* is an expression or saying that states one thing but means another.

1. ________ **to break the ice**
2. ________ **a chip on his shoulder**
3. ________ **out of the frying pan and into the fire**
4. ________ **pie-in-the-sky**
5. ________ **going bananas**
6. ________ **cup of tea**
7. ________ **the cream of the crop**
8. ________ **fly off the handle**

(A) unrealistic

(B) something one enjoys

(C) the best available

(D) to make a start

(E) to lose one's temper

(F) seemingly angry or resentful

(G) go crazy

(H) from a bad situation to a worse one

STOP

Name ______________________________ Date ______________

Reading

1B

For pages 17–27

Mini-Test 2

Read with Understanding and Fluency

DIRECTIONS: Read the passage, then answer the questions.

During the 1700s, America wanted to gain independence from the British. This caused many struggles between the two countries.

The British passed a law in 1765 that required legal papers and other items to have a tax stamp. It was called the Stamp Act. Colonists were forced to pay a fee for the stamp. Secret groups began to work against the requirement of the tax stamp. The law was finally taken away in 1766.

In 1767, the British passed the Townshend Acts. These acts forced people to pay fees for many items, such as tea, paper, glass, lead, and paint. This wasn't fair.

Colonists were furious. On December 16, 1773, they tossed 342 chests of tea over the sides of ships in Boston Harbor. This was later called the Boston Tea Party. Colonists had shown that they would not accept these laws.

1. Which of the following sentences from the story states an opinion?

Ⓐ The British passed a law in 1765 that required legal papers and other items to have a tax stamp.

Ⓑ The law was finally taken away in 1766.

Ⓒ This was later called the Boston Tea Party.

Ⓓ This wasn't fair.

2. What caused the colonists to throw 342 chests of tea into Boston Harbor?

Ⓕ They were angry about the Townshend Acts.

Ⓖ They wanted to make a big pot of tea.

Ⓗ The tea was bad.

Ⓙ They were angry because of the Stamp Act.

3. According to the text, what was the cause of the many struggles?

Ⓐ Secret groups began to work against the requirement of the tax stamp.

Ⓑ Colonists were forced to pay a fee for the stamp.

Ⓒ America wanted to gain independence from the British.

Ⓓ The British passed the Townshend Acts.

4. In what year did the Boston Tea Party occur?

Ⓕ 1767

Ⓖ 1765

Ⓗ 1773

Ⓙ 1766

5. What is the main idea of this passage?

Ⓐ Colonists did not want the tax stamp.

Ⓑ The colonists' desire for independence caused conflict with the British.

Ⓒ Colonists showed they would not accept British laws.

Ⓓ The British passed an act that forced the colonists to pay a fee for items.

Reading Standards

Read with Understanding and Fluency

Goal 1: Read with understanding and fluency.

Learning Standard 1A *(See page 7.)*

Learning Standard 1B *(See page 16.)*

Learning Standard 1C—Students who meet the standard can comprehend a broad range of reading materials.

1. Use evidence in text to modify predictions and questions. *(See page 30.)*
2. Use evidence in text to respond to open-ended questions. *(See page 31.)*
3. Use evidence in text to generate and confirm or reject hypotheses. *(See page 32.)*
4. Compare themes, topics, and story elements of various selections by one author. *(See page 33.)*
5. Interpret concepts or make connections through comparison, analysis, evaluation, and inference. *(See page 34.)*
6. Select reading strategies for text appropriate to the reader's purpose.
7. Make generalizations based on relevant information from expository text. *(See page 35.)*
8. Recognize main ideas and secondary ideas in expository text. *(See page 36.)*
9. Paraphrase/summarize narrative text according to text structure. *(See page 37.)*
10. Recognize how illustrations reflect, interpret, and enhance the text. *(See pages 38–39.)*
11. Recognize similarities and differences when presented with varying styles or points of view. *(See page 40.)*
12. Apply information obtained from age-appropriate fiction and nonfiction materials to simple tables, maps, and charts. *(See page 41.)*
13. Apply appropriate reading strategies to fiction and nonfiction texts within and across content areas.
14. Develop familiarity with available electronic literary forms (e.g., interactive web sites, interactive software, and electronic mail).

Name ________________________________ Date ______________

Reading

1C.1

Modifying Predictions

Read with Understanding and Fluency

DIRECTIONS: Answer the first question before reading the passage. Then, read the passage and answer the remaining questions.

1. **The title of the following passage is** *How the Great Lakes Came to Be.* **Without reading the passage, make a prediction as to how you think the lakes came into existence.**

____

____

____

____

____

____

____

____

How the Great Lakes Came to Be

Have you ever wondered how the Great Lakes came to be? The same elements came together to create Lake Superior, Lake Michigan, Lake Huron, Lake Erie, and Lake Ontario.

Thousands of years ago, glaciers—huge masses of slowly moving ice—covered the earth. More and more snow fell. Temperatures grew colder. Glaciers grew larger and larger.

The movement of glaciers pulled up huge amounts of soil and rocks. These were shoved ahead and to the sides of the glaciers.

Warming temperatures caused the glaciers to melt. The glaciers had taken up space. The soil and rocks that were pulled up and shoved along by the glaciers had taken up space. When the glaciers melted, there were huge holes.

Water from the melting glaciers and from rain filled these huge holes. They were no longer holes. They were lakes!

2. **Now that you have read the passage, briefly describe how the Great Lakes came into existence. Did it differ from your original prediction? In what ways?**

____

____

____

____

____

____

____

____

3. **What caused the glaciers to grow larger?**
   - (A) They pulled up huge amounts of soil and rocks.
   - (B) More snow fell and temperatures got colder.
   - (C) Temperatures grew warmer.
   - (D) Melting water fell on them.

4. **Where did the water come from that filled up the glacier holes?**
   - (F) Native Americans filled up the holes to use them as lakes.
   - (G) It rained a lot.
   - (H) Rivers nearby flowed into the holes.
   - (J) It came from the melting glaciers and rain.

Name ______________________ Date ______________

Reading **1C.2**

Responding to Questions

Read with Understanding and Fluency

DIRECTIONS: Read the passage and answer the questions that follow.

The Origins of the Telegraph

Have you ever watched someone tap a key and send a code for S.O.S.? Perhaps you have seen an old film showing a ship about to sink. Perhaps someone was tapping wildly on a device, trying to send for help.

From where did this system of tapping out dashes and dots come? Who invented this electronic device? Samuel Morse invented the telegraph and the electronic alphabet called *Morse code.*

When Morse was young, he was an artist. People in New York knew his work well and liked it a great deal. Being well known, Morse decided to run for office. He ran for the office of New York mayor and congressman, but he lost these political races.

In 1832, while Morse was sailing back to the United States from Europe, he thought of an electronic telegraph. This would help people communicate across great distances, even from ship to shore. He was anxious to put together his invention as quickly as possible. Interestingly, someone else had also thought of this same idea.

By 1835, he had put together his first telegraph, but it was only experimental. In 1844, he built a telegraph line from Baltimore to Washington, D.C. He later made his telegraph better, and in 1849, was granted a patent by the U.S. government. Within a few years, people communicated across 23,000 miles of telegraph wire.

As a result of Samuel Morse's invention, trains ran more safely. Conductors could warn about dangers or problems across great distances and ask for help. People in business could communicate more easily, which made it easier to sell their goods and services. Morse had changed communication forever.

1. What is the main idea of this passage?

____

____

____

2. Give three details from the passage that helped you answer Question 1.

____

____

____

3. Use your answers to Questions 1 and 2 to write a brief summary of this passage.

____

____

____

____

____

STOP

Name ______________________________ Date ______________

Reading

1C.3

Confirming Hypothesis

Read with Understanding and Fluency

DIRECTIONS: Rebecca has been asked to research and write a report on hydropower. This topic is new to her, but she makes the hypotheses that hydropower is power that comes from water. During her research, she found the following information. Read the passage and answer the questions that follow.

A hypothesis is an assumption, guess, or conjecture that can be proved or disproved by comparison with observed facts.

People around the world use energy every day, and some forms of energy are being used up very quickly. But resources like energy from the sun, energy from ocean waves, and hydroelectric power do not get used up completely. These resources last and last. They are called *renewable resources*. *Hydropower* is a renewable resource that is very common. The beginning of this word, *hydro*, refers to water. So, hydropower refers to power that comes from water.

What makes hydropower work? A dam, which looks like a tall cement wall built across a body of water, raises the level of water in an area by blocking it. This causes the water to fall over the side of the dam. The falling water pushes against a machine called a *turbine*. The force of the falling water makes the blades inside spin. A machine called a *generator* captures the power from the spinning turbines. This makes electrical energy and sends out electricity to people who need it.

1. Does the passage confirm Rebecca's hypothesis? Why or why not?

____

____

____

2. What purpose does the dam serve?

- (A) It blocks the flow of water, raising the level of the water.
- (B) It spins the turbines.
- (C) It captures the power of the spinning turbines.
- (D) It sends the electricity to the people who need it.

3. Resources that last a long time are called __________ .

- (F) hydropower
- (G) energy
- (H) fossil fuels
- (J) renewable resources

4. What produces the electrical energy from the water?

- (A) the generator
- (B) the turbine
- (C) the dam
- (D) ocean waves

Name ______________________________ Date ______________

Reading

1C.4

Comparing Story Elements

Read with Understanding and Fluency

DIRECTIONS: The following stories were written by the same person. Read both stories, then fill in the blank with the correct answer from the parentheses.

Maggie and Isabel went to the park on Saturday. They both headed for the slides. But, they couldn't decide who should go first. Isabel said she should because she was older. Maggie said she should go first because Isabel always got to. Just then, their mother came over and said, "Why don't you each get on one slide and start down at the same time?"

And that's just what they did.

Joel's hockey team had been playing well all season, and this was their chance to win the tournament. He was their best player.

He glanced around at his teammates. "Guys," he said. "Let's skate really hard and show them how great we are!"

The team cheered and started to walk out to the ice. Joel turned around to grab his helmet, but it wasn't there. He looked under the benches and in the lockers, but his helmet wasn't anywhere. He sat down and felt his throat get tight. If he didn't have a helmet, he couldn't play.

Just then, there was a knock on the door. Joel's mom peeked her head around the locker room door. "Thank goodness," she said. "I got here just in time with your helmet."

1. Both of the stories are ____________ .

(fiction / nonfiction)

2. Both stories are about ____________ that gets solved.

(an argument / a problem)

3. The person who solves the problem in both stories is ____________ .

(the coach / the mother)

4. If both of these stories appeared together in a book of similar stories, a good title for the book would be ____________ .

(Sports Bloopers / Mom to the Rescue)

STOP

Name ______________________ Date ______________

Reading

1C.5

Comparing and Contrasting Information

Read with Understanding and Fluency

DIRECTIONS: Read the passages and answer the questions that follow.

Pompeii

Almost 2,000 years ago, Pompeii was a rich and beautiful city in Italy on the Bay of Naples. The city lay close to a great volcano, Mount Vesuvius.

One day, Vesuvius began to rumble and erupt. Lava, steam, and ash burst from the volcano. Soon, the sky was black with ash. The ash rained down on Pompeii. The people tried to hide in buildings or escape to the sea in boats. But the ash fell so quickly that people were buried wherever they were. The city was covered with over 12 feet of ash.

Scientists have found the remains of Pompeii. Much of what they have found is just as it was the day Mount Vesuvius erupted. This discovery has helped us learn more about ancient Roman times.

Rabaul

Rabaul is a small town in Papua, New Guinea. It is located on a huge volcanic crater. People who live there today know that the volcano has erupted before, so they have made an escape plan. In 1994, there was a major volcanic eruption in Rabaul. Just before the eruption, scientists noticed strong earthquakes. They warned the people to leave, or evacuate. There was very little notice, but people were able to begin their escape plan. On the day of the eruption, earthquakes shook Rabaul. More than 50,000 people left the area. Volcanic ash filled the sky. When the smoke cleared, about three-fourths of the houses on the island had been flattened. The island suffered greatly, but because of planning only a few people lost their lives.

1. **Why were their fewer deaths in Rabaul than in Pompeii when the volcanoes erupted?**

____

____

____

2. **Why were the people of Rabaul able to begin their escape before the eruption?**

____

____

____

3. **What is one of the main differences between these stories about volcanic eruptions in Pompeii and Rabaul?**

____

____

____

____

____

Name ______________________ Date ______________

Reading

1C.7

Making Generalizations

Read with Understanding and Fluency

DIRECTIONS: Read the passage and then indicate whether the following statements are true or false.

Making Clay Move

Beginning in about 1990, claymation became very popular. Animators have used this clay animation to make several famous movies and TV commercials. However, claymation is not a new idea. In 1897, a clay-like material called *plasticine* was invented. Moviemakers used plasticine to create clay animation films as early as 1908. Animators could use the plasticine models for scenes that could not be filmed in real life.

Here's how claymation works. First, an artist makes one or more clay models. Moviemakers pose each model, take a picture, and then stop. Next, they move the model a tiny bit to a slightly different pose. Then they take another picture. They continue the pattern of taking pictures, moving the model, and taking pictures again. It can take hundreds of pictures to make a few seconds of film. The idea of moving models and using stop-action photography came from a French animator named George Melier. He had once had a job as a magician and called his work "trick film."

Today's animators use different kinds of clay. They can also use computers to speed up the claymation process. But the basic idea of clay animation has not changed in over a hundred years!

1. Clay holds its shape under studio lighting.

____

2. Claymation is often a time-intensive process.

____

3. Claymation is not widely seen.

____

4. Claymation does not require actors.

____

5. Animators use only clay animation in their films. ______________

6. Claymation will undergo significant changes in the future. ______________

STOP

Name ______________________________ Date ______________

Reading **1C.8**

Main and Secondary Ideas

Read with Understanding and Fluency

DIRECTIONS: Read the passage and answer the questions.

Sound

It is easy to take sounds for granted. But do you really know what sound is? Sound is caused by something quivering back and forth. This shaking motion is called a *vibration.* Vibrations travel through the air and you hear them as sounds. You can hear many sounds at the same time because the air can carry many vibrations at one time. Different sounds are created according to how fast something vibrates. The faster it vibrates, the higher the sound. A slower vibration causes a lower sound.

Unpleasant sounds are called *noise.* Some noise can be harmful to your hearing. Loud noises, such as those from airplanes or machines, can even cause a hearing loss. But other sounds, such as music or talking, are not dangerous—just pleasant.

1. The main idea of this passage is about ____________ .

Ⓐ sound
Ⓑ vibration
Ⓒ noise
Ⓓ hearing loss

2. Noise, as discussed in this passage, is ____________ .

Ⓕ pleasant
Ⓖ a secondary idea
Ⓗ not dangerous
Ⓙ the main idea

3. Sound is caused by ____________ .

Ⓐ music and talking
Ⓑ vibrations in the air
Ⓒ airplanes and machines
Ⓓ the air carrying noise

4. Vibrations ____________ .

Ⓕ cause higher sounds
Ⓖ always cause unpleasant sounds
Ⓗ never cause hearing loss
Ⓙ travel through the air several at a time

5. Different sounds are made ____________ .

Ⓐ according to how fast something vibrates
Ⓑ according to how hot the air becomes
Ⓒ according to how noisy something is
Ⓓ by your hearing

Name ______________________________ Date ______________

Reading

1C.9

Summarizing Text

Read with Understanding and Fluency

DIRECTIONS: Read the passage. Then, create a summary of the passage by answering the questions that follow.

Glue

Glue is an adhesive. It is used to stick things together. There are three basic kinds of glue: hide glue, bone glue, and fish glue. Glues are made of gelatin, which comes from boiling animal parts and bones.

Long ago, people used other materials as glue. Ancient people used sticky juices from plants and insects. This was mixed with vegetable coloring and used as paint on rocks and caves. Egyptians learned to boil animal hides and bones to make glue. This was much like the glue that is used today.

Today, there are many special kinds of glue. Epoxy glue is made to stick in high temperatures, even if it becomes wet. "Super" glue is the strongest of glues. It can stick even with two tons of pressure against it.

1. Complete the summary by adding phrases from the passage.

Glue is used to ______________________________

____

Glues are made of ______________________________

____

Long ago, ancient people used

______________________________ from

______________________________ and

______________________________ for

______________________________. Today,

there are ______________ kinds of glue.

2. What are the three basic kinds of glue?

______________________________ glue

______________________________ glue

______________________________ glue

3. Which is the best definition of glue?

- (A) useful for repairs or art activities
- (B) an adhesive used to stick things together
- (C) something that sticks in high temperatures
- (D) mixture of vegetable coloring and bones

STOP

Name ______________________________ Date ______________

Reading **1C.10**

Illustrations

Read with Understanding and Fluency

DIRECTIONS: Read the passage and answer the questions on the next page.

Minnie the Mole

Minnie the Mole and her five children live in a cozy burrow under Mr. Smith's garden. Minnie works hard gathering insects and worms, her five children's favorite treats. It is not an easy job since moles eat their own weight in food each day.

Mr. Smith did not like the raised roofs of Minnie's tunnels in his garden. One hot summer day, as Minnie was digging through the bean patch with her sharp claws, she heard a new sound. Although she has no external ears, Minnie can hear very well. Mr. Smith was pounding a trap into position at the front entrance to her burrow.

Minnie hurried home and gathered her children around her. "We are in danger! We must move quickly. Get in line and follow me," demanded Minnie. The little moles with their short, stocky bodies and long snouts did as their mother told them.

Minnie started digging a tunnel in the soft soil as fast as she could. "We're going to Uncle Marty Mole's burrow. We'll be safer there," Minnie said. She and the children worked tirelessly for two hours. They were far from Mr. Smith's garden now. Tired, but safe, the little group rested in the comfort of Uncle Marty's living room.

"You were busy as beavers today," said Uncle Marty.

"I'd say we were more like a 'mole machine'!" laughed Minnie.

Name ______________________________ Date ______________

1. **How does the illustration on the previous page help you to interpret the story?**

2. **What emotion does Minnie appear to be showing in the first illustration? Why do you think this?**

3. **How does the second illustration at the bottom of this page help you to interpret the story?**

4. **Did the illustrations add to your understanding or enjoyment of the story? Why or why not?**

STOP

Name ______________________ Date ______________________

Reading

1C.11

Identifying Points of View

Read with Understanding and Fluency

DIRECTIONS: Read the passages and then answer the questions.

Samantha's Birthday

A. I knew it would be a great day from the minute I woke up. Piled beside my bed was a stack of presents. I jumped out of bed. I was so excited. When I came downstairs carrying the presents, everyone shouted, "Happy birthday!"

B. Before Samantha woke up, I left her presents beside her bed. I knew she would like the surprise from her father and me. When we saw Samantha on the stairs, we surprised her by saying, "Happy birthday!"

C. I bought Samantha a book about dinosaurs for her birthday. Mom and Dad let me do extra chores to earn the money. I had to wake up early to surprise her, but it was worth it to see her face when we all said, "Happy birthday!"

1. **Who is the writer of passage A?**

   ____

   What special day is it for this person?

   ____

2. **Who is the writer of passage B?**

   ____

   How did you guess?

   ____

3. **Who is the writer of passage C?**

   ____

   How did you guess?

   ____

4. **All of these passages are written from what point of view?**

   Ⓐ first person
   Ⓑ second person
   Ⓒ third person
   Ⓓ None of these.

Name ______________________ Date ______________

Reading

1C.12

Applying Information to Tables

Read with Understanding and Fluency

DIRECTIONS: Read the passage, then fill in the chart below to compare the Fahrenheit and Celsius scales.

Temperature Rising

Can you imagine a hot summer day with a temperature of 30 degrees? Or having a fever of 38 degrees that sends you to the doctor? If you're thinking in degrees Fahrenheit, you're probably confused. Another way to measure temperature is in degrees Celsius. The temperature scales on most thermometers show both Fahrenheit and Celsius.

An early version of a thermometer was made in 1593. Gabriel Fahrenheit invented the first mercury thermometer in 1714. The Fahrenheit scale is named after him. On the Fahrenheit scale, water freezes at 32°F, water boils at 212°F, and normal body temperature is 98.6°F.

Anders Celsius was a Swedish astronomer born in 1701. He experimented with a scale based on 100 degrees. On the Celsius scale, water freezes at 0°C, water boils at 100°C, and normal body temperature is 37°C.

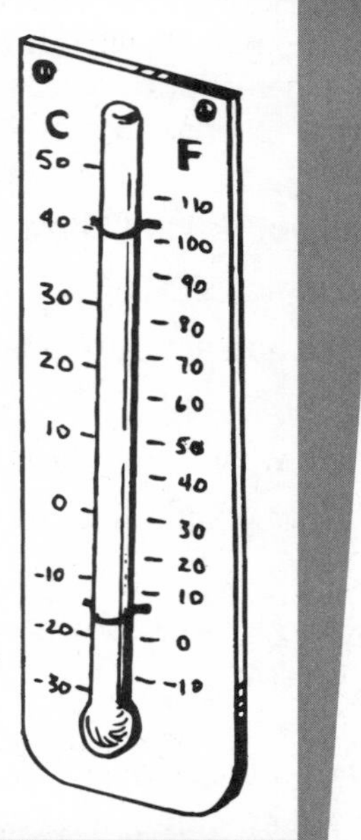

	Fahrenheit	Celsius
invented by		
water freezes		
normal body temperature		
water boils		

STOP

Name ______________________ Date ______________

Reading

1C

For pages 30–41

Mini-Test 3

Read with Understanding and Fluency

DIRECTIONS: Read the passage and answer the question that follows.

Bobby saw Dad lying on the sofa. He looked peaceful with his eyes closed and his hands resting on his stomach. Bobby took his roller skates and quietly left the room. A few minutes later, Bobby's mother asked where Bobby was. His dad said that Bobby had gone roller skating.

1. **How did Bobby's dad know where he was?**
   - (A) He has ESP.
   - (B) He had set up a video camera to watch him.
   - (C) He wasn't really asleep on the couch.
   - (D) Bobby left a note for him.

DIRECTIONS: Read the passage and answer the questions that follow.

Brian went zooming to the park to meet his buddies for an afternoon of hoops. It would have been a perfect day, but he had to drag his little brother Pete along.

"Wait for me, Brian," whined Pete.

Brian walked Pete over to a nearby tree, handed him his lunch, and said, "Sit here and eat. Don't move until I come back and get you." Brian ran off to meet his buddies.

As Pete began eating, he heard the pitter-patter of rain falling around him. When Pete saw lightning, he ran for shelter. Suddenly, a loud crack of lightning sounded. Looking behind him, Pete saw the top of the tree come crashing down right where he had been sitting. Brian saw it too, from the other side of the park.

"Pete!" Brian screamed as he ran. At the moment the lightning struck, Brian thought, "Pete's not the drag I always thought he was."

2. **What is the main conflict in this story?**
   - (F) Brian has to drag his brother along to the park.
   - (G) There is a lightning storm.
   - (H) The tree crashes down.
   - (J) Brian thinks Pete is hurt.

3. **This passage is written from what point of view?**
   - (A) first person
   - (B) second person
   - (C) third person
   - (D) None of these.

4. **Why does Brian realize that Pete is not such a drag?**
   - (F) They have fun together.
   - (G) He didn't have to save him.
   - (H) Pete turns out to be a great runner.
   - (J) He realizes that he had been taking his little brother for granted.

Reading Standards

Read and Understand Literature

Goal 2: Read and understand literature representative of various societies, eras, and ideas.

Learning Standard 2A—Students who meet the standard can understand how literary elements and techniques are used to convey meaning.

1. Read a wide range of fiction.
2. Identify and compare themes or messages in various selections. *(See pages 44–45.)*
3. Compare one or more story elements (e.g., character, plot, setting) and points of view in a variety of works by a variety of authors from different times and cultures. *(See page 46.)*

What it means:

- Students should be able to compare literary works from different cultures and identify similarities in structure, purpose, and character traits. For example, in some Native American tales, the wolf is often portrayed as a trickster. He plays tricks on other characters to get his way. That same character type is often found in Aesop's fables, as well as in literary works of other cultures.

4. Identify and discuss the elements of plot and subplot. *(See pages 47–48.)*
5. Identify/compare characters' attributes and motives. *(See page 49.)*
6. Make inferences about character traits and check text for verifications. *(See pages 50–51.)*
7. Analyze unfamiliar vocabulary. *(See page 52.)*
8. Identify metaphor, simile, onomatopoeia, and hyperbole in text. *(See pages 53–54.)*
9. Discuss and respond to a variety of literature (e.g., folktales, legends, myths, fiction, nonfiction, poems). *(See page 55.)*
10. Identify rhythm and rhyme in original work. *(See page 56.)*
11. Identify poetic devices (e.g., alliteration, assonance, consonance, onomatopoeia, rhyme scheme). *(See page 57.)*

Learning Standard 2B—Students who meet the standard can read and interpret a variety of literary works.

1. Make inferences, draw conclusions, make connections from text to text, text to self, text to world. *(See page 58.)*
2. Read a wide range of nonfiction (e.g., books, newspapers, magazines, textbooks, visual media).
3. Support plausible interpretations with evidence from the text. *(See pages 59–60.)*
4. Support an interpretation by citing the text. *(See pages 59–60.)*
5. Compare works by the same author. *(See pages 61–62.)*
6. Analyze several works that have a common theme. *(See pages 61–62.)*

Name ______________________ Date ______________

Reading

2A.2

Identifying Themes and Morals

Read and Understand Literature

DIRECTIONS: Read both stories and then answer the questions on the next page.

One Afternoon in March

One afternoon in March, I went for a walk. After being cooped up all winter, it felt good to wander around outside. It was still cold, but some of the snow was beginning to melt.

I was walking down the street when something caught my eye. I leaned down and found two silver dollars shining in a half-melted snow bank. *Buried treasure!* was my first thought. So, I dug through the snow looking for more. Of course, I just ended up with really cold hands. I slipped the two coins into my pocket and went home colder but richer.

I began to think about how to spend the money. I could add it to my skateboard fund. Or I could use it to buy a soda and hot pretzel, my favorite snack. The possibilities were exciting.

Two days later, Mary Ann and her little sister were searching the snow banks. *Finders keepers*, was my first thought. I didn't need to get to the losers weepers part since Suzy was already crying for real.

"I dropped them right here," she said between tears. Her hands were cold and red from digging in the snow.

"Maybe they got shoved down the street with the snow plow. Let's dig over here." Mary Ann's voice sounded optimistic.

They'll never know, was my second thought, and I walked past them toward Wisser's house.

"Phil, have you seen two silver dollars?" asked Mary Ann. Suzy looked up from digging. Her eyes were hopeful.

"Coins?" *Look innocent,* was my third thought.

"Yeah, Suzy dropped two silver dollars along here last week."

"Silver dollars?"

"Yeah," said Suzy. "They're thick and big." She brushed the snow off her red hands and wiped the tears from her face. Her eyes were as red as her hands.

Lie, was my fourth thought. "As a matter of fact," I hesitated, "I dug two coins out of that snow bank just a few days ago. I wondered who might have lost them."

Suzy leaped on me, hugging me. "Oh, thank you, thank you."

Name ______________________ Date ______________

It's Not My Fault

Almost every day at school, I eat lunch with Heather. Tracy is my friend, too, but she usually eats with Melody and Jordan. Every now and then, I eat lunch at their table, but not this time. Tracy was angry at me. I needed Heather's advice.

"You be the judge. I need an objective opinion. Tracy says I'm a liar," I said as I took a bite of my ham sandwich.

"About what?" Heather asked.

"It doesn't matter. I'm honest, right?"

"Honest about what?" Heather took a sip of milk.

"Honest. You know, trustworthy, direct, truthful," I smiled.

Heather hesitated and then nodded. "Yeah, you're pretty honest. Except the time you lied to your folks about your math grade. And then the time you . . ."

"Math grades don't count, and the time I went shopping with Tracy doesn't count either."

"Shopping? What about the time you went shopping with Tracy?" Heather looked confused.

"It's not my fault that Tracy didn't want you to come. I didn't want to hurt your feelings. So, she told me to tell you I was sick."

"So, you lied to me," Heather accused, raising her voice. I could tell she was really upset. She was usually very quiet.

"I didn't lie. Tracy made up the lie."

"Don't blame Tracy because you lied to me," Heather said as she ripped the cellophane covering off her brownie.

"It's not my fault. Plus, you're way too sensitive," I said. Then, I gulped my milk.

"Cheryl, the point is simple. You lie to your friends and then blame them for your mistakes," Heather said. "So, no, you're not really honest."

"Forget it," I said. I could see that Heather was still hurt about Tracy. She wouldn't understand my problem. "I gotta go. I'll see you tomorrow."

1. Explain in a few words what theme both of these stories have in common.

____

____

____

2. Who is probably the better friend, Phil or Cheryl? Why?

____

____

____

3. The moral of "It's Not My Fault" should be

____

____

____

4. The moral of "One Afternoon in March" should be

____

____

____

STOP

Name ______________________________ Date ______________

Reading **2A.3**

Comparing Literature

Read and Understand Literature

DIRECTIONS: Read the stories and then answer the questions.

Walks All Over the Sky

Back when the sky was completely dark, there was a chief with two sons, a younger son, One Who Walks All Over the Sky, and an older son, Walking About Early. The younger son was sad to see the sky always so dark so he made a mask out of wood and pitch (the sun) and lit it on fire. Each day, he travels across the sky. At night, he sleeps below the horizon, and when he snores sparks fly from the mask and make the stars. The older brother became jealous. To impress their father, he smeared fat and charcoal on his face (the moon) and makes his own path across the sky.

–From the *Tsimshian of the Pacific Northwest*

The Porcupine

Once, Porcupine and Beaver argued about the seasons. Porcupine wanted five winter months. He held up one hand and showed his five fingers. He said, "Let the winter months be the same in number as the fingers on my hand." Beaver said, "No," and held up his tail, which had many cracks or scratches on it. He said, "Let the winter months be the same in number as the scratches on my tail." They argued more and Porcupine got angry and bit off his thumb. Then, holding up his hand with the four fingers, he said, "There must be only four winter months." Beaver was afraid and gave in. For this reason, today porcupines have four claws on each foot.

–From the *Tahltan: Teit, Journal of American Folk-Lore, xxxii, 226*

Both of these stories are from different cultures. However, they both try to explain something.

1. **What is explained in the first story?**

____

____

2. **What is explained in the second story?**

____

____

3. **Who are the two characters in the first story? In the second story?**

____

____

4. **How is the relationship between the characters in the first story and the characters in the second story alike?**

____

____

____

Name ______________________________ Date ______________

Reading

2A.4

Identifying Plot

Read and Understand Literature

DIRECTIONS: Read the story and then fill in the web diagram on the next page.

Bits's Bad Summer

Bits was a small, gray squirrel who lived in a big maple tree on Alten Road. She had a nice, dry nest in the tree. She had lots of trees around her where she could find nuts and seeds. There was a little stream for water. Bits had a happy life . . . until a new guest came to stay in the yellow house for the summer. This person had red hair, and she owned a big, black cat. The cat spent all day, every day, outside.

Bits knew by instinct that the cat scared her, but she didn't know why. A cat bite, even a little nip, can kill a squirrel in a single day. Cats are fast and silent when they hunt. Even a cat that has been fed will hunt small animals. That's the cat's instinct.

Most of the people on Alten Road kept their cats indoors. But, the guest at the yellow house let her cat out every morning.

The cat created other dangers for Bits. Squirrels are usually careful when they cross streets, but not if a cat is chasing them. Bits had almost been hit by a truck one day when the black cat was chasing her.

Bits grew very hungry and thirsty. All of her food was buried in the ground. But, the cat was looking for someone to hunt. So, Bits could not dig up the food she had stored. She could not go to the stream for water. Bits needed to dig for the nuts and seeds she had buried, but with the cat outside all day, she couldn't. The cat went inside at night, and that is when Bits had to go back to her nest. Squirrels do this to keep away from other hunters, such as owls.

Sometimes, Bits was able to race down her tree and find a nut before the cat saw her. Bits was scared. She knew she had to be careful all the time.

Then one day, just as the leaves were falling from the big maple trees, Bits saw the red-haired woman carrying a basket to her car. The woman put the basket with her other bags into the car and drove away. Bits's bad summer was over. She had survived.

GO

Name ______________________________ Date ______________

Bits's street

Bits's tree

Bits's life

The new guest

Bits's home

The new guest's pet

Bits's problem

The new guest's bad habit

Bits was hungry because ______________________________.

Bits was thirsty because ______________________________.

Bits was scared because ______________________________.

Bits had to be careful of...

Bits's solution

Way in which the problem was solved

Time of year the problem was solved

STOP

Name ______________________ Date ______________________

Reading

2A.5

Identifying Character Attributes and Motives

Read and Understand Literature

DIRECTIONS: Read the story and then answer the questions.

Ralph

Ralph was a dirty mutt. His once-white hair was gray and brown with grime. He wore a dirty collar around his neck that had an old identification tag.

Right now, Ralph was on his belly. His bright, black eyes were glued on a plate at the edge of the table. On it was a ham sandwich. His moist, black nose twitched with the smell. Ralph knew he would get a swat with the broom or spray with the hose if the lady of the house caught him in the yard again.

His empty belly made him brave. The screen door slammed as the lady went back for other goodies. Ralph flew like a bullet to the edge of the table. The plate tipped onto the ground. Ralph grabbed the sandwich with his teeth and he was off. As he dove through a hole in the bushes, water from the hose whitened the back half of his body and his dirty tail.

1. What is Ralph?

____

____

2. Is Ralph living in a home with people the day he steals the sandwich?

____

____

3. Did Ralph have a home at one time? Explain your answer.

____

____

4. What was Ralph's motive for stealing the sandwich?

____

____

5. How does the lady in the passage feel about Ralph? Why do you think this?

____

____

Name ______________________________ Date ______________

Reading

2A.6

Inferring Character Traits

Read and Understand Literature

DIRECTIONS: Read the passage and answer the questions on the next page.

Volcano Adventure

"OK," said Sara. "Let's take this experiment one step at a time. First, we have to build a sand volcano with this film can inside of it."

"Let's make it really tall!" said Abdul. "I'll help!"

"Are you sure this won't blow up?" asked Tim, looking worried. "I've read that science labs blow up all the time."

Valerie yawned. "Oh, come on, Tim! Don't be silly." She studied her nails while the other three students built the sand volcano.

"Good," said Sara. "Now, we mix the red food coloring into this vinegar. The volcano won't be red, but the 'lava' will."

"That's great! This is going to be the coolest thing!" said Abdul. "I got to see a real volcano in Hawaii." He bent over to watch Sara mixing the liquids together.

"Really, Abdul?" asked Tim. "Weren't you afraid it would blow up while you were standing there?"

"No," said Abdul. "It wasn't scary."

"Abdul, would you please hold this funnel?" asked Sara. "Valerie, will you put the baking soda in the volcano?"

"Oh, how thrilling," said Valerie, rolling her eyes. "I think I'll just stand here and watch the rest of you scientists."

"Here, Tim, you can do it," said Sara. "Just fill it halfway."

"This isn't going to blow up in my face, is it?" Tim looked nervous as he spooned the powder into the volcano. Sara read the instruction sheet. "No, there's no reaction until we pour the vinegar on it," she said.

Tim jumped back. "Don't pour yet!"

"The film can is like the underground chamber of the volcano," said Abdul. "The red lava is really melted rock that's forced to the surface by hot gases. That's why the lava is red . . . it's red hot. After it cools down, it turns back into a solid again. Then, it's called *pumice.*"

Valerie yawned and looked out the window. Sara said, "Is everyone ready? I'm going to pour in the vinegar now."

Tim moved back against the bookshelves. Abdul leaned forward to watch. He grinned as the soda "erupted" over the top of the volcano. "Wow! It looks like the real thing!" he said. "Let's do it again!"

Name ______________________________ Date ____________

Each student went home and told his or her parents about the science lab. Write the name of each character above each description.

1. ______________________

"We did an experiment where a volcano actually erupted right in class! But it was OK. Nobody was hurt."

2. ______________________

"We did an experiment and built a volcano model. It was very important that we followed the instructions to make it work."

3. ______________________

"We built a model of a volcano that worked like the real thing! We actually made a mixture that was red like lava. Then we made the volcano erupt! It was so great, I wanted to do it again!"

4. ______________________

"We did some kind of science thing. I don't really remember."

5. Which character seems most excited?

____

6. Which character seems least interested?

____

7. Which character seems fearful?

____

8. Which character seems calm?

____

9. Which character seems the most organized?

____

10. Which character seems bored by school?

____

STOP

Name ______________________________ Date ______________

Reading

2A.7

Analyzing Unfamiliar Vocabulary

Read and Understand Literature

DIRECTIONS: Read the passage. Then, answer the questions that follow.

Snakes

How much do you know about snakes? Read these snake facts and find out.

A snake skeleton has numerous ribs. A large snake may have as many as 400 pairs!

Most snakes have poor eyesight. They track other animals by sensing their body heat.

Snakes can't blink! They sleep with their eyes open.

Although all snakes have teeth, very few of them—only the venomous ones—have fangs.

Many snakes are very docile and unlikely to bite people.

Pet snakes recognize their owners by smell. They flick their tongues in the air to detect smells.

Snakes have special ways of hearing. Sound vibrations from the earth pass through their bellies to receptors in their spines. Airborne sounds pass through snakes' lungs to receptors in their skin.

1. *Numerous* **means about the same as ___________ .**
   - Ⓐ number
   - Ⓑ many
   - Ⓒ few
   - Ⓓ special

2. **In this passage, *poor* means the opposite of ___________ .**
   - Ⓕ rich
   - Ⓖ good
   - Ⓗ happy
   - Ⓙ broke

3. **What does *track* mean as it is used in this passage?**
   - Ⓐ the rails on which a train moves
   - Ⓑ a sport that includes running, jumping, and throwing
   - Ⓒ to follow the footprints of
   - Ⓓ to find and follow

4. **What does the word *venomous* mean as it is used in this passage?**
   - Ⓕ vicious
   - Ⓖ sharp
   - Ⓗ poisonous
   - Ⓙ huge

5. **Which word means the opposite of *docile*?**
   - Ⓐ vicious
   - Ⓑ shy
   - Ⓒ gentle
   - Ⓓ active

6. **Which word means the same as *detect*?**
   - Ⓕ enjoy
   - Ⓖ arrest
   - Ⓗ find
   - Ⓙ hide

7. **A receptor ___________ something.**
   - Ⓐ throws
   - Ⓑ takes in
   - Ⓒ gives
   - Ⓓ sees

8. **Airborne sounds are ___________ .**
   - Ⓕ carried through the air
   - Ⓖ carried through the earth
   - Ⓗ always made by wind
   - Ⓙ louder than other sounds

Name ______________________ Date ______________

Reading **2A.8**

Identifying Hyperbole

Read and Understand Literature

DIRECTIONS: Read the poem and answer the questions about **hyperbole** (exaggeration). Then, write your own hyperbole.

My Backpack

My backpack's so heavy
It must weigh a ton.
With thousands of books—
My work's never done.

My arms are so sore
I can't lift a pen.
My breath is so short
I need oxygen.

When I stoop over,
It makes me fall down.
I think I'll just stay here
All squashed on the ground.

1. **Which of the following phrases is an example of hyperbole?**
   - (A) It makes me fall down.
   - (B) My work's never done.
   - (C) My breath is so short.
   - (D) It must weigh a ton.

2. **The poet decided there were too many exaggerations in the poem. Which of the following revised lines still contains a hyperbole?**
   - (F) My backpack is so heavy, it's hard to lift.
   - (G) My arms are so sore, I can't lift a pen.
   - (H) With four small textbooks, my work's almost done.
   - (J) My breath is so short, I need to rest.

3. **Write your own hyperboles. Remember that you should include exaggeration as part of your description.**

   My dog is so ugly,

   ____

   ______________________________.

   I am so tired,

   ____

   ______________________________.

STOP

Name ______________________ Date ______________

Reading

2A.8

Identifying Metaphors

Read and Understand Literature

DIRECTIONS: Read the poem and answer the questions about **metaphors.** Then, write your own metaphors, comparing two different things without using the words *like* or *as.*

Sunset

At the end of the day
Sank the sun in the sky.
The colors were children,
Alive and bright-eyed.

The clouds were the pillows
For each child to rest,
Ready to sleep
Now so colorfully dressed.

The lake was the glass
Reflecting their play.
How gorgeous this close,
This end to the day.

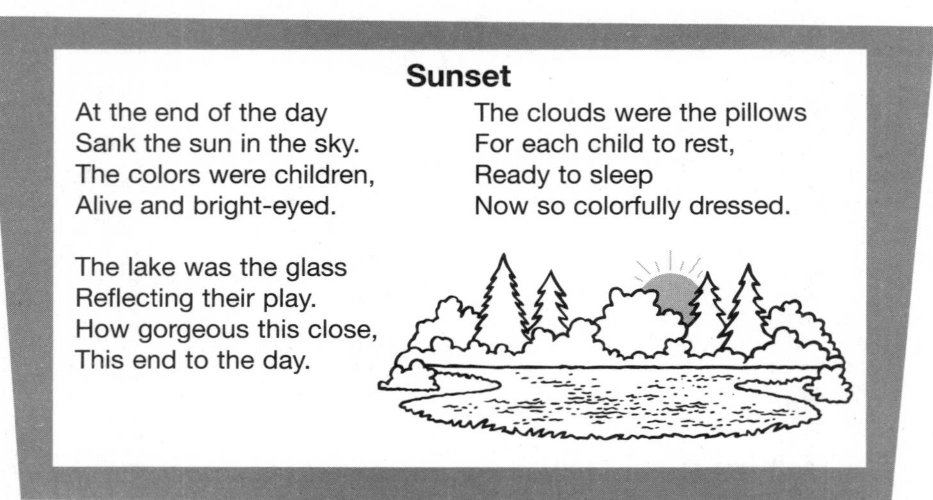

1. **In this poem, the clouds are compared to ______________.**

2. **The colors of the sunset are compared to ______________ in the poem.**

3. **The lake in the poem is compared to ______________.**

4. **Write your own metaphors by filling in the blanks below with a comparison. For a challenge, use these metaphors to create your own poem about the sunset.**

The lake was a ______________.

The clouds were ______________.

The sun was a ______________.

The sky was a ______________.

STOP

Name ______________________ Date ______________

Reading **2A.9**

Responding to Literature

Read and Understand Literature

DIRECTIONS: Read the passage and then answer the questions.

The Un-Birthday

In my family, we don't celebrate birthdays—at least not like most families. My friends say I have an "un-birthday."

The tradition started with my grandmother. She and grandfather grew up in Poland. They escaped before World War II and made their way to America. When they got here, they were so grateful that they decided to share what they had with others. On their birthdays, they gave each other just one small gift. Then, they each bought a gift for someone who needed it more than they did.

As the years passed and the family grew, the tradition continued. On my last birthday, I got a backpack for school. We had a little party with cake and all of that, and then we headed off to the Lionel School for disabled kids. Some of the children are in electric wheelchairs, and only a few can walk. I picked this school because a friend has a sister there.

When we walked in with our arms full of gifts, the kids were really excited. Even though we gave them little things—like sticker books and puzzles—all the presents were wrapped and had bows.

I gave Maggie, my friend's sister, a floppy, stuffed animal. Maggie can't talk, but she hugged her stuffed animal and looked at me so I knew she was grateful.

I don't get as much stuff as my friends, but it's okay, even though I want a new skateboard. Seeing Maggie and the others receive their gifts was a lot better than getting a bunch of presents myself.

1. How do you think the narrator feels about this unusual family tradition?

____

____

____

____

2. How does the narrator know that Maggie liked her gift?

____

____

____

3. Why does the narrator call this family tradition an "un-birthday"?

____

____

____

4. Would the narrator agree with the saying, "It is better to give than to receive"? Explain your answer.

____

____

____

STOP

Name ______________________________ Date ______________

Reading

2A.10

Rhyme

Read and Understand Literature

DIRECTIONS: Poets who set up a pattern of rhymes at the end of each line are creating a **rhyme scheme.** In a rhyme scheme, the first line is designated **a,** and all lines that rhyme with that word are also designated **a.** If the next line does not rhyme with the first, it is designated with a **b.**

Example:

Each day I walk to school and see **(a)**
A lot of people driving cars. **(b)**
Why don't they choose to walk, like me? **(a)**

1. At the end of each line, label the "By the Ocean" poem with the correct rhyme scheme. Then, fill in the following chart, placing words that rhyme together.

By the Ocean

As she walked along the sandy shore
with delight as nature's wonders she did see
starfish, whitecaps, conch shells, and more.
She knew that she would never fly free
like the tissue-paper seagulls above
or swim with the dolphins she did love.

a	b	c

2. Make a list of your own rhyming words about the ocean. Use them as a starting point for writing a poem.

____

____

____

____

Name ______________________ Date ______________

Reading

2A.11

Identifying Onomatopoeia

Read and Understand Literature

DIRECTIONS: The following story is full of words whose sounds make you think of what they mean, such as *zooming* and *fizzing.* Words like these are examples of **onomatopoeia.** Use the clues to write the correct word from the story on the line. Each word will be an example of onomatopoeia.

Summer Storm

Brian went zooming to the park on his bike. It started out as a perfect day, until Brian's mom made him drag his little brother Pete along.

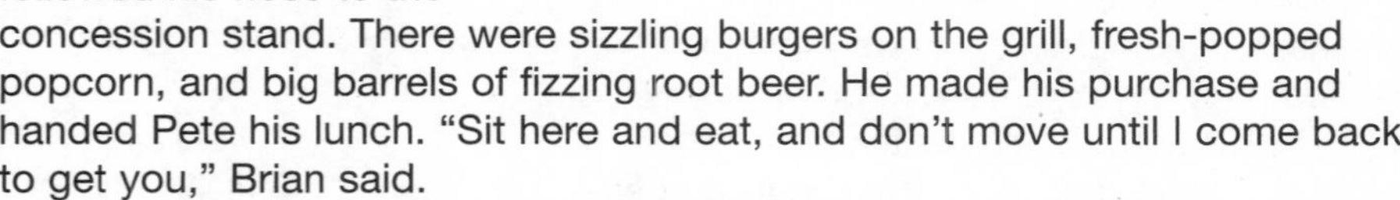

"Wait for me, Brian," whined Pete as he tried to keep up.

Brian parked his bike and followed his nose to the concession stand. There were sizzling burgers on the grill, fresh-popped popcorn, and big barrels of fizzing root beer. He made his purchase and handed Pete his lunch. "Sit here and eat, and don't move until I come back to get you," Brian said.

As Pete began eating, he heard the pitter-patter of rain falling around him, but he stayed dry under the large tree. As the rain increased, the wind began to howl. With the leaves rustling above his head, it sounded as though it was raining harder. Then he heard the plink of the hail on the roof of the concession stand. When Pete saw lightning in the distance, he knew he should move from under the tree. Brian would just have to look for him.

When the storm got worse, Brian knew he had to find Pete. Brian thought he heard his name as he ran, but then wondered if it was the wind playing tricks on him. There it was again. "Brian!" That voice had never sounded so good.

1. **moving rapidly**

   ____

2. **sharp metallic sound**

   ____

3. **soft crackling sound**

   ____

4. **a series of light, quick tapping sounds**

   ____

5. **a hissing noise**

   ____

6. **Write a clue for two other examples of onomatopoeia used in the story.**

   ____

   ____

STOP

Name ______________________ Date ______________

Reading **2B.1**

Drawing Conclusions

Read and Understand Literature

DIRECTIONS: Read the passage and then answer the questions.

The North Star

The North Star is one of the most famous stars. Its star name is *Polaris*. It is called the North Star because it shines almost directly over the North Pole. If you are at the North Pole, the North Star is overhead. As you travel farther south, the star seems lower in the sky. Only people in the Northern Hemisphere can see the North Star.

Because the North Star is always in the same spot in the sky, it has been used for years to give direction to people at night. Sailors used the North Star to navigate through the oceans.

Polaris, like all stars, is always moving. Thousands of years from now, another star will get to be the North Star. Vega was the North Star thousands of years before it moved out of position and Polaris became the North Star.

1. The North Star might be one of the most famous stars because __________ .

- Ⓐ it is near the North Pole
- Ⓑ it is always moving
- Ⓒ it is always in the same spot in the sky
- Ⓓ it is difficult to find in the sky

2. Another star will someday get to be the North Star because __________ .

- Ⓕ stars are always moving
- Ⓖ there are many stars in the sky
- Ⓗ earth will turn to the South Pole
- Ⓙ scientists rename it every 50 years

3. The name *Polaris* most likely comes from which name?

- Ⓐ polecat
- Ⓑ polar bear
- Ⓒ Poland
- Ⓓ North Pole

4. Only people in the __________ Hemisphere can see the North Star.

- Ⓕ Eastern
- Ⓖ Western
- Ⓗ Northern
- Ⓙ Southern

Name ______________________________ Date ______________

Reading

2B.3/2B.4

Supporting Interpretations

Read and Understand Literature

DIRECTIONS: Read the passage then answer the questions on the next page.

A bicycle of the future may look very different from the one you ride now. One day, you may be riding around on a recumbent bicycle—or even a tricycle!

On a recumbent cycle, the rider sits in a reclining position in a comfortable, slung fabric seat, similar to a hammock. This position, with the legs extended forward, lets the cyclist use the greater strength in the upper legs to pedal.

Racers like these cycles because the streamlined position allows the rider to attain greater speeds. On an ordinary upright bicycle, air pushes against the rider's body to create wind resistance, which slows the rider down. To go faster, the rider puts his or her head down and straightens into as much of a horizontal position as possible. The recumbent cycle is more streamlined than an ordinary bicycle. The rider's reclined body position lowers wind resistance, and the cyclist goes faster.

Some people like three-wheeled recumbent cycles because they are steadier and safer than two-wheeled bicycles. That's important when a parent is transporting a small child on the back. Three-wheeled recumbent cycles can also carry heavy loads without falling over as easily as regular cycles.

Most recumbent cycles are lightweight, ride smoothly, and use standard parts. Many cyclists and bicycle designers believe that recumbent cycles will someday replace today's upright bicycles in popular use. They may look strange now, but what may seem strange today may not seem so strange tomorrow.

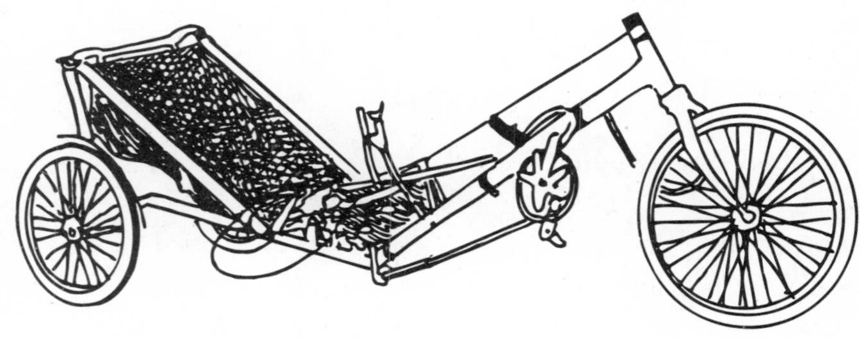

GO

Name ______________________________ Date ______________

1. Find the best ending to the sentence. The author's purpose for writing this passage is to ________ .

- (A) protect small children from bicycle accidents
- (B) alarm the reader about the dangers of bike riding
- (C) make the reader laugh
- (D) inform the reader about an unusual bicycle

2. Which sentence tells the author's opinion?

- (F) Change can be hard.
- (G) How we do things today may not be the way we do them in the future.
- (H) Small children can get hurt on bicycles.
- (J) Bicycle designers don't like three-wheelers.

3. What title do you think the author would give to this passage?

- (A) "Slow but Popular"
- (B) "Bicycle of the Future"
- (C) "The History of Bicycles"
- (D) "Two Wheels are Better than Three"

4. Does the author think people will start riding recumbent cycles more in the future? Support your answer with clues from the passage.

____

____

____

____

____

____

____

____

____

5. Do you agree with the author's view about the use of recumbent cycles in the future? Explain your answer.

____

____

____

____

____

____

Name ______________________ Date ______________

Reading

2B.5/2B.6

Comparing Works and Themes

Read and Understand Literature

DIRECTIONS: Read the journal entries and answer the questions on the next page.

Ben's Journal

February 9

Tomorrow is the big day. I've studied so hard for the past three weeks that I think I could spell these words in my sleep.

But what if I get nervous and mess up? What if someone else knows more words than I know? Rebecca always wins when we practice at school. I just want to do the best that I can.

Mom has helped me every night after supper. She says that studying and learning are more important, in the long run, than winning. I guess she's right. But, I still really hope I win.

February 10

I did it! Well, I didn't win first place, but I came in second. And, I'm really proud of that.

At first, I was scared when I looked out and saw all those people in the audience. I was afraid I'd forget everything. But then I told myself, "You studied hard. You know all those words. Come on, you can do it!"

My first word was *indicate:* i-n-d-i-c-a-t-e. It was easy. Then, I knew I could do the rest of them, too. The only word that really stumped me was *cannibal.* I spelled it c-a-n-n-i-b-l-e—oops. Rebecca spelled it right, along with her last word: *hydraulics.*

Oh well, I won a dictionary and had my picture taken for the newspaper. When I came home, my family had a party to celebrate! Tomorrow, I start studying for next year's contest.

Name ______________________ Date ______________

1. **What is the common theme of the two journal entries?**

2. **Describe how Ben was feeling when he wrote the first entry.**

3. **Have Ben's emotions changed from the first to the second entry? Explain.**

4. **Ben mentioned Rebecca in his first journal entry. Did what he say there predict what happened the next day? Explain.**

STOP

Name ______________________________ Date ______________

Reading

2

For pages 44–62

Mini-Test 4

Read and Understand Literature

DIRECTIONS: Read the passage and answer the questions that follow.

A Bumpy Ride

When we first climbed into the car and strapped on our safety belts, I wasn't very nervous. I was sitting right next to my big brother, and he had done this many times before. As we started to climb the hill, however, I could feel my heart jump into my throat. "Brian?" I asked nervously. "Is this supposed to be so noisy?" "Sure, Matthew," Brian answered. "It always does that." A minute later, we whooshed so fast down the hill I didn't have time to think. With a twist, a loop, and a bunch of fast turns, everyone on board screamed in delight. No wonder this was one of the most popular rides in the park. By the time the car pulled into the station and we got off the ride, I was ready to do it again!

1. Which of the following best describes the setting of this story?

- (A) a car ride to school
- (B) a train ride
- (C) a ride on a roller coaster
- (D) a trip to the grocery store

2. From the beginning to end of this story, Matthew went from being _________ .

- (F) nervous to calm to scared
- (G) calm to nervous to bored
- (H) bored to excited to scared
- (J) calm to nervous to excited

3. What might have happened if this story had taken place in a regular car?

- (A) Brian might have lost his license for careless driving.
- (B) Brian might have started a taxi business.
- (C) Matthew might have wanted to drive with Brian again.
- (D) Matthew might not have been nervous.

4. The word *whooshed* is an example of what type of figurative language?

- (F) simile
- (G) metaphor
- (H) onomatopoeia
- (J) hyperbole

STOP

How Am I Doing?

Mini-Test 1 Page 15 **Number Correct**	**8–9** answers correct	**Great Job!** Move on to the section test on page 66.
	5–7 answers correct	**You're almost there!** But you still need a little practice. Review the practice pages 8–14 before moving on to the section test on page 66.
	0–4 answers correct	**Oops!** Time to review what you have learned and try again. Review the practice section on pages 8–14. Then retake the test on page 15. Now move on to the section test on page 66.
Mini-Test 2 Page 28 **Number Correct**	**5** answers correct	**Awesome!** Move on to the section test on page 66.
	3–4 answers correct	**You're almost there!** But you still need a little practice. Review the practice pages 17–27 before moving on to the section test on page 66.
	0–2 answers correct	**Oops!** Time to review what you have learned and try again. Review the practice section on pages 17–27. Then retake the test on page 28. Now move on to the section test on page 66.

How Am I Doing?

Mini-Test 3 Page 42 **Number Correct**	**4** answers correct	**Great Job!** Move on to the section test on page 66.
	3 answers correct	**You're almost there!** But you still need a little practice. Review the practice pages 30–41 before moving on to the section test on page 66.
	0–2 answers correct	**Oops!** Time to review what you have learned and try again. Review the practice section on pages 30–41. Then retake the test on page 42. Now move on to the section test on page 66.
Mini-Test 4 Page 63 **Number Correct**	**4** answers correct	**Awesome!** Move on to the section test on page 66.
	2–3 answers correct	**You're almost there!** But you still need a little practice. Review the practice pages 44–62 before moving on to the section test on page 66.
	0–1 answers correct	**Oops!** Time to review what you have learned and try again. Review the practice section on pages 44–62. Then retake the test on page 63. Now move on to the section test on page 66.

Name ______________________________ Date ______________

Final Reading Test

for pages 8–63

DIRECTIONS: Choose the word that correctly completes both sentences.

1. **Someone bought the ________ on the corner.**
   A new house costs a ________ of money.
   - (A) bunch
   - (B) lot
   - (C) house
   - (D) property

2. **Inez bought a ________ of soda.**
   The doctor said it was a difficult ________ .
   - (F) case
   - (G) carton
   - (H) disease
   - (J) situation

3. **It's not safe to ________ a boat.**
   This ________ is too heavy to move.
   - (A) sink
   - (B) stone
   - (C) push
   - (D) rock

4. **What _____ does Carl work?**
   Help me _____ the box to that side.
   - (F) shift
   - (G) time
   - (H) move
   - (J) job

DIRECTIONS: Read the paragraph. Find the word below the paragraph that fits best in each numbered blank.

It takes a great deal of ___5___ to become a champion in any sport. Many hours of practice are ___6___, and you must often ___7___ other aspects of your life.

5.
   - (A) inflammation
   - (B) dedication
   - (C) restriction
   - (D) location

6.
   - (F) required
   - (G) deflected
   - (H) extracted
   - (J) expanded

7.
   - (A) include
   - (B) neglect
   - (C) locate
   - (D) construct

DIRECTIONS: Choose the best answer.

8. **What prefix can you add to the root word *satisfied* to make a word that means "not satisfied."**
   - (F) *re-*
   - (G) *anti-*
   - (H) *dis-*
   - (J) *pre-*

Name ______________________________ Date ______________

DIRECTIONS: Choose the word that means the same or about the same as the underlined word.

9. high fence

- Ⓐ tall
- Ⓑ happy
- Ⓒ long
- Ⓓ wide

10. paste the paper

- Ⓕ fold
- Ⓖ attach
- Ⓗ patch
- Ⓙ glue

11. chilly day

- Ⓐ long
- Ⓑ frozen
- Ⓒ cold
- Ⓓ unpleasant

DIRECTIONS: Choose the word that means the opposite of the underlined word.

12. valuable painting

- Ⓕ strange
- Ⓖ expensive
- Ⓗ worthless
- Ⓙ humorous

13. loose tie

- Ⓐ tight
- Ⓑ lost
- Ⓒ plain
- Ⓓ ill fitting

DIRECTIONS: Read the passage, then answer the questions.

Helping the Mountain Gorilla

Mountain gorillas live in the rain forests in Rwanda, Uganda, and the Democratic Republic of the Congo. These large, beautiful animals are becoming very rare. They have lost much of their habitat as people move in and take over gorillas' lands. Although there are strict laws protecting gorillas, poachers continue to hunt them.

Scientists observe gorillas to learn about their habits and needs. Then, scientists write about their findings in magazines. Concerned readers sometimes contribute money to help safeguard the mountain gorillas.

Many other people are working hard to protect the mountain gorillas. Park rangers patrol the rain forest and arrest poachers. Tourists bring much-needed money into the area, encouraging local residents to protect the gorillas, too.

14. What is this passage mainly about?

- Ⓕ mountain gorillas' family relationships
- Ⓖ scientists who study mountain gorillas
- Ⓗ ways that gorillas are threatened and helped
- Ⓙ poachers and wars that threaten gorillas' survival

15. Which words help you figure out the meaning of *habitat*?

- Ⓐ "large, beautiful animals"
- Ⓑ "gorillas' lands"
- Ⓒ "the human population"
- Ⓓ "recent civil wars"

16. In this passage, *poacher* means __________ .

- Ⓕ park ranger
- Ⓖ mountain gorilla
- Ⓗ unlawful hunter
- Ⓙ scientist

Name ______________________________ Date ______________

17. **The author of the passage thinks that tourism _________ .**
   - (A) is very harmful to mountain gorillas
   - (B) is one cause of civil wars in Africa
   - (C) can be helpful to mountain gorillas
   - (D) is one cause of overpopulation in Africa

18. **The author's purpose for writing this passage is _________ .**
   - (F) to entertain readers
   - (G) to inform readers about mountain gorillas
   - (H) to motivate readers to visit Rwanda
   - (J) to explain to readers where Africa is

19. **Which of the following is a fact?**
   - (A) Mountain gorillas are beautiful animals.
   - (B) Mountain gorillas live in the rain forests in Rwanda, Uganda, and the Democratic Republic of the Congo.
   - (C) Everyone should send money to help the gorillas.
   - (D) Scientists work to arrest poachers.

DIRECTIONS: Read the passage, then answer the questions.

Home Alone

"Are you sure you're going to be all right at home alone?" Yong's mother asked.

"Yes, Mom," Yong replied, trying not to roll her eyes. "I'm old enough to stay here alone for three hours." Yong's mom and dad were going to a barbecue that afternoon. Since kids weren't invited, Yong was staying home alone. It was the first time her parents had left her home by herself. Yong was a little nervous, but she was sure she could handle it.

"Let me give you a last-minute quiz to make sure," her dad said. Yong's father was a teacher, and he was always giving her little tests. "What happens if somebody calls and asks for your mom or me?"

"I tell them that you are busy and can't come to the phone right now," Yong said. "Then, I take a message."

"What if there is a knock on the door?" asked her dad.

"I don't answer it, because I can't let anyone in anyway."

"Okay, here's a tough one." Her father looked very serious. "What if you hear ghosts in the closets?"

"Dad!" Yong giggled. "Our house isn't haunted. I'll be fine. Look, I have the phone number of the house where you'll be, so I can call if I need to. I've got the numbers for the police, the fire department, and the poison control center. I won't turn on the stove or leave the house. And, I'll double lock the doors behind you when you leave."

Yong's parents were satisfied. They hugged her goodbye and left for the afternoon. Yong sat for a few minutes and enjoyed the quiet of the empty house. Then, she went to the kitchen to fix herself a snack. She opened the cupboard door. Then, she jumped back, startled. There was a ghost in the cupboard! Yong laughed and laughed. Her dad had taped up a picture of a ghost. It said, "BOO! We love you!"

20. **Which answer shows the best summary of this story?**
   - (F) Yong is staying home by herself for the first time and must remember all the important safety rules.
   - (G) Yong cannot go to the barbecue with her mom and dad.
   - (H) Yong's parents play a trick on her by hiding a paper ghost in the cupboard.
   - (J) Yong enjoys a peaceful afternoon at home alone.

21. **What is the setting of this story?**
   - (A) the beach
   - (B) a barbecue
   - (C) Yong's house
   - (D) a haunted house

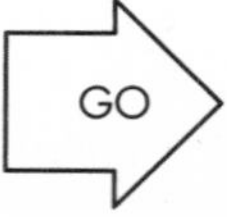

Name ______________________________ Date ______________

22. What is the main reason Yong's dad keeps asking her questions?

- (F) He wants to make sure she knows all the emergency phone numbers.
- (G) He wants to make sure she will be safe while they are gone.
- (H) He likes giving her quizzes.
- (J) He played a trick on her.

23. What should Yong do if someone knocks at the door?

- (A) She should answer it.
- (B) She should call her dad.
- (C) She should not answer it and not let anyone in.
- (D) She should see who it is before letting the person in.

24. What do you think Yong will do if she spills drain cleaner and the dog accidentally licks some up?

- (F) She will call her friend Sam to tell him.
- (G) She will call the fire department.
- (H) She will do nothing.
- (J) She will call the poison control center and then her parents.

25. Because kids are *not* invited to the barbecue, __________ .

- (A) they won't have any fun
- (B) the parents will not go
- (C) Yong must stay home alone
- (D) Yong will not get any dinner

26. Who are the main characters in this story?

- (F) Yong, her mom, and her dad
- (G) Yong and her friend Sam
- (H) Yong, her dad, and the dog
- (J) Yong and her dad

27. What do you learn about Yong's dad?

- (A) He has a good sense of humor.
- (B) He is very serious.
- (C) He is very quiet.
- (D) He has a good job.

28. Which of the following would *not* have been a logical ending for the story.

- (F) Yong enjoys her afternoon alone eating popcorn and watching a movie.
- (G) Yong's parents decide to stay home because she doesn't want to be alone.
- (H) Yong thinks of a good trick to play on her dad when he gets home.
- (J) Yong's parents come home and find her fast asleep on the couch.

STOP

Name ______________________ Date ______________

Final Reading Test

Answer Sheet

1 Ⓐ Ⓑ Ⓒ Ⓓ
2 Ⓕ Ⓖ Ⓗ Ⓙ
3 Ⓐ Ⓑ Ⓒ Ⓓ
4 Ⓕ Ⓖ Ⓗ Ⓙ
5 Ⓐ Ⓑ Ⓒ Ⓓ
6 Ⓕ Ⓖ Ⓗ Ⓙ
7 Ⓐ Ⓑ Ⓒ Ⓓ
8 Ⓕ Ⓖ Ⓗ Ⓙ
9 Ⓐ Ⓑ Ⓒ Ⓓ
10 Ⓕ Ⓖ Ⓗ Ⓙ

11 Ⓐ Ⓑ Ⓒ Ⓓ
12 Ⓕ Ⓖ Ⓗ Ⓙ
13 Ⓐ Ⓑ Ⓒ Ⓓ
14 Ⓕ Ⓖ Ⓗ Ⓙ
15 Ⓐ Ⓑ Ⓒ Ⓓ
16 Ⓕ Ⓖ Ⓗ Ⓙ
17 Ⓐ Ⓑ Ⓒ Ⓓ
18 Ⓕ Ⓖ Ⓗ Ⓙ
19 Ⓐ Ⓑ Ⓒ Ⓓ
20 Ⓕ Ⓖ Ⓗ Ⓙ

21 Ⓐ Ⓑ Ⓒ Ⓓ
22 Ⓕ Ⓖ Ⓗ Ⓙ
23 Ⓐ Ⓑ Ⓒ Ⓓ
24 Ⓕ Ⓖ Ⓗ Ⓙ
25 Ⓐ Ⓑ Ⓒ Ⓓ
26 Ⓕ Ⓖ Ⓗ Ⓙ
27 Ⓐ Ⓑ Ⓒ Ⓓ
28 Ⓕ Ⓖ Ⓗ Ⓙ

Illinois Mathematics Content Standards

The mathematics section of the state test measures knowledge in five different areas.

Goal 3: **Demonstrate and apply a knowledge and sense of numbers, including numeration and operations, patterns, ratios, and proportions.**

Goal 4: **Estimate, make, and use measurement of objects, quantities, and relationships and determine acceptable levels of accuracy.**

Goal 5: **Use algebraic and analytical methods to identify and describe patterns and relationships in data, solve problems, and predict results.**

Goal 6: **Use geometric methods to analyze, categorize, and draw conclusions about points, lines, planes, and space.**

Goal 7: **Collect, organize, and analyze data using statistical methods; predict results; and interpret certainty using concepts of probability.**

Illinois Mathematics Table of Contents

Mathematics Standards

Number Sense

Goal 3: Demonstrate and apply a knowledge and sense of numbers, including numeration and operations, patterns, ratios, and proportions.

Learning Standard 3A—Students who meet the standard can demonstrate knowledge and use of numbers and their many representations in a broad range of theoretical and practical settings. *(Representations)*

1. Represent, order, and compare decimals to demonstrate understanding of the place-value structure in the base-ten number system. *(See page 73.)*
2. Identify prime numbers through 100. *(See page 74.)*
3. Recognize equivalent representation for decimals and generate them by composing and decomposing numbers (e.g., 0.15 = 0.1 + 0.05). *(See page 75.)*
4. Represent fractions as parts of unit wholes, as parts of a set, as locations on a number line, and as divisions of whole numbers. *(See page 76.)*
5. Explore numbers less than zero by extending a number line and familiar applications. *(See page 77.)*

Learning Standard 3B—Students who meet the standard can investigate, represent, and solve problems using number facts, operations, and their properties, algorithms, and relationships. *(Operations and properties)*

1. Describe classes of numbers according to characteristics, such as factors and multiples. *(See page 78.)*
2. Solve addition or subtraction number sentences and word problems using fractions with like denominators. *(See pages 79–80.)*
3. Solve multi-step number sentences and word problems using whole numbers and the four basic operations. *(See pages 81–82.)*
4. Select and use one of various algorithms to multiply and divide. *(See page 83.)*

Learning Standard 3C—Students who meet the standard can compute and estimate using mental mathematics, paper-and-pencil methods, calculators, and computers. *(Choice of method)*

1. Develop and use strategies (e.g., compatible numbers, front-end estimation) to estimate the results of whole number computations and to judge the reasonableness of such results. *(See page 84.)*
2. Estimate the sum or difference of a number sentence containing decimals using a variety of strategies. *(See page 85.)*

Learning Standard 3D—Students who meet the standard can solve problems using comparison of quantities, ratios, proportions, and percents.

1. Determine 50% and 100% of a given group in context. *(See page 86.)*

Name ______________________________ Date ______________

Mathematics **Number Sense**

3A.1

Comparing and Ordering Decimals

DIRECTIONS: Choose the best answer.

1. **Which decimal below names the smallest number?**
   - (A) 0.06
   - (B) 0.6
   - (C) 0.64
   - (D) 6.40

2. **Which decimal below names the largest number?**
   - (F) 2.15
   - (G) 2.05
   - (H) 2.50
   - (J) 2.21

3. **What is the correct sign to complete the equation $426.10 ■ $416.19?**
   - (A) =
   - (B) <
   - (C) >
   - (D) None of these

4. **Which decimal below names the smallest number?**
   - (F) 1.90
   - (G) 1.21
   - (H) 1.09
   - (J) 1.18

5. **Which group of numbers is in order from smallest to largest?**
   - (A) 21.009, 21.09, 21.9, 22.001, 22.10
   - (B) 21.09, 21.009, 21.9, 22.10, 22.001
   - (C) 21,009, 21.09, 21.9, 22.10, 22.001
   - (D) 21.9, 21.09, 21.009, 22.10, 22,001

6. **Which group of numbers is in order from greatest to least?**
   - (F) 0.99, 0.95, 0.59, 0.059, 0.095
   - (G) 0.099, 0.059, 0.59, 0.99, 0.95
   - (H) 0.99, 0.95, 0.59, 0.095, 0.059
   - (J) 0.95, 0.99, 0.59, 0.095, 0.059

7. **What is the correct sign to complete the equation 18.58 ■ 18.85?**
   - (A) =
   - (B) <
   - (C) >
   - (D) None of these

8. **Which decimal below names the largest number?**
   - (F) 3.17
   - (G) 3.07
   - (H) 3.71
   - (J) 3.10

STOP

Name ______________________ Date ______________

Mathematics **Number Sense**

3A.2

Identifying Prime Numbers

DIRECTIONS: Choose the best answer.

Read each question carefully. Look for key words and numbers that will help you find the answers.

1. Prime numbers are numbers whose factors ________.

- (A) are less than 10.
- (B) are greater than 10.
- (C) are the number and 1.
- (D) are multiples of each other.

2. Which of the following numbers is *not* prime?

- (F) 13
- (G) 23
- (H) 33
- (J) 43

3. Which of the following numbers is *not* prime?

- (A) 37
- (B) 47
- (C) 57
- (D) 67

4. Which of the following numbers is *not* prime?

- (F) 59
- (G) 69
- (H) 79
- (J) 89

5. Which of the following numbers is *not* prime?

- (A) 21
- (B) 31
- (C) 41
- (D) 61

6. Which of the following numbers is *not* prime?

- (F) 51
- (G) 19
- (H) 11
- (J) 31

7. Which of the following numbers is prime?

- (A) 56
- (B) 57
- (C) 58
- (D) 59

8. Which of the following numbers is prime?

- (F) 81
- (G) 83
- (H) 85
- (J) 87

STOP

Name ______________________________ Date ______________

Mathematics

3A.3

Number Sense

Composing and Decomposing Decimals

DIRECTIONS: Build each number.

1. **7 ones**
   6 tenths
   2 tens
   3 hundreds

			.	

2. **4 hundredths**
   5 tens
   4 tenths
   9 ones

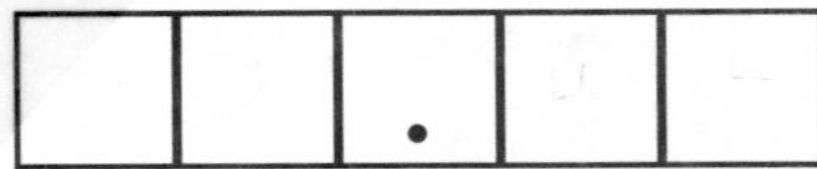

3. **6 ones**
   9 thousandths
   8 tenths
   7 hundredths

4. **7 thousandths**
   5 hundreds
   3 tenths
   1 one
   0 hundredths
   2 tens
   4 thousands

   Insert the decimal point in the correct square.

DIRECTIONS: Choose the best answer.

5. **How is 1.593 written in expanded notation?**
   (A) 1 + .5 + .09 + .003
   (B) 1 + .5 + . 093
   (C) 1 + .05 + .009 + .0003
   (D) 1 + 5 + .9 + .03

6. **What is the standard form of 20 + 8 + .6 + .08 + .002?**
   (F) 20.8682
   (G) 28.862
   (H) 28.286
   (J) 28.682

7. **How is 18.604 written in expanded notation?**
   (A) 10 + 8 + .06 + .004
   (B) 10 + 8 + .6 + .004
   (C) 10 + 8 + .6 + .04
   (D) 10 + 8 + .06 + .04

8. **What is the standard form of 4 + .03 + .0007?**
   (F) 4.0307
   (G) 4.037
   (H) 4.3007
   (J) 4.7003

9. **How is 238.6 written in expanded notation?**
   (A) 20 + 3 + .8 + .06
   (B) 200 + 30 + .8 + .006
   (C) 200 + 38 + .6
   (D) 200 + 30 + 8 + .6

STOP

Name ______________________ Date ______________

Mathematics **Number Sense**

3A.4

Fractions

DIRECTIONS: Choose the best answer.

Pay close attention to the numbers in the problem and in the answer choices. If you misread even one number, you will probably choose the wrong answer.

1. What picture shows a fraction equivalent to $\frac{3}{10}$?

Ⓐ 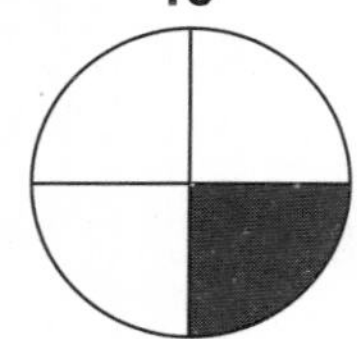

Ⓑ 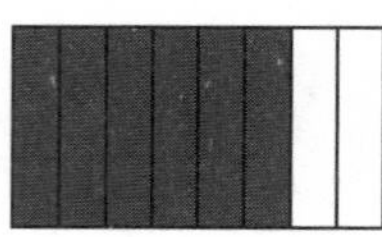

Ⓒ 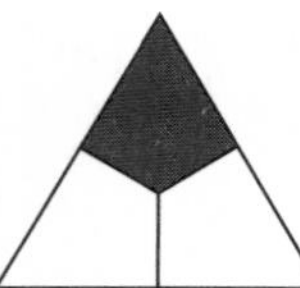

Ⓓ 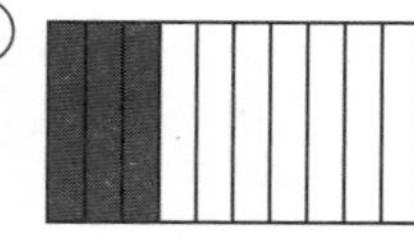

DIRECTIONS: Use the number line for exercises 2 and 3.

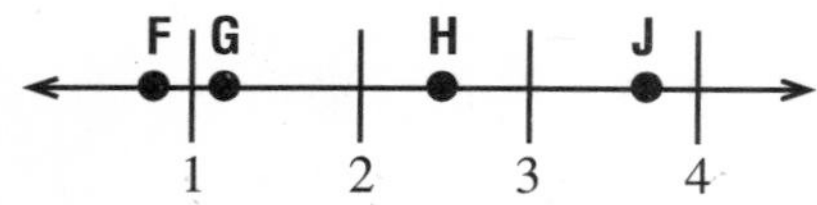

2. What point represents $\frac{3}{4}$?

Ⓕ F

Ⓖ G

Ⓗ H

Ⓙ J

3. What point represents $2\frac{1}{2}$?

Ⓐ F

Ⓑ G

Ⓒ H

Ⓓ J

DIRECTIONS: Choose the best answer.

4. Which fraction represents 4 divided by 5?

Ⓕ $\frac{5}{4}$

Ⓖ $\frac{3}{5}$

Ⓗ $\frac{4}{5}$

Ⓙ $\frac{5}{5}$

5. Which fraction tells how much of this figure is shaded?

Ⓐ $\frac{2}{3}$

Ⓑ $\frac{3}{4}$

Ⓒ $\frac{1}{4}$

Ⓓ $\frac{5}{8}$

6. Which fraction shows how many of the shapes are shaded?

Ⓕ $\frac{1}{6}$

Ⓖ $\frac{3}{5}$

Ⓗ $\frac{7}{10}$

Ⓙ $\frac{1}{2}$

STOP

Name ______________________ Date ______________

Mathematics

Number Sense

3A.5

Negative Numbers

DIRECTIONS: Use the number line for numbers 1 and 2.

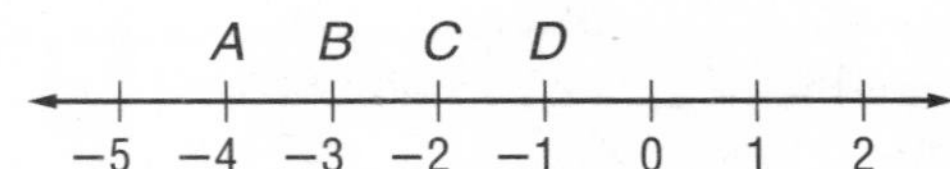

1. **Which letter is at −1 on the number line?**
   - (A) A
   - (B) B
   - (C) C
   - (D) D

2. **Which letter is at −4 on the number line?**
   - (F) A
   - (G) B
   - (H) C
   - (J) D

DIRECTIONS: Choose the best answer.

3. **Which number is not greater than −3?**
   - (A) 4
   - (B) 0
   - (C) −2
   - (D) −4

4. **Which statement represents losing $5?**
   - (F) 5
   - (G) 0
   - (H) −5
   - (J) 10

5. **Which temperature is coldest?**
   - (A) −4
   - (B) 0
   - (C) −2
   - (D) 4

6. **Which statement represents a loss of 3 yards?**
   - (F) −3
   - (G) 0
   - (H) 3
   - (J) +3

DIRECTIONS: Use the thermometer for numbers 7 and 8.

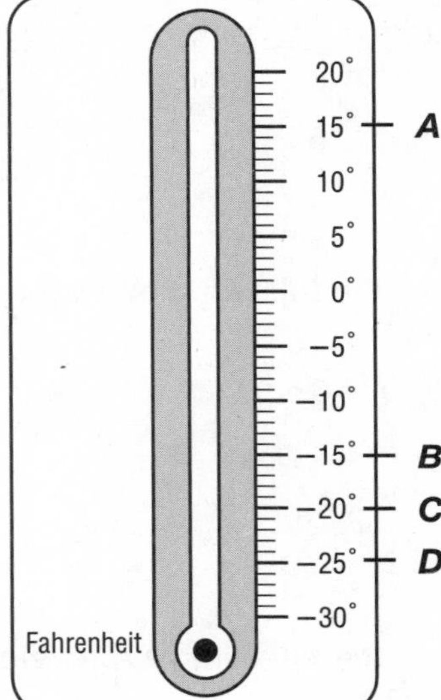

7. **Which letter on the thermometer represents −15°?**
   - (A) A
   - (B) B
   - (C) C
   - (D) D

8. **Which letter on the thermometer represents −25°?**
   - (F) A
   - (G) B
   - (H) C
   - (J) D

STOP

Name ______________________ Date ______________

Mathematics | Number Sense

3B.1

Factors and Multiples

DIRECTIONS: Choose the best answer.

A **factor** is a number that divides evenly into another number. A **multiple** is the result of a number multiplied by any whole number.

1. **Which of the following expressions does *not* equal 12?**
   - Ⓐ 4×3
   - Ⓑ 6×6
   - Ⓒ 2×6
   - Ⓓ $2 \times 2 \times 3$

2. **Which of the following expressions does *not* equal 54?**
   - Ⓕ 9×6
   - Ⓖ 5×4
   - Ⓗ 3×18
   - Ⓙ 2×27

3. **Which of the following expressions does *not* equal 20?**
   - Ⓐ 20×1
   - Ⓑ 4×5
   - Ⓒ 2×10
   - Ⓓ $2 \times 2 \times 4$

4. **Which of the following expressions does *not* equal 48?**
   - Ⓕ 3×18
   - Ⓖ 6×8
   - Ⓗ 2×24
   - Ⓙ 4×12

5. **Which of the following expressions does *not* equal 36?**
   - Ⓐ 3×11
   - Ⓑ 2×18
   - Ⓒ 6×6
   - Ⓓ $2 \times 2 \times 3 \times 3$

6. **List all factors of 15.**
   - Ⓕ 1, 15
   - Ⓖ 1, 3, 15
   - Ⓗ 1, 3, 5, 15
   - Ⓙ 5, 10, 15, 20

7. **List all factors of 24.**
   - Ⓐ 1, 2, 6
   - Ⓑ 1, 2, 3, 4, 6, 12
   - Ⓒ 1, 2, 3, 4, 6, 8, 12, 24
   - Ⓓ 0, 1, 2, 3, 4, 5, 6, 12, 14, 24

8. **Complete the table of multiples.**

Multiples of 3	15	18		24			33
Multiples of 4	12	16			28	32	

What common multiple of 3 and 4 is in the table?
   - Ⓕ 21
   - Ⓖ 24
   - Ⓗ 30
   - Ⓙ 33

9. **Complete the table of multiples.**

Multiples of 6	30	36			54	60	
Multiples of 9		27	36			63	

What common multiples of 6 and 9 are in the table?
   - Ⓐ 36 and 54
   - Ⓑ 36 and 63
   - Ⓒ 27 and 54
   - Ⓓ 42 and 54

Name ______________________ Date ______________

Mathematics **Number Sense**

3B.2

Adding and Subtracting Fractions

DIRECTIONS: Choose the correct answer to each equation in simplest form. Choose "None of these" if the correct answer is not given.

Examples:

$\frac{4}{5} + \frac{4}{5} =$

Ⓐ $\frac{5}{8}$
Ⓑ $1\frac{3}{5}$
Ⓒ 1
Ⓓ None of these

Answer: Ⓑ

$1\frac{4}{7} - \frac{3}{7}$

Ⓕ 2
Ⓖ $1\frac{1}{7}$
Ⓗ $\frac{17}{7}$
Ⓙ None of these

Answer: Ⓖ

Look closely at the operation sign. Add whole numbers together first, then fractions. Remember to reduce to simplest form.

1. $2\frac{1}{5} + 1\frac{3}{5}$

Ⓐ 4
Ⓑ $3\frac{4}{5}$
Ⓒ $3\frac{2}{5}$
Ⓓ None of these

2. $\frac{3}{4} - \frac{1}{4} =$

Ⓕ $\frac{4}{4}$
Ⓖ 1
Ⓗ $\frac{1}{2}$
Ⓙ None of these

3. $\frac{1}{10} + \frac{5}{10} =$

Ⓐ $\frac{10}{6}$
Ⓑ $\frac{3}{5}$
Ⓒ $\frac{6}{10}$
Ⓓ None of these

4. $\frac{5}{8} + \frac{7}{8} + \frac{1}{8} =$

Ⓕ $1\frac{3}{8}$
Ⓖ $1\frac{3}{24}$
Ⓗ $1\frac{5}{8}$
Ⓙ None of these

5. $\frac{6}{6} - \frac{6}{6} =$

Ⓐ 0
Ⓑ $\frac{12}{6}$
Ⓒ $\frac{0}{6}$
Ⓓ None of these

6. $\square - \frac{2}{9} = \frac{5}{9}$

Ⓕ $1\frac{1}{9}$
Ⓖ $\frac{3}{9}$
Ⓗ $\frac{7}{9}$
Ⓙ None of these

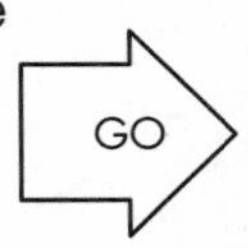

Name ______________________ Date ____________

7. $\begin{array}{r} \frac{7}{9} \\ -\ \frac{6}{9} \\ \hline \end{array}$

- Ⓐ $1\frac{4}{9}$
- Ⓑ $\frac{13}{9}$
- Ⓒ $\frac{1}{9}$
- Ⓓ None of these

8. $\begin{array}{r} \frac{5}{6} \\ +\ \square \\ \hline 1\frac{2}{3} \end{array}$

- Ⓕ $\frac{5}{6}$
- Ⓖ 1
- Ⓗ $\frac{7}{6}$
- Ⓙ None of these

9. $\square - \frac{2}{3} = 0$

- Ⓐ $\frac{2}{3}$
- Ⓑ $1\frac{2}{3}$
- Ⓒ 0
- Ⓓ None of these

10. $\begin{array}{r} 1\frac{3}{14} \\ -\ \frac{1}{14} \\ \hline \end{array}$

- Ⓕ $1\frac{2}{7}$
- Ⓖ $1\frac{1}{7}$
- Ⓗ $\frac{1}{7}$
- Ⓙ None of these

11. $\frac{11}{12} - \frac{9}{12} =$

- Ⓐ $\frac{1}{6}$
- Ⓑ $\frac{1}{12}$
- Ⓒ $1\frac{1}{2}$
- Ⓓ None of these

12. $\begin{array}{r} 1\frac{7}{9} \\ +\ \frac{5}{9} \\ \hline \end{array}$

- Ⓕ $2\frac{2}{9}$
- Ⓖ $1\frac{12}{9}$
- Ⓗ $2\frac{1}{3}$
- Ⓙ None of these

13. $\frac{2}{3} - \square = \frac{1}{3}$

- Ⓐ $\frac{3}{3}$
- Ⓑ $\frac{1}{3}$
- Ⓒ 1
- Ⓓ None of these

14. $\frac{1}{24} + \frac{5}{24} =$

- Ⓕ $\frac{1}{4}$
- Ⓖ $\frac{4}{24}$
- Ⓗ $\frac{6}{24}$
- Ⓙ None of these

15. $\frac{3}{11} + \frac{9}{11} + \frac{1}{11} =$

- Ⓐ $\frac{13}{11}$
- Ⓑ $1\frac{2}{11}$
- Ⓒ $\frac{5}{11}$
- Ⓓ None of these

16. $\frac{2}{4} + \square = 1$

- Ⓕ $\frac{1}{4}$
- Ⓖ $\frac{2}{4}$
- Ⓗ $1\frac{1}{2}$
- Ⓙ None of these

STOP

Name ______________________________ Date ______________

Mathematics

3B.3

Number Sense

Solving Multi-Step Problems

DIRECTIONS: Choose the best answer.

Remember the order of operations: parentheses, multiplication, division, addition, and subtraction.

1. **Find 3 + (51 ÷ 3).**
   - (A) 17
   - (B) 20
   - (C) 57
   - (D) 54

2. **Find (2 × 1,000) + (6 × 100) + (9 × 1).**
   - (F) 2,690
   - (G) 2,609
   - (H) 269
   - (J) 2,069

3. **Find (8 × 2) + 4.**
   - (A) 10
   - (B) 14
   - (C) 20
   - (D) 23

4. **Find 3 × (4 + 1).**
   - (F) 13
   - (G) 15
   - (H) 9
   - (J) 16

5. **Find (3 × 4) + 1.**
   - (A) 13
   - (B) 15
   - (C) 9
   - (D) 16

6. **Find 5 + (2 × 3) − 2.**
   - (F) 19
   - (G) 13
   - (H) 11
   - (J) 9

7. **Find (4 × 2) + (3 × 3).**
   - (A) 17
   - (B) 12
   - (C) 23
   - (D) 60

8. **Find 1 + (5 × 4) + 2.**
   - (F) 26
   - (G) 23
   - (H) 21
   - (J) 60

9. **Find 2 × (278 + 3).**
   - (A) 562
   - (B) 281
   - (C) 559
   - (D) 1,668

10. **Find (4 × 4) + (7 × 3) + (8 − 2).**
    - (F) 27
    - (G) 43
    - (H) 39
    - (J) 37

GO

Name ______________________________ Date ______________

11. **Find 9 − (4 × 2).**
   - (A) 10
   - (B) 1
   - (C) 7
   - (D) 17

12. **Find (9 − 4) × 2.**
   - (F) 10
   - (G) 1
   - (H) 7
   - (J) 17

13. **Find (9 − 4) × (2 × 1).**
   - (A) 17
   - (B) 7
   - (C) 10
   - (D) 1

14. **Find 48 − [42 − (3 × 9)].**
   - (F) 27
   - (G) 9
   - (H) 21
   - (J) 33

15. **Find 63 − [(8 ÷ 2) + (14 − 10)].**
   - (A) 63
   - (B) 55
   - (C) 59
   - (D) 71

16. **Find 800 ÷ (200 × 4).**
   - (F) 16
   - (G) 150
   - (H) 1,600
   - (J) 1

17. **Find 28 + [10 − (4 + 2)].**
   - (A) 32
   - (B) 36
   - (C) 34
   - (D) 20

18. **Find (11 − 5) × (10 + 14).**
   - (F) 25
   - (G) 74
   - (H) 144
   - (J) 60

19. **The school play sold out every night. The play ran for 3 nights, and 345 people attended each night. Tickets cost $4.25 each. How much money did the school play make?**
   - (A) $1,239.50
   - (B) $1,466.25
   - (C) $1,035.00
   - (D) $4,398.75

20. **A store manager ordered 4 cases of juice boxes. There are 6 boxes in each package and 12 packages in a case. How many juice boxes did he order all together?**
   - (F) 24 boxes
   - (G) 288 boxes
   - (H) 48 boxes
   - (J) 72 boxes

STOP

Name ______________________ Date ______________

Mathematics

3B.4

Number Sense

Multiplying and Dividing

DIRECTIONS: Choose the best answer.

You can check your answers in a division problem by multiplying your answer by the divisor.

1. Find 777 ÷ 7.

- (A) 10
- (B) 11
- (C) 100
- (D) 111

2. Find 185 ÷ 5.

- (F) 37
- (G) 36
- (H) 180
- (J) 190

3. Find 88 ÷ 8.

- (A) 8
- (B) 0
- (C) 1
- (D) 11

4. Find 46 × 82.

- (F) 3,772
- (G) 3,672
- (H) 3,662
- (J) 128

5. Find 444 ÷ 6.

- (A) 78
- (B) 63
- (C) 74
- (D) 64

6. Find 12 × 12.

- (F) 240
- (G) 144
- (H) 140
- (J) 24

7. Find 304 × 57.

- (A) 361
- (B) 247
- (C) 17,328
- (D) 19,380

8. Find 42 ÷ 7.

- (F) 49
- (G) 294
- (H) 35
- (J) 6

9. Find 145 × 32.

- (A) 4,640
- (B) 725
- (C) 177
- (D) 4,760

10. Find 464 ÷ 4.

- (F) 460
- (G) 468
- (H) 116
- (J) 232

STOP

Name ______________________ Date ______________

Mathematics

3C.1

Number Sense

Estimating Whole Number Computations

DIRECTIONS: Choose the best answer.

Example:

Each of the 4 members of a relay team runs 440 yards. What is the approximate total distance the team will run?

- (A) 800 yards
- (B) 444 yards
- (C) 1,600 yards
- (D) 2,000 yards

Answer: (C)

1. Benjamin delivers 165 papers each day. Approximately how many papers does he deliver in a week?

- (A) 1,400
- (B) 700
- (C) 900
- (D) 1,500

2. A plane travels 922 kilometers in 2 hours. The same distance was traveled each hour. Approximately how far did the plane travel each hour?

- (F) 922 kilometers
- (G) 400 kilometers
- (H) 450 kilometers
- (J) 500 kilometers

3. There are 158 nails in a 1-pound pack. Approximately how many nails will be in a 5-pound pack?

- (A) 1,000
- (B) 500
- (C) 2,000
- (D) 50

4. It takes 1,212 photographs to fill 6 photo albums. Approximately how many photos are in each album?

- (F) 60
- (G) 100
- (H) 50
- (J) 200

5. A contractor estimated that it would take 2,032 bricks to build each of the 4 walls of a new house. Approximately how many bricks would it take to build all 4 walls?

- (A) 2,072
- (B) 2,000
- (C) 9,000
- (D) 8,000

6. There are 7 boxes on a truck. Each box weighs about 680 kilograms. Approximately what is the weight of all the boxes?

- (F) 4,900 kilograms
- (G) 490 kilograms
- (H) 4,200 kilograms
- (J) 4,000 kilograms

Name ______________________ Date ______________

Mathematics

Number Sense

3C.2

Estimating Decimal Computations

DIRECTIONS: Estimate the answers of the following number sentences to the nearest whole number.

1. 4.2 + 5.2 = __________
2. 6.4 + 1.5 = __________
3. 3.1 + 7.8 = __________
4. 4.7 + 3.2 = __________
5. 4.9 + 2.0 = __________
6. 5.9 – 3.2 = __________
7. 6.7 – 5.6 = __________
8. 7.8 – 2.5 = __________
9. 5.8 – 3.3 = __________
10. 3.9 – 1.5 = __________

DIRECTIONS: Estimate the following to one decimal place.

11. .23 + .25 = __________
12. .43 + .16 = __________
13. .26 + .42 = __________
14. .64 + .15 = __________
15. .68 – .31 = __________
16. 5.34 – 2.43 = __________

STOP

Name ______________________________ Date ______________

Mathematics Number Sense

3D.1

Determining Percentages

DIRECTIONS: Mrs. Brett's fourth grade class has 16 girls and 12 boys. Use this information to answer the following questions.

1. What number is 50% of the girls in the class?

Ⓐ 6
Ⓑ 8
Ⓒ 12
Ⓓ 14

2. What number is 50% of the boys in the class?

Ⓕ 6
Ⓖ 8
Ⓗ 12
Ⓙ 14

3. What number is 50% of all students in the class?

Ⓐ 8
Ⓑ 12
Ⓒ 14
Ⓓ 16

4. What number is 100% of all students in the class?

Ⓕ 12
Ⓖ 24
Ⓗ 28
Ⓙ 26

DIRECTIONS: During the school year, Mrs. Brett has four new boys transfer in and two girls transfer out of her class. Use this information to answer the following questions.

5. What number is now 100% of the class?

Ⓐ 34
Ⓑ 24
Ⓒ 30
Ⓓ 32

6. What number is 50% of the girls in the class?

Ⓕ 7
Ⓖ 8
Ⓗ 6
Ⓙ 9

7. What number is 50% of the boys in the class?

Ⓐ 6
Ⓑ 8
Ⓒ 9
Ⓓ 7

8. What number is 50% of all students in the class?

Ⓕ 15
Ⓖ 14
Ⓗ 17
Ⓙ 16

STOP

Name ______________________ Date ______________

Mathematics

3

For pages 73–86

Mini-Test 1

Number Sense

DIRECTIONS: Answer each question.

1. **Write seventy one hundredths as a decimal.**

____

2. **On a number line, is $-\frac{2}{3}$ to the right or left of $-\frac{1}{2}$?**

____

DIRECTIONS: Choose the best answer.

3. **Joaquim is eating a pizza. The pizza has eight slices and Joaquim eats five. What fraction of the pizza did Joaquim eat?**

   Ⓐ $\frac{1}{8}$

   Ⓑ $\frac{3}{8}$

   Ⓒ $\frac{2}{8}$

   Ⓓ $\frac{5}{8}$

4. **Find (14 + 5) + (9 × 3) − 1.**

   Ⓕ 30

   Ⓖ 31

   Ⓗ 46

   Ⓙ 45

5. **Find 5 − (2 × 2).**

   Ⓐ 0

   Ⓑ 1

   Ⓒ 2

   Ⓓ 3

6. **Which of the following expressions does not equal 24?**

   Ⓕ 8 × 3

   Ⓖ 4 × 6

   Ⓗ 2 × 12

   Ⓙ 2 × 2 × 3

7. **Which of the following expressions does not equal 40?**

   Ⓐ 4 × 10

   Ⓑ 2 × 20

   Ⓒ 5 × 7

   Ⓓ 2 × 2 × 2 × 5

8. **Which of the following numbers is *not* prime?**

   Ⓕ 19

   Ⓖ 29

   Ⓗ 49

   Ⓙ 59

9. **Which of the following numbers is prime?**

   Ⓐ 87

   Ⓑ 89

   Ⓒ 91

   Ⓓ 93

10. **What are the factors of 47?**

   Ⓕ 6, 8

   Ⓖ 9, 5

   Ⓗ 1, 47

   Ⓙ 2, 23

STOP

Mathematics Standards

Estimate, Make, and Use Measurement

Goal 4: Estimate, make, and use measurement of objects, quantities, and relationships and determine acceptable levels of accuracy.

Learning Standard 4A—Students who meet the standard can measure and compare quantities using appropriate units, instruments, and methods. *(Performance and conversion of measurements)*

1. Measure angles using a protractor or angle ruler. *(See page 89.)*
2. Measure with a greater degree of accuracy. *(See page 89.)*
3. Convert U.S. customary measurements into larger or smaller units with the help of conversion charts. *(See pages 90–91.)*
4. Convert linear metric measurements into larger or smaller units with the help of a conversion chart. *(See page 92.)*

Learning Standard 4B—Students who meet the standard can estimate measurements and determine acceptable levels of accuracy. *(Estimation)*

1. Develop and discuss strategies for estimating the perimeters, areas, and volumes of regular and nonregular shapes. *(See pages 93–94.)*
2. Develop and use common referents for volume, weight/mass, capacity, area, and angle measures to make comparisons and estimates. *(See pages 95–96.)*

Learning Standard 4C—Students who meet the standard can select and use appropriate technology, instruments, and formulas to solve problems, interpret results, and communicate findings. *(Progression from selection of appropriate tools and methods to application of measurements to solve problems)*

1. Select and apply appropriate standard units and tools to measure the size of angles. *(See page 97.)*
2. Determine the volume of a cube or rectangular prism using concrete materials. *(See pages 98–99.)*
3. Create an accurate representation of a polygon with a given perimeter or area. *(See page 100.)*

Name ______________________________ Date ______________

Mathematics

4A.1/4A.2

Measuring Angles

Estimate, Make, and Use Measurement

DIRECTIONS: Use a protractor or angle ruler to measure the following angles.

1. ____________

2. ____________

3. ____________

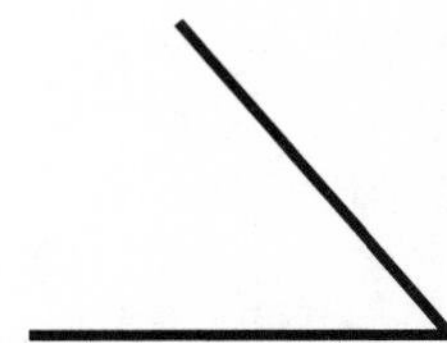

4. ____________

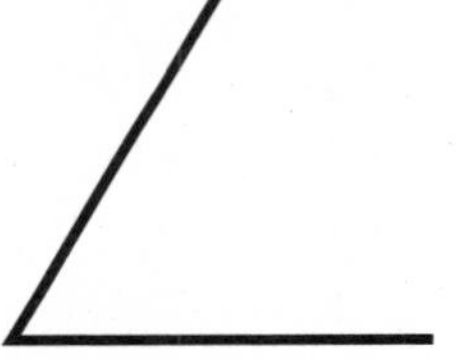

5. ____________

6. ____________

7. ____________

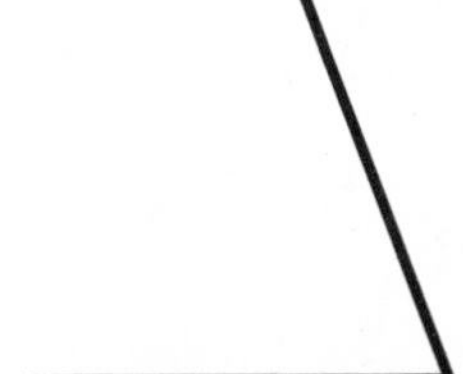

8. ____________

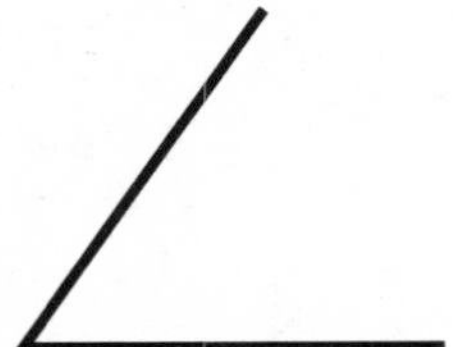

9. ____________

STOP

Name ______________________________ Date ______________

Mathematics

4A.3

Converting U.S. Customary Measurements

Estimate, Make, and Use Measurement

DIRECTIONS: Fill in the blanks with the equivalent measurement. Use the conversion chart below to help you find your answers.

Length:
1 foot = 12 inches
1 yard = 3 feet
1 mile = 5,280 feet

1. 7 yards = _______ feet
2. 24 inches = _______ feet
3. 6 feet = _______ yard(s)
4. 10 miles = _______ feet
5. 60 inches = _______ feet
6. 30 feet = _______ yard(s)
7. 5 feet + 2 inches = _______ inches
8. 3 feet = _______ inches
9. 1 yard + 4 inches = _______ inches
10. 1/2 mile = _______ feet
11. 1 yard − 1 foot = _______ feet
12. 46 inches − 10 inches = _______ yard(s)
13. 4 yards = _______ feet
14. 7 feet − 4 feet = _______ yard(s)
15. 1 yard + 3 inches = _______ inches

Name ______________________________ Date ______________

DIRECTIONS: Fill in the blanks with the equivalent measurement. Use the conversion chart below to help you find your answers.

Capacity:
1 tablespoon = 3 teaspoons
1 cup = 16 tablespoons = 8 fluid ounces
1 pint = 2 cups
1 quart = 2 pints
1 gallon = 4 quarts

16. 18 pints = _______ quarts

17. 28 quarts = _______ pints

18. 10 pints = _______ cups

19. 18 cups = _______ quarts

20. 4 tablespoons = _______ teaspoons

21. 24 quarts = _______ gallons

22. 5 pints = _______ fluid ounces

23. 1 quart = _______ fluid ounces

24. 2 cups = _______ tablespoons

DIRECTIONS: Fill in the blanks with the equivalent measurement. Use the conversion chart below to help you find your answers.

Weight:
1 pound (lb.) = 16 ounces (oz.)
1 ton (t.) = 2,000 pounds (lbs.)

25. 2 lbs. = _______ oz.

26. 160 oz. = _______ lbs.

27. 15 lbs. = _______ oz.

28. 16,000 lbs. = _______ t.

29. 10 lbs. = _______ oz.

30. 5,000 lbs. = _______ t.

31. 6 t. = _______ lbs.

32. 20 lbs. = _______ oz.

33. 64 oz. = _______ lbs.

STOP

Name ______________________________ Date ______________

Mathematics

4A.4

Converting Linear Metric Measurements

Estimate, Make, and Use Measurement

DIRECTIONS: Use the conversion chart below to help you answer the questions.

Length:
1 centimeter (cm) = 10 millimeters (mm)
1 meter (m) = 100 centimeters (cm)
1 kilometer (km) = 1,000 meters (m)

1. Jodi measured her tomato plant. It is 34 centimeters. How many millimeters is this?

____

2. Meg has a plastic case that is 4 centimeters long. She found a shell that is 34 millimeters long. Will it fit in her case?

____

3. Kifa jumped 3 meters. How many centimeters is this?

____

4. Jordan's desk is 1 meter by 1 meter. He would like to put his science project inside his desk. The science project is on poster board that is 95 centimeters by 110 centimeters. Will it fit inside his desk without sticking out?

____

5. Anna is walking in a 5-kilometer charity event. How many meters will she walk by the time she reaches the finish line?

____

6. Jonathan is running in the 10,000-meter race. How many kilometers is the race?

____

7. Amar's room measures 10 meters by 12 meters. What is the room's measurements in centimeters?

____

Name ____________________ Date ____________________

Mathematics

4B.1

Estimating Area and Perimeter

Estimate, Make, and Use Measurement

DIRECTIONS: For each of the following figures, estimate the area. Circle the number choice that is most likely the area (in square units) beneath each figure.

You can estimate the area of an irregular shape by looking at the squares around it. In the example to the right, you know that 4 full squares are covered, so the area will be greater than 4 square units. You also know that the total figure is not larger than 16 square units (4 units × 4 units). You can estimate the area of the figure is between 4 and 16 square units.

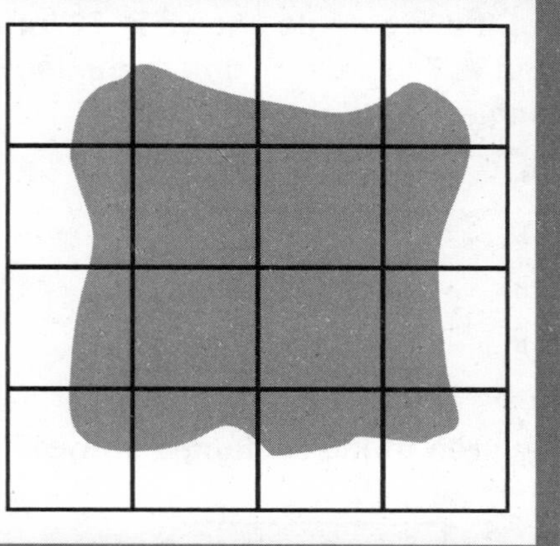

1.

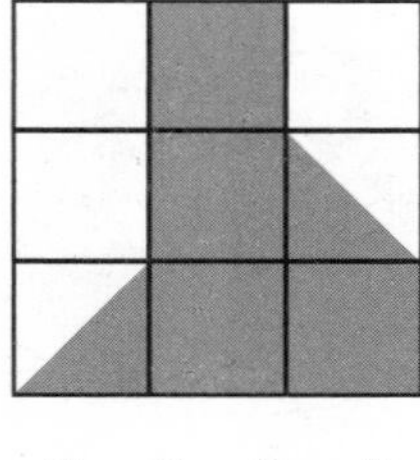

3 5 9 2

2.

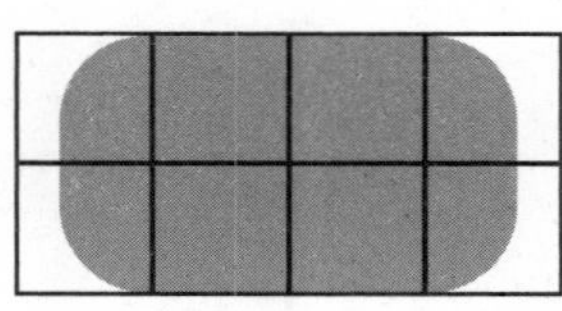

9 8 6 4

3.

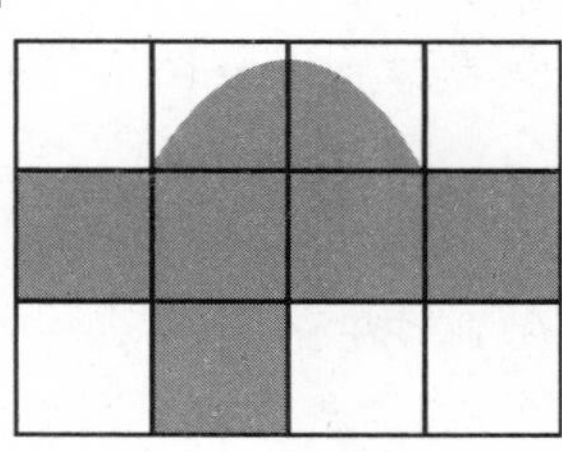

5 6 12 4

4.

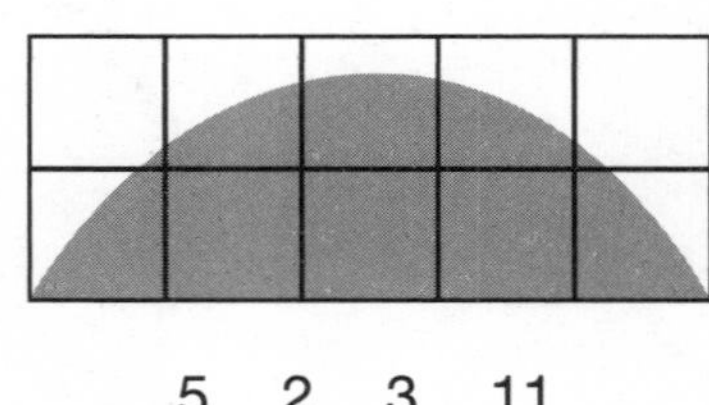

5 2 3 11

5.

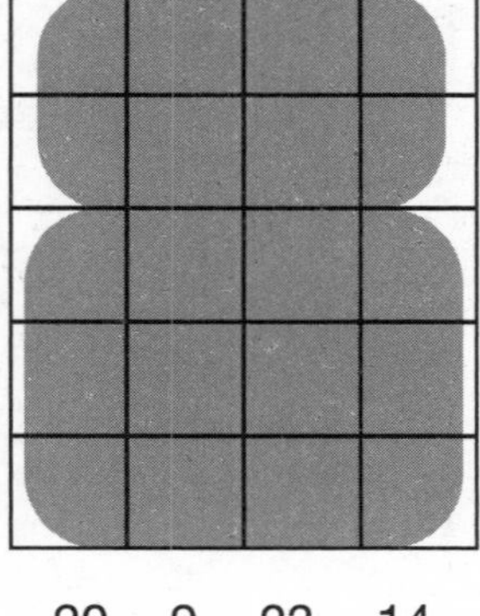

20 9 23 14

6.

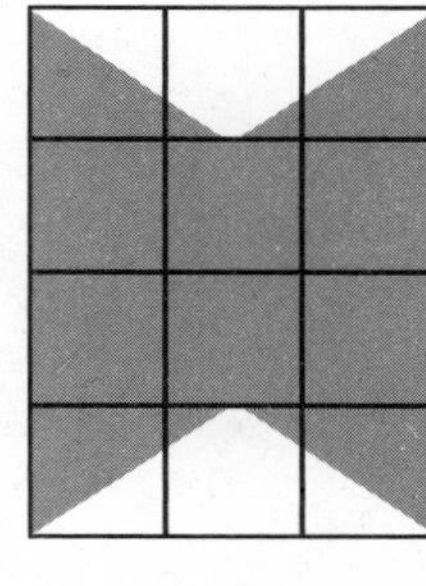

5 9 6 14

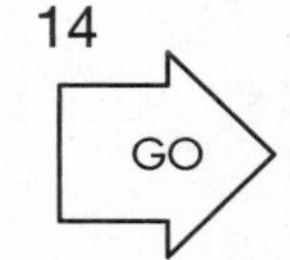

Name ______________________ Date ______________

DIRECTIONS: Choose the best answer.

7. Estimate the area of the square shown.

Ⓐ 32 yd.^{2}
Ⓑ 64 yd.^{2}
Ⓒ 100 yd.^{2}
Ⓓ 900 yd.^{2}

32 yd.
32 yd.

8. If the area of the rectangle shown is 72 in.^{2} and the width is 7 inches, estimate the length of the rectangle.

Ⓕ 5 in.
Ⓖ 6 in.
Ⓗ 10 in.
Ⓙ 20 in.

7 in.

9. Estimate the area of the rectangle shown.

51 cm
140 cm

Ⓐ 7,000 cm^2
Ⓑ 3,000 cm^2
Ⓒ 500 cm
Ⓓ 80 cm

10. A square has sides measuring 41 centimeters. Estimate the square's perimeter.

Ⓕ 80 cm
Ⓖ 100 cm
Ⓗ 160 cm
Ⓙ 400 cm

11. A square has sides measuring 152 inches. Estimate the square's perimeter.

Ⓐ 300 in.
Ⓑ 600 in.
Ⓒ 1,800 in.
Ⓓ 15,000 in.

12. A rectangle has sides measuring 31 centimeters and 98 centimeters. Estimate the rectangle's perimeter.

Ⓕ 130 cm
Ⓖ 320 cm
Ⓗ 240 cm
Ⓙ 260 cm

STOP

Name ______________________________ Date ______________

Mathematics

4B.2

Measuring Objects

Estimate, Make, and Use Measurement

DIRECTIONS: Choose the best answer.

1. **For which of the following would a quart be an appropriate unit of measure?**
   - (A) bananas
   - (B) breakfast cereal
   - (C) paper
   - (D) motor oil

2. **For which of the following would a pound be an appropriate unit of measure?**
   - (F) fruit punch
   - (G) bunch of bananas
   - (H) milk
   - (J) cooking oil

3. **Which of the following shows the units of measurement in correct order from least to greatest?**
   - (A) gallon, quart, pint, cup
   - (B) cup, gallon, pint, quart
   - (C) cup, pint, quart, gallon
   - (D) quart, gallon, cup, pint

4. **Which of the following is *not* a measure of liquid capacity?**
   - (F) ton
   - (G) gallon
   - (H) cup
   - (J) pint

5. **If you were ordering fruit punch for a party with 120 people, which unit of measurement would you most likely be using?**
   - (A) cups
   - (B) pints
   - (C) pounds
   - (D) gallons

DIRECTIONS: Show which metric units would be best to measure these common items and events by writing the letter of the appropriate units next to each item. Each unit should be used only once.

A. grams

B. milligrams

C. kilograms

D. liters

E. milliliters

F. kiloliters

_______ **6. weight of one apple**

_______ **7. dose of liquid baby medicine**

_______ **8. amount of water in a water tower**

_______ **9. amount of milk in a jug**

_______ **10. towing capacity of a truck**

_______ **11. weight of one pill**

GO

Name ______________________ Date ______________

DIRECTIONS: Circle the best unit of capacity or mass for measuring the objects and containers below.

12. mL L kL	**13.** mL L kL	**14.** mL L kL
15. mL L kL	**16.** mL L kL	**17.** mL L kL
18. g kg	**19.** g kg	**20.** g kg
21. g kg	**22.** g kg	**23.** g kg

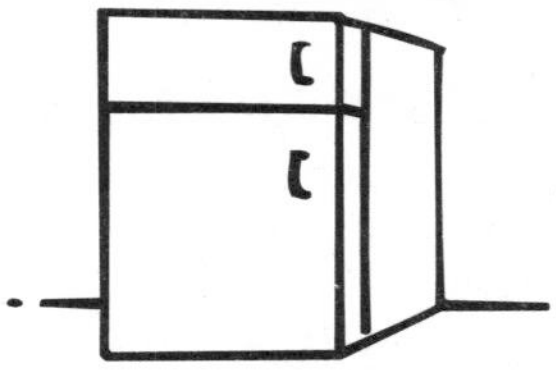

STOP

Name ______________________________ Date ______________

Mathematics

4C.1

Time Angles

Estimate, Make, and Use Measurement

DIRECTIONS: The size of an angle is measured in many ways. One method is to use degrees. The degrees tell you how far you rotated to make the angle. Think of the minute hand on a clock. In one hour, the hand sweeps around in one full circle, ending back where it started. It has made one full turn, which equals 360 degrees, or 360°. This chart shows angles measured by the rotation of a circle, the minutes on a clock, and degrees. Use it to help you with the questions below.

Rotation	Minutes	Degrees
$\frac{1}{4}$ turn	15	90
$\frac{1}{2}$ turn	30	180
$\frac{3}{4}$ turn	45	270
full turn	60	360

For each problem, write the degree measure of the angle made when the minute hand on a clock travels from the first time to the second time.

1. **3:15 to 3:30** 90 degrees
2. **7:45 to 8:15** ______
3. **4:15 to 5:15** ______
4. **2:00 to 2:45** ______
5. **6:30 to 7:00** ______
6. **11:15 to 11:45** ______
7. **9:30 to 10:00** ______
8. **5:45 to 6:30** ______
9. **4:15 to 5:00** ______
10. **1:30 to 2:00** ______
11. **8:45 to 9:00** ______
12. **4:25 to 4:40** ______
13. **9:30 to 10:30** ______
14. **3:30 to 3:45** ______
15. **4:20 to 4:50** ______
16. **7:03 to 7:48** ______
17. **5:10 to 5:25** ______
18. **2:15 to 2:30** ______
19. **6:04 to 6:49** ______
20. **7:48 to 8:48** ______

STOP

Name ______________________ Date ______________

Mathematics

4C.2

Finding Volume

Estimate, Make, and Use Measurement

DIRECTIONS: Find the number of cubes and volume for each figure below.

Example:

Volume—the amount of space inside a three-dimensional figure.

The volume of 1 cube is 1 cubic unit.

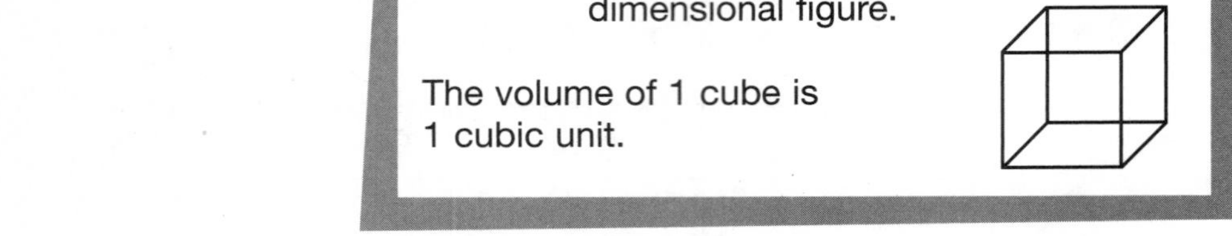

1. Number of cubes ______

Volume = ______ **cubic units**

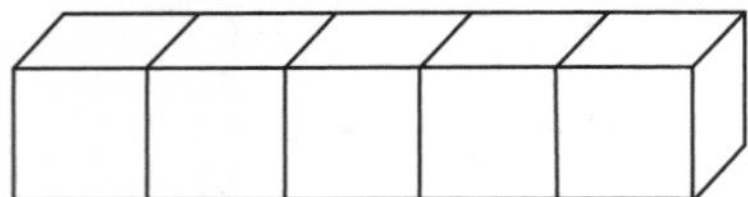

2. Number of cubes ______

Volume = ______ **cubic units**

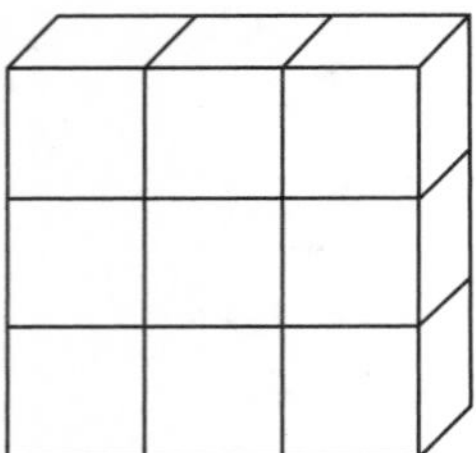

3. Number of cubes ______

Volume = ______ **cubic units**

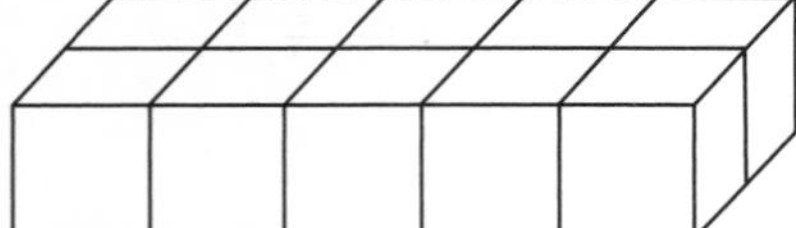

4. Number of cubes ______

Volume = ______ **cubic units**

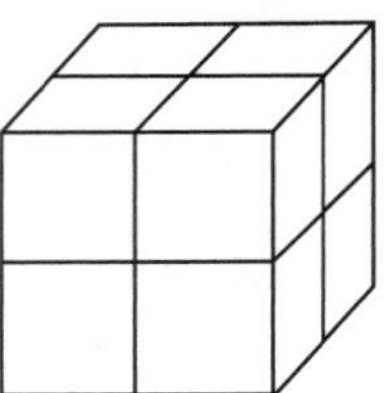

5. Number of cubes ______

Volume = ______ **cubic units**

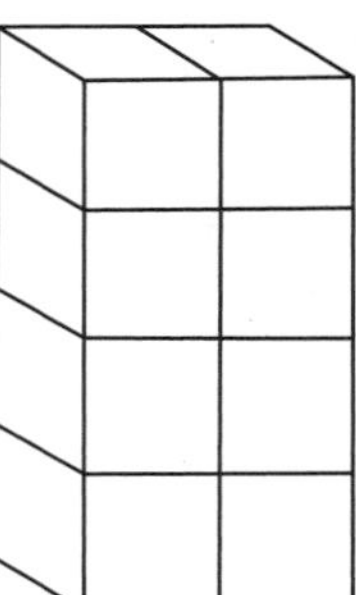

6. Number of cubes ______

Volume = ______ **cubic units**

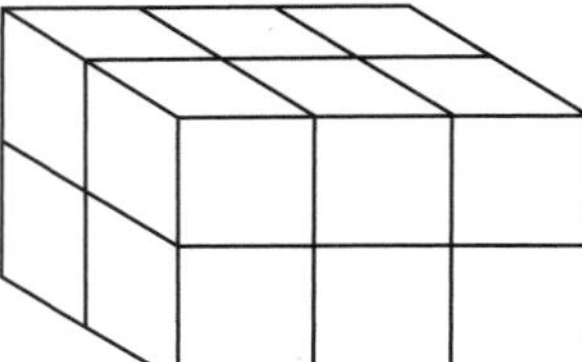

Name ______________________________ Date ______________

DIRECTIONS: Use the formula to determine the volume of the figures below. Match each figure to its correct volume.

Another way to find volume is to use the following rule:

Volume = length × width × height

7.

height = ______

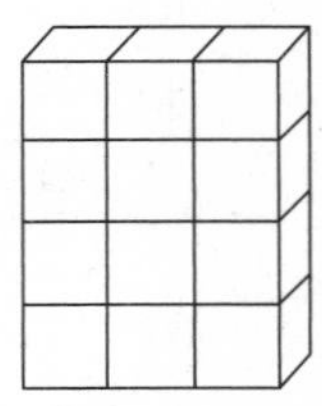

width = ______

length = ______

10 cubic units

8.

height = ______

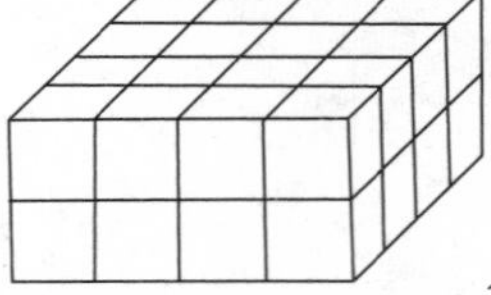

width = ______

length = ______

6 cubic units

9.

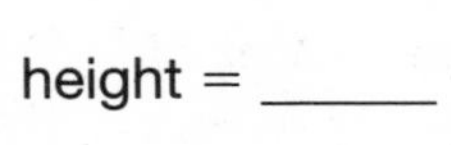

height = ______

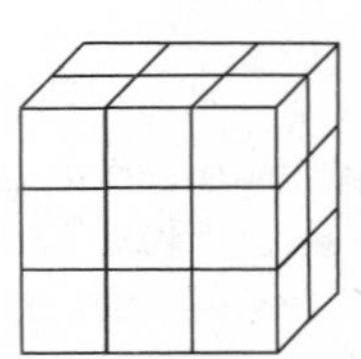

width = ______

length = ______

12 cubic units

10.

height = ______

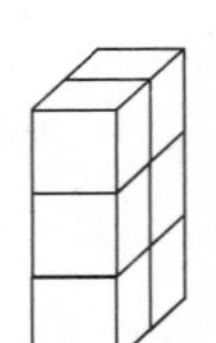

width = ______

length = ______

18 cubic units

11.

height = ______

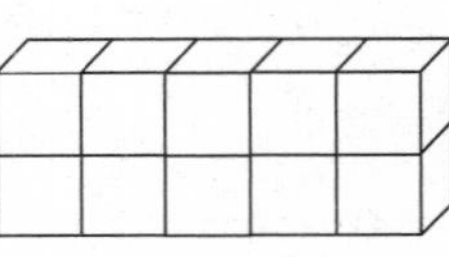

width = ______

length = ______

32 cubic units

STOP

Name ______________________________ Date ______________

Mathematics

4C.3

Creating Polygons

Estimate, Make, and Use Measurement

DIRECTIONS: Draw the polygons described.

1. **A polygon with a perimeter of 8 inches and four equal sides.**

2. **A three-sided polygon with a perimeter of 8 inches, having two sides of equal length.**

3. **A polygon with a perimeter of 19 centimeters and five sides.**

4. **A four-sided polygon with a perimeter of 6 inches; one set of two sides are of equal length, and the other set of two sides are a different equal length.**

Name ______________________________ Date ______________

Mathematics

4

For pages 89–100

Mini-Test 2

Estimate, Make, and Use Measurement

DIRECTIONS: Choose the best answer.

1. **A truck has 6 tons of cargo. How many pounds is that?**
   - (A) 12,000 pounds
   - (B) 1,200 pounds
   - (C) 120 pounds
   - (D) 12 pounds

2. **9 kilograms is how many grams?**
   - (F) 90,000 grams
   - (G) 90 grams
   - (H) 900 grams
   - (J) 9,000 grams

3. **Barb used 8 quarts of water when she washed her hands and face. How many pints of water did she use?**
   - (A) 8 pints
   - (B) 16 pints
   - (C) 24 pints
   - (D) 32 pints

4. **How many quarts of water would be needed to fill a 10-gallon aquarium?**
   - (F) 4 quarts
   - (G) 40 quarts
   - (H) 20 quarts
   - (J) 60 quarts

5. **The length of a rectangle is 41 inches and the width is 29 inches. Estimate the area of the rectangle.**
   - (A) 80 in.^{2}
   - (B) 800 in.^{2}
   - (C) 1,200 in.^{2}
   - (D) 140 in.^{2}

6. **Estimate the area of the following figure.**

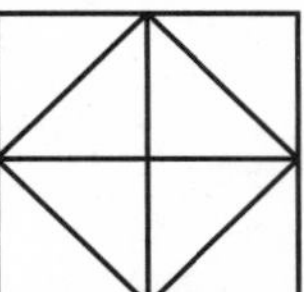

   - (F) 4 square units
   - (G) 5 square units
   - (H) 6 square units
   - (J) 8 square units

7. **What is the volume of this figure?**

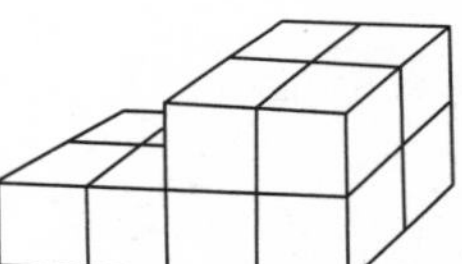

   - (A) 8 cubic units
   - (B) 10 cubic units
   - (C) 12 cubic units
   - (D) 14 cubic units

8. **What is the degree measure of the angle made when the minute hand on a clock travels from 2:25 to 3:10?**
   - (F) 90 degrees
   - (G) 180 degrees
   - (H) 270 degrees
   - (J) 360 degrees

STOP

Mathematics Standards

Use Algebraic and Analytical Methods

Goal 5: Use algebraic and analytical methods to identify and describe patterns and relationships in data, solve problems, and predict results.

Learning Standard 5A—Students who meet the standard can describe numerical relationships using variables and patterns. *(Representations and algebraic manipulations)*

1. Identify a number pattern, both increasing and decreasing, and extend the number sequence. *(See page 103.)*
2. Determine the missing number(s) in a complex repeating pattern. *(See page 104.)*
3. Construct and solve simple number sentences using a symbol for a variable. *(See page 105.)*
4. Make generalizations given a specific pattern. *(See page 106.)*
5. Create, describe, and extend patterns. *(See page 107.)*
6. Describe a pattern with one operation, verbally and symbolically, given a table of input/output numbers. *(See page 108.)*

Learning Standard 5B—Students who meet the standard can interpret and describe numerical relationships using tables, graphs, and symbols. *(Connections of representations including the rate of change)*

1. Create a table that describes a function rule for a single operation. *(See page 109.)*
2. Demonstrate, in simple situations, how a change in one quantity results in a change in another quantity (e.g., increase the measure of the side of a square and the perimeter increases). *(See page 110.)*
3. Identify situations with varying rates of change using words, tables, and graphs (e.g., growth of a plant). *(See pages 111–112.)*

Learning Standard 5C—Students who meet the standard can solve problems using systems of numbers and their properties. *(Problem solving: number systems, systems of equations, inequalities, algebraic functions)*

1. Solve problems with whole numbers using appropriate field properties. *(See page 113.)*

Learning Standard 5D—Students who meet the standard can use algebraic concepts and procedures to represent and solve problems.

1. Solve one-step linear equations with one missing value in isolation and in problem-solving situations. *(See page 114.)*

Name ________________________ Date ____________

Mathematics

5A.1

Identifying and Extending Number Patterns

Use Algebraic and Analytical Methods

DIRECTIONS: Find the pattern in each row of numbers. Continue the pattern to fill in the blanks. Then match the pattern to the correct rule.

Pattern	Rule
1. 1, 3, 5, ___, ___, 11, 13	−11
2. 70, ___, 50, ___, ___, 20, 10	+12
3. 1, 8, 15, 22, ___, ___, ___	+8
4. 36, 33, 30, ___, ___, ___, ___	−9
5. 115, 100, 85, ___, ___, ___, ___	+2
6. 64, 55, 46, ___, ___, ___, ___	−10
7. 17, 25, 33, ___, ___, ___, ___	−3
8. 96, ___, 84, 78, ___, ___, ___	−15
9. 88, ___, 66, ___, 44, ___, ___	−6
10. 12, 24, 36, ___, ___, ___, ___	+7

11. If you were to continue pattern 3, what would be the next three numbers in the pattern?

____

12. If you were to continue pattern 8, what would be the next three numbers in the pattern?

____

STOP

Name ______________________ Date ______________

Mathematics

5A.2

Finding Missing Numbers in Patterns

Use Algebraic and Analytical Methods

DIRECTIONS: Find the pattern in each row of numbers. Fill in the missing number and explain the rule for each pattern.

1. **1, 2, 3, 5, 8, 13, ______, 34**

   Rule: ______________________

2. **4, 5, 7, 10, 14, 19, 25, ______**

   Rule: ______________________

3. **80, 77, 71, ______, 50, 35, 17**

   Rule: ______________________

4. **20, 21, 19, 22, 18, 23, ______, 24**

   Rule: ______________________

5. **12, 23, ______, 89, 177, 353, 705**

   Rule: ______________________

6. **4, 8, 16, 28, ______, 64, 88, 116**

   Rule: ______________________

7. **______, 88, 86, 83, 79, 74, 68, 61**

   Rule: ______________________

8. **15, 17, 21, 27, 35, 45, 57, ______**

   Rule: ______________________

9. **56, 53, 55, 52, 54, ______, 53, 50**

   Rule: ______________________

10. **76, 81, 73, ______, 70, 75, 67, 72**

    Rule: ______________________

STOP

Name ______________________________ Date ______________

Mathematics

5A.3

Working With Variables

Use Algebraic and Analytical Methods

DIRECTIONS: Choose a variable for the unknown amount. Then, write a number sentence to represent the problem. Finally, find the solution.

Example:

Kyle made a dozen cookies. His little sister ate 5 of them. How many cookies are left?

Variable: Let c = number of cookies left
Number sentences: $c + 5 = 12$
Solution: $c = 7$

A **variable** is an amount that is not known. It is often represented by a letter. Variables are used in number sentences to represent a situation.

1. **Julie is playing a board game. She rolls a 3 on the first die. What must she roll on the second die to move 9 spaces?**

   Variable: ______________________________

   Number sentence: ______________________________

   Solution: ______________________________

2. **Jacob has a bag with 4 pieces of candy. His father puts another handful into the bag. Jacob then has 13 pieces. How many pieces did his father give him?**

   Variable: ______________________________

   Number sentence: ______________________________

   Solution: ______________________________

3. **A factory has 314 workers. The owner gave a total bonus of $612,300 to all of the workers. Each worker got the same amount. What amount of the bonus did each worker receive?**

   Variable: ______________________________

   Number sentence: ______________________________

   Solution: ______________________________

4. **Kayla's cat had 7 kittens. So far she has given away 5 of them. How many kittens are left?**

   Variable: ______________________________

   Number sentence: ______________________________

   Solution: ______________________________

STOP

Name ______________________ Date ______________

Mathematics

5A.4

Making Generalizations From Patterns

Use Algebraic and Analytical Methods

DIRECTIONS: Choose the best answer. Mr. Pontario's students are making number charts and labeling the squares from 1 to 100.

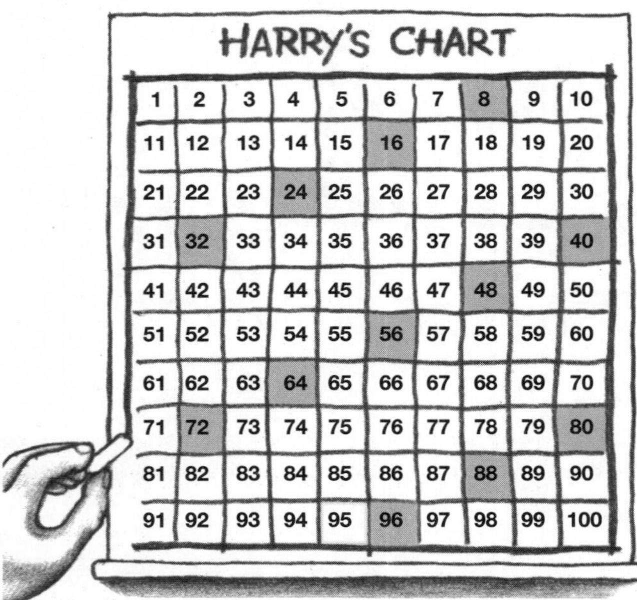

1. Liza is making a number chart. If she shades only the multiples of 4, her chart will have ________ .

Ⓐ about three-fourths as many shaded numbers as Harry's

Ⓑ about two-thirds as many shaded numbers as Harry's

Ⓒ about one-half as many shaded numbers as Harry's

Ⓓ about twice as many shaded numbers as Harry's

2. Tenisha just made a number chart on which she shaded all the multiples of 5. Which pattern shows the shading on her number chart?

Ⓕ 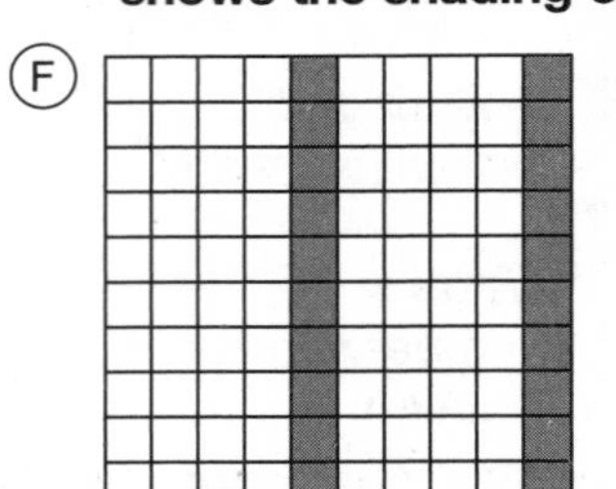

Ⓗ 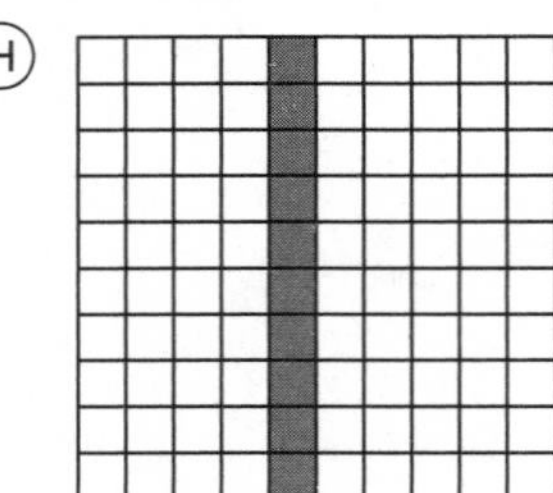

Ⓖ 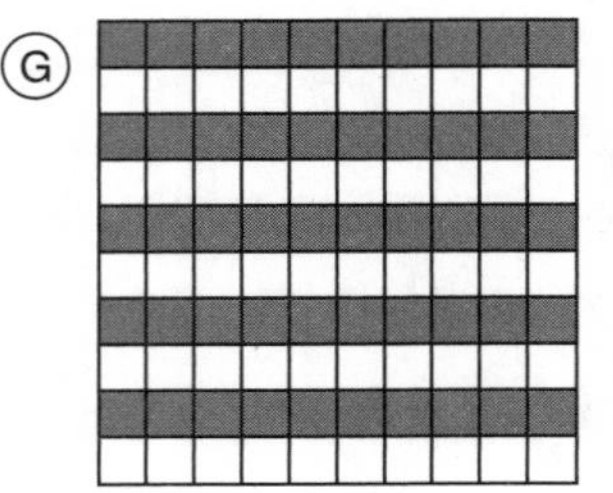

Ⓙ 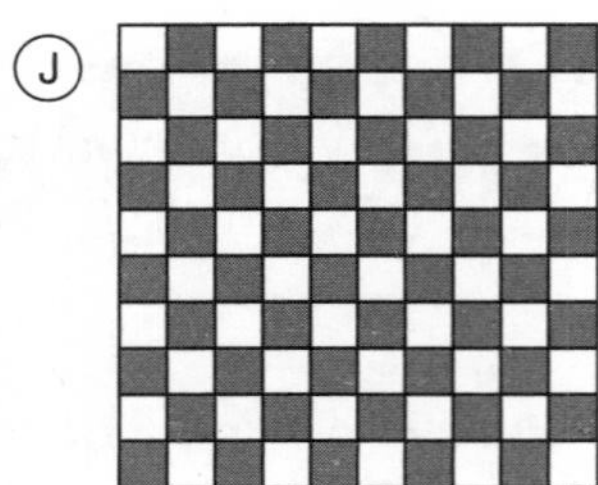

3. Which of these number sentences would help you find the total number of flags?

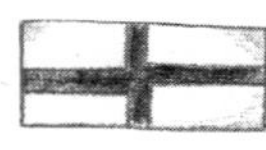
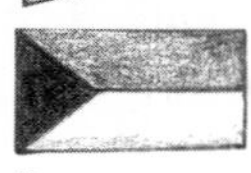

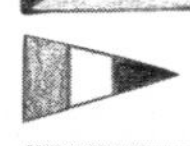

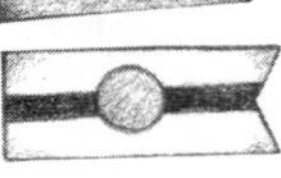
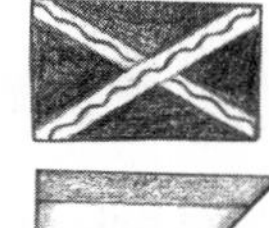
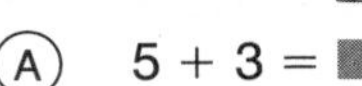

Ⓐ $5 + 3 = \blacksquare$

Ⓑ $5 - 3 = \blacksquare$

Ⓒ $5 \times 3 = \blacksquare$

Ⓓ $5 \div 3 = \blacksquare$

STOP

Name ______________________ Date ______________

Mathematics

5A.5

Creating Patterns

Use Algebraic and Analytical Methods

DIRECTIONS: Create a pattern following the directions given. Give eight numbers for each pattern.

Example:

Start with the number 3 and add 2 to each number.

Pattern: 3, 5, 7, 9, 11, 13, 15, 17

1. **Start with the number 80 and subtract 8 from each number.**

   Pattern: ______________________

   ____

2. **Start with the number 9 and add 13 to each number.**

   Pattern: ______________________

   ____

3. **Start with the number 16 and add consecutive integers (starting with 1) to each number.**

   Pattern: ______________________

   ____

4. **Start with the number 123 and subtract consecutive odd integers (starting with 1) from each number.**

   Pattern: ______________________

   ____

5. **Start with the number 53, add 9 to get the next number, subtract 3 for the next result, repeat.**

   Pattern: ______________________

   ____

6. **Start with the number 23 and add consecutive even integers (starting with 2) to each number.**

   Pattern: ______________________

   ____

7. **Start with the number 74 and subtract decreasing consecutive integers (starting with 12) from each number.**

   Pattern: ______________________

   ____

STOP

Name ______________________________ Date ______________

Mathematics

Using Input/Output Tables

Use Algebraic and Analytical Methods

DIRECTIONS: The function machine uses rules to change numbers. Look for a pattern in the IN and OUT numbers in each table. Fill in the table. Write the rule using variables (e.g., IN + 2 = OUT).

1.

IN	78	15	41	22	37		55
OUT	65	2	28			3	

Rule: ______________________________

2.

IN	2	9	81	76	37		
OUT	11	18		85		34	51

Rule: ______________________________

3.

IN	82	16	70	34	44		60
OUT	41	8			22	25	

Rule: ______________________________

4.

IN	23	7	15		42		
OUT	69	21		33		81	18

Rule: ______________________________

Name ______________________________ Date ______________

Mathematics

5B.1

Linear Function Rules

Use Algebraic and Analytical Methods

DIRECTIONS: Complete the table for each function rule given below.

Example:

Rule: $m = n + 3$

IN (n)	12	14	16	18	20	22
OUT (m)	15	17	19			

Answer: 21, 23, 25

1. Rule: $m = 3n$

IN (n)	0	1	2	3	4	5
OUT (m)						

2. Rule: $m = 3n - 3$

IN (n)	2	4	6	8	10	12
OUT (m)						

3. Rule: $m = n + 4$

IN (n)	6	7	9	11	14	16
OUT (m)						

4. Rule: $m = n \times 4$

IN (n)	1	3	6	8	10	13
OUT (m)						

5. Rule: $m = n - 2$

IN (n)	10	13	16	19	22	25
OUT (m)						

STOP

Name ____________________ Date ____________

Mathematics

5B.2

Quantity and Change

Use Algebraic and Analytical Methods

DIRECTIONS: This is Chris's favorite sugar cookie recipe. Use it to answer the questions.

Sugar Cookies

1/3 cup butter or margarine, softened
1/3 cup shortening
3/4 cup sugar
1 teaspoon baking powder
pinch salt
1 egg
1 teaspoon vanilla
2 cups all-purpose flour

Beat butter and shortening thoroughly. Add sugar, baking powder and a pinch of salt and mix until well combined. Beat in egg and vanilla and flour.
Cover and chill for at least 1 hour. Split the dough in 1/2 and roll one half at a time. Cut out with cookie cutters.
Bake at 325° on ungreased cookie sheets for about 7 to 8 minutes, until edges are firm and bottoms are lightly browned (don't over cook).
Makes 36 cookies.

1. If Chris bakes 36 cookies, how much flour does he need?

- (A) 1 cup
- (B) $1\frac{1}{2}$ cups
- (C) 2 cups
- (D) 3 cups

2. If Chris bakes 2 batches of cookies, how many cookies will he bake?

- (F) 66
- (G) 72
- (H) 76
- (J) 84

3. How much flour will he need to bake the 2 batches of cookies?

- (A) 2 cups
- (B) $2\frac{1}{2}$ cups
- (C) 3 cups
- (D) 4 cups

4. Chris needs to bake 3 batches of cookies for a party. How much butter or margarine does he use?

- (F) $\frac{1}{3}$ cup
- (G) $\frac{2}{3}$ cup
- (H) 1 cup
- (J) 3 cups

STOP

Name ______________________ Date ______________

Mathematics

5B.3

Rates of Change

Use Algebraic and Analytical Methods

DIRECTIONS: Answer the following.

1. **Look for a pattern in the following shapes. Fill in the table.**

Pattern A:

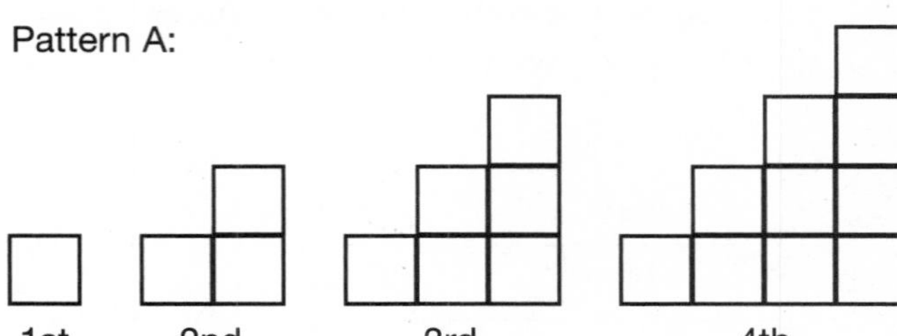

Shape	Number of Tiles
1st	1
2nd	3
3rd	6
4th	10
5th	
6th	
7th	
8th	

2. **Explain how the pattern grows.**

____

____

____

____

____

____

3. **If the pattern continues, how many tiles will be in the 10th shape?** ________

4. **Doug is planning a party. He has to plan where to seat people. He can seat one guest on each open end of a table. He must group the tables in rectangles. Look for a pattern and fill in the table below.**

Pattern B:

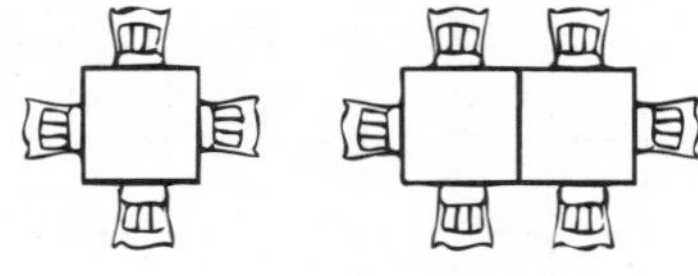

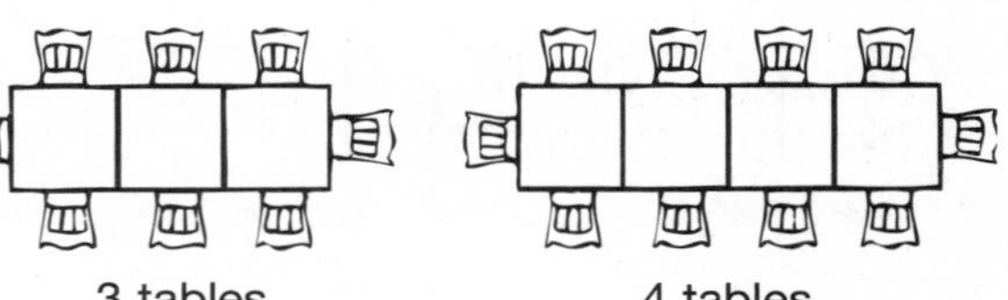

Number of Tables	1	2	3	4	5	6	7	8
Number of Guests	4	6	8	10				

5. **Explain how the pattern grows.**

____

____

____

____

____

____

6. **If the pattern continues, how many guests will be able to sit at 10 tables?** ________

GO

Name ______________________________ Date ______________

7. **For pattern A, make a graph showing how the number of tiles increases for each shape. On the coordinate grid below, plot a point for each ordered pair (shape, number of tiles) in your table from problem 1. You may have to estimate the location of the point.**

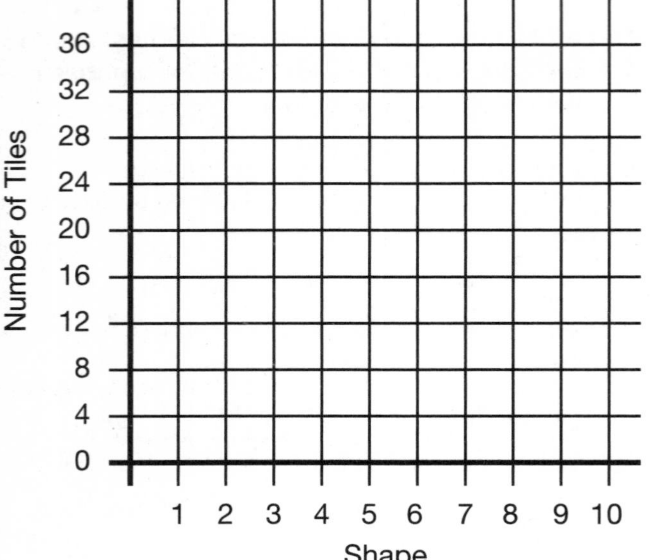

8. **For pattern B, make a graph showing how the number of tiles increases for each shape. Plot a point to represent each ordered pair (number of tables, number of guests) in your table from problem number 4. You may have to estimate the location of the point.**

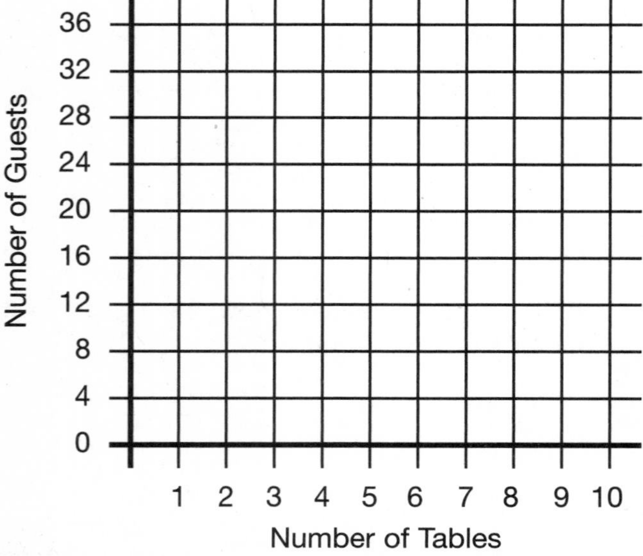

9. **Which pattern has higher values at the beginning? ______________ The end? ______________**

10. **Look at the tables and the graphs and compare the two patterns. Does one grow faster or slower, or do they grow at the same rate? Write a sentence or two comparing the growth of the two patterns.**

____

____

____

____

____

____

____

____

STOP

Name ______________________ Date ______________

Mathematics

5C.1

Associative and Distributive Properties

Use Algebraic and Analytical Methods

DIRECTIONS: Choose the best answer.

Examples:

The **associative property** means you can change the grouping of numbers and still get the same answers. The associative property only works with equations of addition or multiplication. For example:

$$(12 + 3) + 5 = 12 + (3 + 5) \text{ or}$$
$$(12 \times 3) \times 5 = 12 \times (3 \times 5)$$

The **distributive property** is used when there is a combination of multiplication over addition or subtraction. The number being multiplied is distributed to each number that is being added or subtracted. For example:

$$12(3 + 5) = (12 \times 3) + (12 \times 5)$$

1. Which of the following expressions is equal to the expression $3(2 + 4)$?

- (A) $2 + 4$
- (B) $2 + (3 \times 4)$
- (C) $(3 \times 2) + (3 \times 4)$
- (D) $(3 \times 2) + 4$

2. Which of the following expressions is equal to the expression $2 \times (3 \times 6) \times 4$?

- (F) $(2 \times 3) \times 6 \times 4$
- (G) $2 \times 3 \times (6 \times 4)$
- (H) $(2 \times 3) \times (6 \times 4)$
- (J) All of the above

3. Which of the following expressions is equal to the expression $(8 \times 2) - (3 \times 2)$?

- (A) 16×6
- (B) $(8 - 3)2$
- (C) $(8 \times 3) - 2$
- (D) None of the above

4. Which of the following expressions is equal to the expression $(7 + 8) + 6$?

- (F) $7 + (8 + 6)$
- (G) $7(8 + 6)$
- (H) $(7 + 8)6$
- (J) None of the above

5. Which of the following expressions is equal to the expression $4(9 - 5)$?

- (A) $9 - (4 \times 5)$
- (B) $9 - 5 \times 4$
- (C) $(4 \times 9) - 5$
- (D) $(4 \times 9) - (4 \times 5)$

6. $2(6 + 3) =$ ______

- (F) 11
- (G) 12
- (H) 15
- (J) 18

7. $(15 - 3)2 =$ ______

- (A) 27
- (B) 24
- (C) 9
- (D) 14

8. $3 \times (8 \times 2) \times 6 =$ ______

- (F) 288
- (G) 54
- (H) 99
- (J) 146

STOP

Name ______________________ Date ______________

Mathematics

5D.1

Solving Equations

Use Algebraic and Analytical Methods

To solve two-variable equations, substitute the given value for x and evaluate the equation to get y.

DIRECTIONS: Choose the best answer. For numbers 1–4, let $y = 5x + 8$.

1. What is *y* when *x* is 2?

- (A) 15
- (B) 13
- (C) 18
- (D) 21

2. What is *y* when *x* is 3?

- (F) 23
- (G) 7
- (H) 16
- (J) 8

3. What is *y* when *x* is 5?

- (A) 18
- (B) 17
- (C) 2
- (D) 33

4. What is *y* when *x* is 10?

- (F) 23
- (G) 58
- (H) 7
- (J) 18

DIRECTIONS: Choose the best answer. For numbers 5–8, let $y = 3x - 2$.

5. What is *y* when *x* is 2?

- (A) 8
- (B) 3
- (C) 4
- (D) 2

6. What is *y* when *x* is 4?

- (F) 10
- (G) 12
- (H) 14
- (J) 15

7. What is *y* when *x* is 12?

- (A) 36
- (B) 32
- (C) 40
- (D) 34

8. What is *y* when *x* is 9?

- (F) 27
- (G) 29
- (H) 25
- (J) 23

STOP

Name ______________________________ Date ______________

Mathematics

5

For pages 103–114

Mini-Test 3

Use Algebraic and Analytical Methods

DIRECTIONS: Choose the best answer.

1. **Extend the number pattern.**
   3, 5, 7, 8, 3, 5, 7, 8, 3, 5, ___
   - (A) 8
   - (B) 3
   - (C) 7
   - (D) 5

2. **Extend the number pattern.**
   1, 4, 7, 10, 13, 16, 19, ___
   - (F) 1
   - (G) 22
   - (H) 20
   - (J) 16

DIRECTIONS: Use the following shape for questions 3–4.

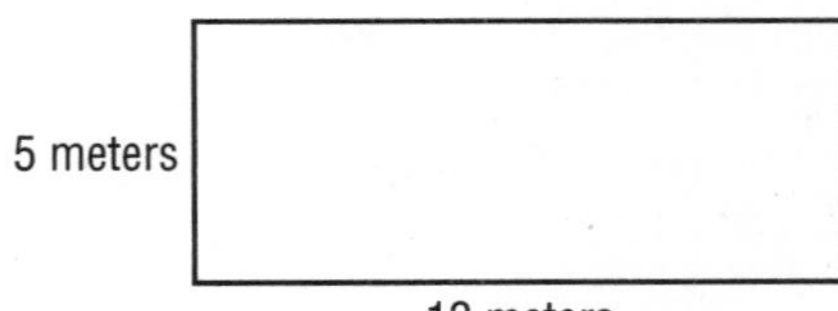

3. **If the length of the shape changes from 12 to 15 meters, what happens to the area of the shape?**
   - (A) It increases by 3 square meters.
   - (B) It decreases by 10 square meters.
   - (C) It increases by 15 square meters.
   - (D) It increases by 16 square meters.

4. **If the width of the shape is changed to 3 meters, what happens to the perimeter of the shape?**
   - (F) It decreases by 4 meters.
   - (G) It increases by 4 meters.
   - (H) It increases by 2 meters.
   - (J) It increases by 1 meter.

5. **The function table below shows input and output numbers. The rule used to change the numbers is shown. What number completes the table?**

   Rule: Multiply by 2, then add 7.

IN	OUT
3	13
4	?
5	17

   - (A) 14
   - (B) 16
   - (C) 15
   - (D) None of these

6. **In the equation $y = 2x$, what is y when x is 10?**
   - (F) 10
   - (G) 20
   - (H) 40
   - (J) 60

7. **In the equation $y = x + 8$, what is x when y is 17?**
   - (A) 8
   - (B) 9
   - (C) 10
   - (D) 11

STOP

Mathematics Standards

Use Geometric Methods

Goal 6: Use geometric methods to analyze, categorize, and draw conclusions about points, lines, planes, and space.

Learning Standard 6A—Students who meet the standard can demonstrate and apply geometric concepts involving points, lines, planes, and space. *(Properties of single figures, coordinate geometry, and constructions)*

1. Identify, draw, and label lines, line segments, rays, parallel lines, intersecting lines, perpendicular lines, acute angles, obtuse angles, right angles, and acute, obtuse, right, scalene, isosceles, and equilateral triangles. *(See pages 117–119.)*
2. Identify, draw, and build regular, irregular, convex, and concave polygons. *(See page 120.)*
3. Read and plot ordered pairs of numbers in the positive quadrant of the Cartesian plane. *(See pages 121–122.)*
4. Describe paths and movement using coordinate systems. *(See page 123.)*
5. Differentiate between polygons and nonpolygons. *(See page 124.)*
6. Identify and label radius, diameter, chord, and circumference of a circle. *(See page 125.)*
7. Explore and describe rotational symmetry of two- and three-dimensional shapes. *(See page 126.)*
8. Construct a circle with a specified radius or diameter using a compass. *(See pages 127–128.)*

Learning Standard 6B—Students who meet the standard can identify, describe, classify, and compare relationships using points, lines, planes, and solids. *(Connections between and among multiple geometric figures)*

1. Determine congruence and similarity of given shapes. *(See pages 129–130.)*
2. Explore polyhedra using concrete models. *(See page 131.)*

Learning Standard 6C—Students who meet the standard can construct convincing arguments and proofs to solve problems. *(Justifications of conjectures and conclusions)*

1. Make and test conjectures about mathematical properties and relationships and justify the conclusions.

Name ____________________ Date ____________________

Mathematics

Use Geometric Methods

6A.1 Lines, Line Segments, and Rays

DIRECTIONS: Match the name to the correct drawing.

Examples:

Letters are used in geometry to identify a particular figure.

A **line** goes on forever in both directions. It is drawn with an arrow on either end.

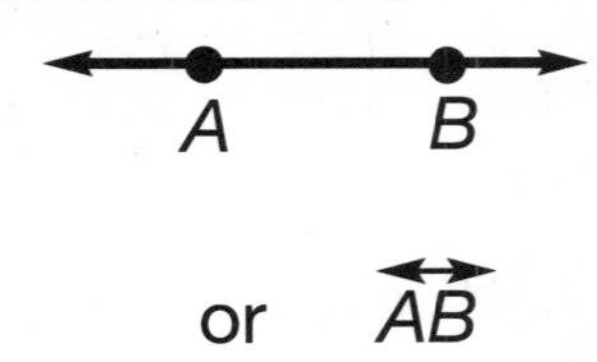

or $\overleftrightarrow{AB}$

A **line segment** is a specific portion of a line. It has two endpoints.

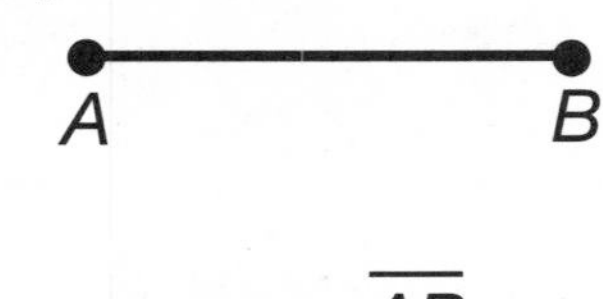

or $\overline{AB}$

A **ray** goes on forever in one direction from a fixed point. It is drawn with one endpoint and one arrow.

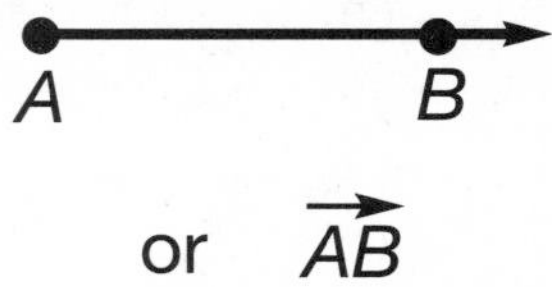

or $\overrightarrow{AB}$

1. $\overline{AB}$ and $\overrightarrow{BD}$

2. $\overleftrightarrow{DE}$ and $\overline{CB}$

3. $\overleftrightarrow{CD}$ and $\overline{BD}$

4. $\overrightarrow{AC}$ and $\overline{AD}$

5. $\overleftrightarrow{EF}$ and $\overrightarrow{EG}$

A.

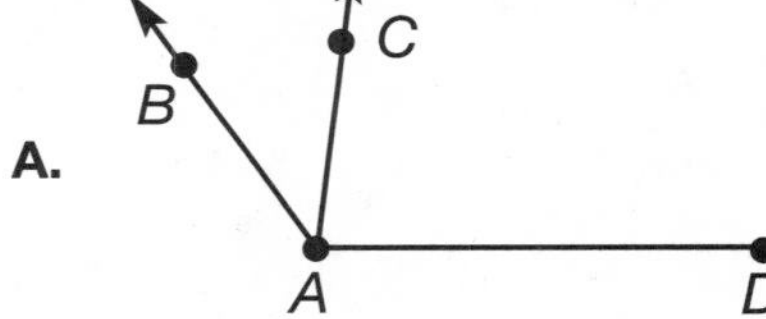

B.

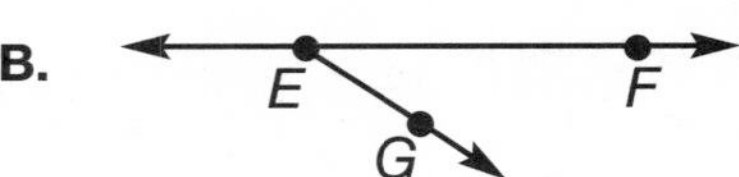

C. A, C, E, B, D

D. A, B, C, D

E. A, B, C, D

STOP

Name ______________________________ Date ______________

Mathematics

6A.1

Identifying Lines and Angles

Use Geometric Methods

DIRECTIONS: Choose the best answer.

Look at all the answer choices before you mark the one you think is correct.

1. These lines are ________ .

(A) parallel
(B) perpendicular
(C) right
(D) None of the above

2. These lines are ________ .

(F) obtuse
(G) perpendicular
(H) parallel
(J) None of the above

3. These lines are ________ .

(A) parallel
(B) perpendicular
(C) obtuse
(D) None of the above

4. These lines are ________ .

(F) right
(G) perpendicular
(H) parallel
(J) None of the above

5. These lines are ________ .

(A) parallel
(B) perpendicular
(C) right
(D) None of the above

6. These lines are ________ .

(F) obtuse
(G) perpendicular
(H) parallel
(J) None of the above

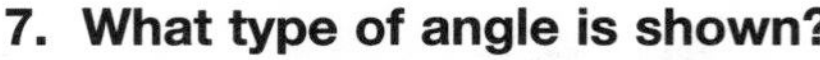

7. What type of angle is shown?

(A) acute
(B) right
(C) obtuse
(D) None of the above

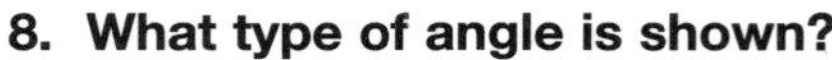

8. What type of angle is shown?

(F) acute
(G) right
(H) obtuse
(J) None of the above

9. What type of angle is shown?

(A) acute
(B) right
(C) obtuse
(D) None of the above

10. What type of angle is shown?

(F) acute
(G) right
(H) obtuse
(J) None of the above

STOP

Name ______________________________ Date ______________

Mathematics

6A.1

Identifying Triangles

Use Geometric Methods

DIRECTIONS: Choose the best answer.

Be sure the answer circle you fill in is the same letter as the answer you think is correct.

1. This is a(n) ________ triangle.

- (A) equilateral
- (B) isosceles
- (C) scalene
- (D) None of the above

2. This is a(n) ________ triangle.

- (F) equilateral
- (G) isosceles
- (H) scalene
- (J) None of the above

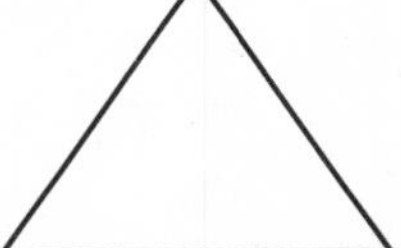

3. This is a(n) ________ triangle.

- (A) equilateral
- (B) isosceles
- (C) scalene
- (D) None of the above

4. This is a(n) ________ triangle.

- (F) equilateral
- (G) isosceles
- (H) scalene
- (J) None of the above

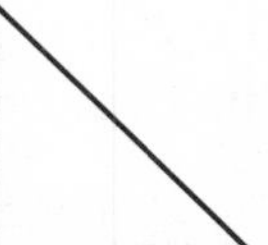

5. This is a(n) ________ triangle.

- (A) equilateral
- (B) isosceles
- (C) scalene
- (D) None of the above

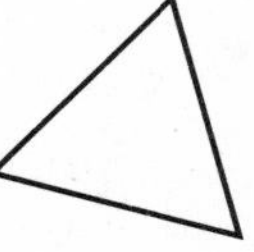

6. An equilateral triangle has ________ sides equal.

- (F) 0
- (G) 1
- (H) 2
- (J) 3

7. An isosceles triangle has ________ sides equal.

- (A) 0
- (B) 1
- (C) 2
- (D) 3

8. A scalene triangle has ________ sides equal.

- (F) 0
- (G) 1
- (H) 2
- (J) 3

STOP

Name ______________________ Date ______________

Mathematics

6A.2

Use Geometric Methods

Identifying Regular and Irregular Polygons

DIRECTIONS: Classify each of the following polygons as regular or irregular.

A **regular polygon** is a polygon where all sides are the same length and all interior angles are the same. An **irregular polygon** has sides of differing length and angles of differing measure.

1. 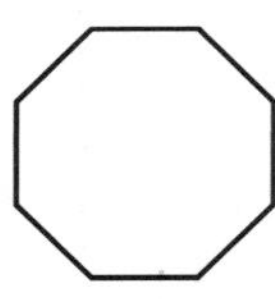

____

2. 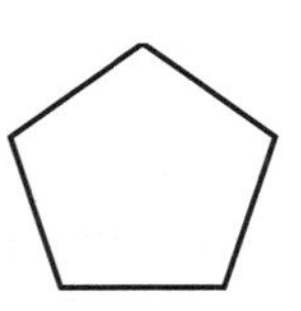

____

3. 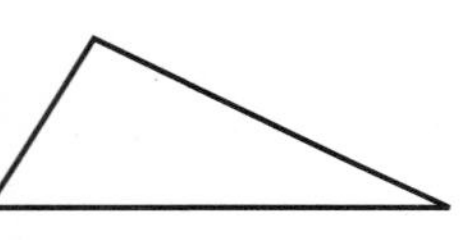

____

4. 

____

5. 

____

6. 

____

7. 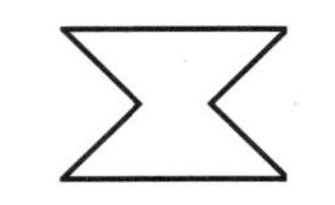

____

DIRECTIONS: Draw the figure described.

8. **Draw a regular 3-sided polygon.**

9. **Draw a regular 4-sided polygon.**

10. **Draw an irregular 5-sided polygon.**

STOP

Name ______________________________ Date ______________

Mathematics

Use Geometric Methods

Reading and Plotting Ordered Pairs

Clue: Remember that the first number of an ordered pair is the number on the x-axis.

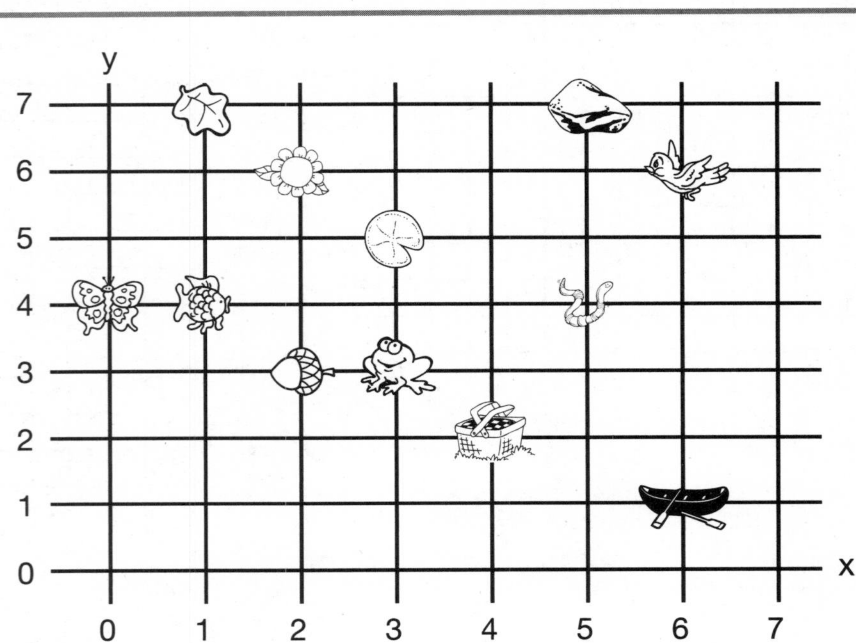

DIRECTIONS: The students in Room 14 are going on a scavenger hunt at Willow Lake. Each team needs to find the objects below. Give the item from the word list that is found at each coordinate.

1. __________ **(6, 1)**

2. __________ **(4, 2)**

3. __________ **(2, 3)**

4. __________ **(3, 3)**

5. __________ **(0, 4)**

6. __________ **(1, 4)**

7. __________ **(5, 4)**

8. __________ **(3, 5)**

9. __________ **(2, 6)**

10. __________ **(6, 6)**

11. __________ **(1, 7)**

12. __________ **(5, 7)**

DIRECTIONS: After the scavenger hunt, the students will have a picnic. Help them get ready for the picnic by drawing the given shapes at each coordinate.

13. banana (0, 0)

14. sandwich (7, 7)

15. milk carton (3, 4)

16. carrot (0, 7)

Name ______________________________ Date ______________

DIRECTIONS: Plot the ordered pairs on the graph. Connect the points in the order given.

17.

13
12
11
10
9
8
7
6
5
4
3
2
1

1 2 3 4 5 6 7 8 9 10 11 12 13

(6, 11)
(4, 9)
(5, 9)
(3, 7)
(4, 7)
(2, 5)
(3, 5)
(1, 3)
(5, 3)
(5, 1)
(7, 1)
(7, 3)
(11, 3)
(9, 5)
(10, 5)
(8, 7)
(9, 7)
(7, 9)
(8, 9)
(6, 11)

18. What shape did you make?

Ⓐ triangle
Ⓑ stop sign
Ⓒ evergreen tree
Ⓓ car

19.

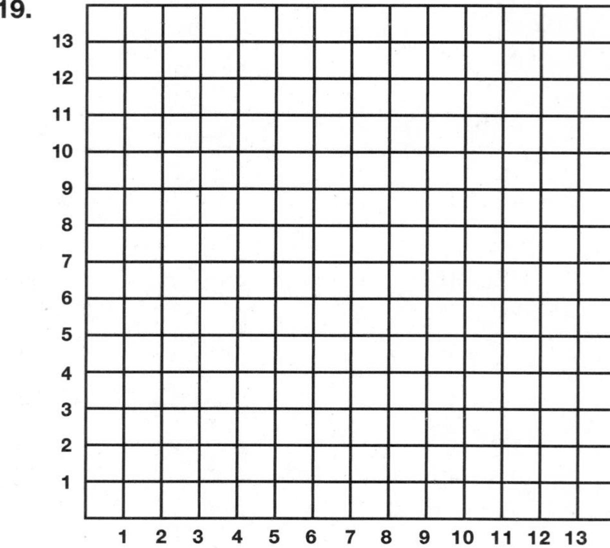

(1, 0)
(3, 0)
(3, 3)
(5, 4)
(6, 6)
(6, 7)
(5, 9)
(3, 10)
(1, 10)
(1, 8)
(1, 6)
(1, 4)
(1, 2)
(1, 0)

20. What letter did you make?

Ⓕ P
Ⓖ R
Ⓗ Q
Ⓙ T

STOP

Name ______________________ Date ______________

Mathematics

6A.4

Using Graphs

Use Geometric Methods

DIRECTIONS: Draw the lines on the graph provided. Label each line clearly.

1. Draw four points on the graph of the equation $y = 3x + 1$. Connect them using a straight line.

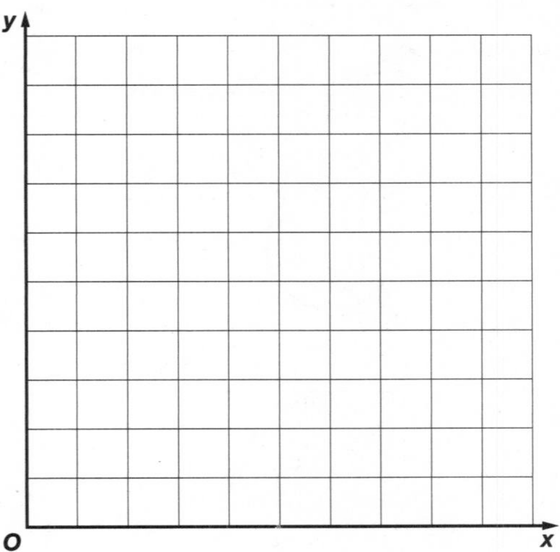

2. Draw four points on the graph of the equation $y = 2x - 1$. Connect them using a straight line.

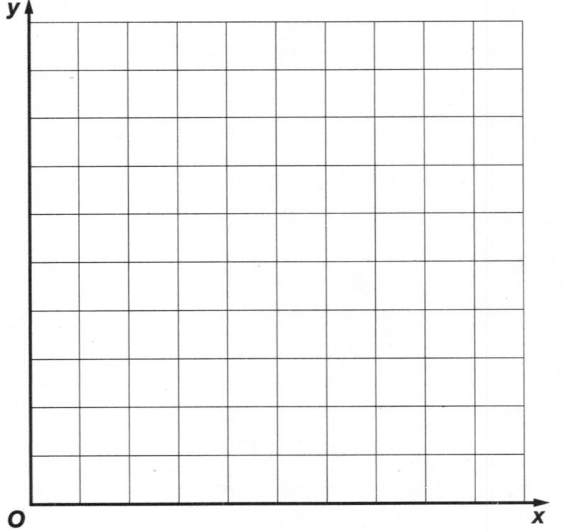

3. Draw four points on the graph of the equation $y = x + 1$. Connect them using a straight line.

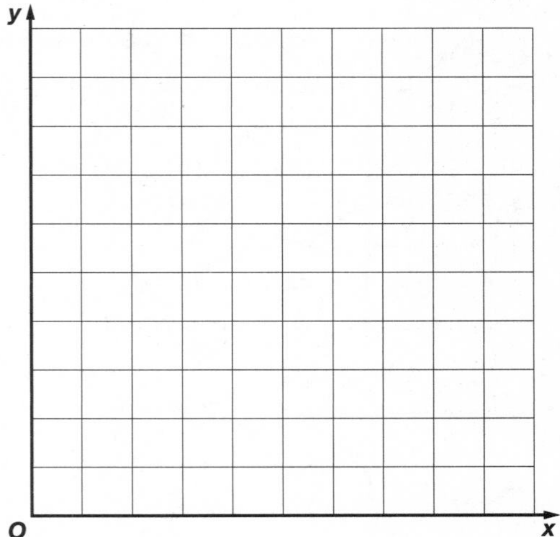

4. Draw four points on the graph of the equation $y = 2x$. Connect them using a straight line.

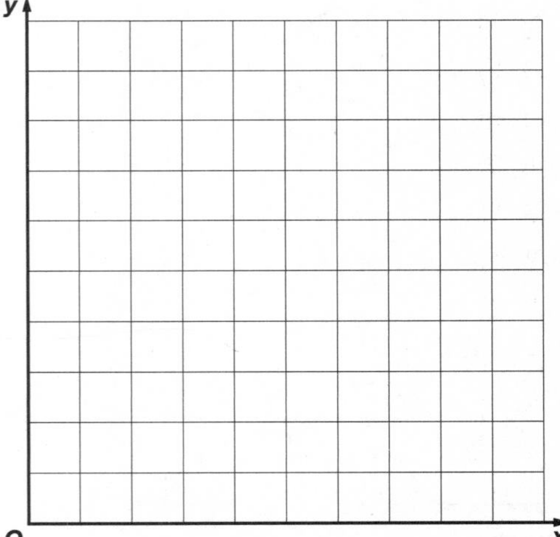

STOP

Name ______________________ Date ______________

Mathematics

6A.5

Use Geometric Methods

Identifying Polygons and Nonpolygons

DIRECTIONS: Classify each of the following as a polygon or nonpolygon.

A **polygon** is a closed figure made up of straight lines.

1.

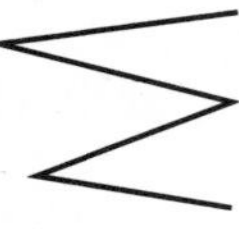

____

2.

____

3.

____

4.

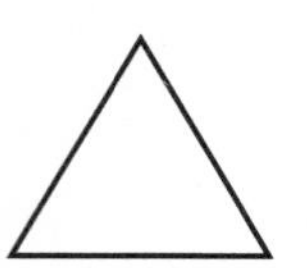

____

5.

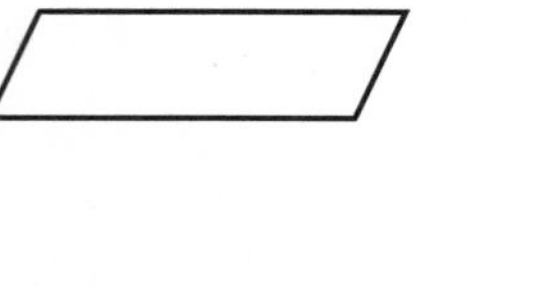

____

6.

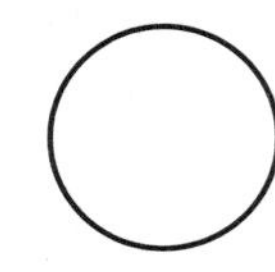

____

7.

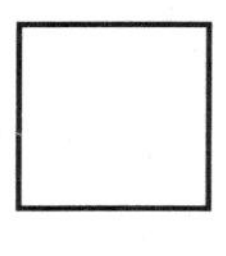

____

8.

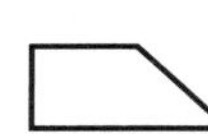

____

9.

____

10.

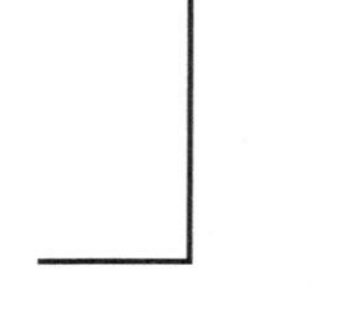

____

STOP

Name ______________________________ Date ______________

Mathematics

6A.6

Identifying Parts of a Circle

Use Geometric Methods

DIRECTIONS: Identify the part(s) of a circle shown for each pair.

Examples:

A **circle** is a closed two-dimensional figure. All of the points on a circle are the same distance from the center point of the circle. There are different ways to talk about parts of a circle in geometry.

A **chord** is a line segment that connects two points on a circle. *AB* is a chord.

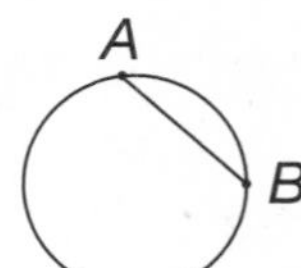

The **radius** of a circle is a line segment from the center point of the circle to any other point in the circle. *CD* is a radius.

The **diameter** of a circle is a chord that goes through the center of the circle. The diameter of a circle is twice the length of the radius. *EF* is the diameter.

1.

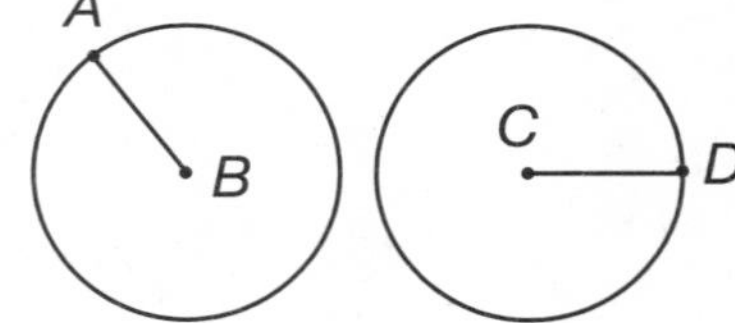

____

2.

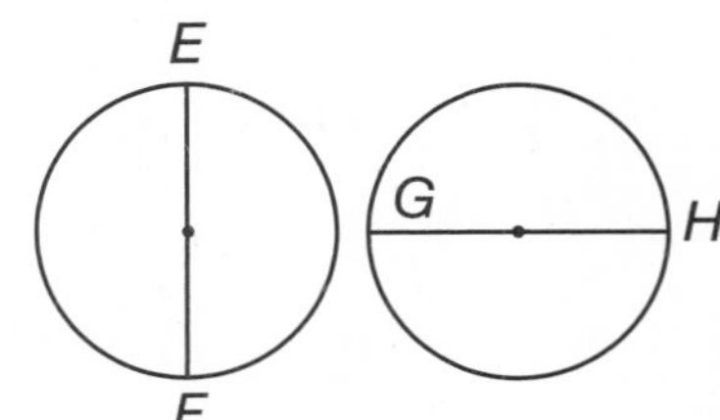

____

3.

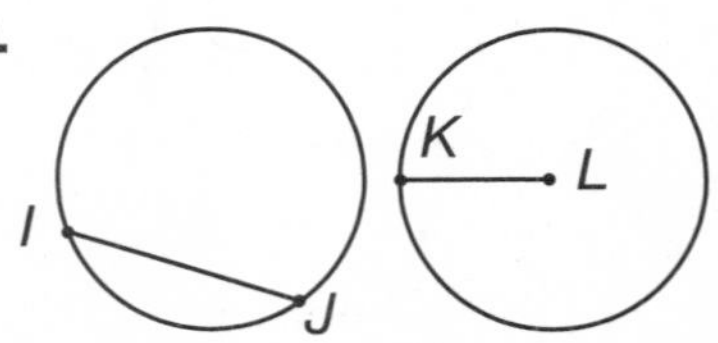

____

4.

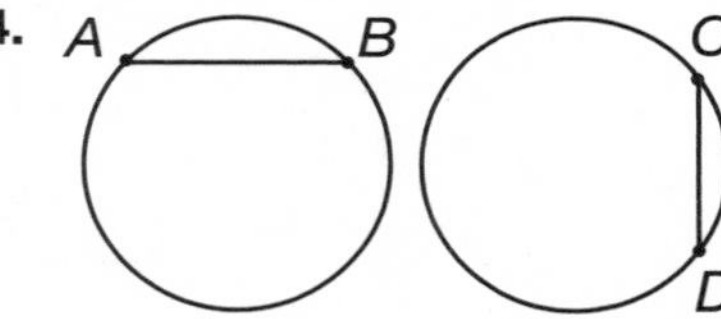

____

5.

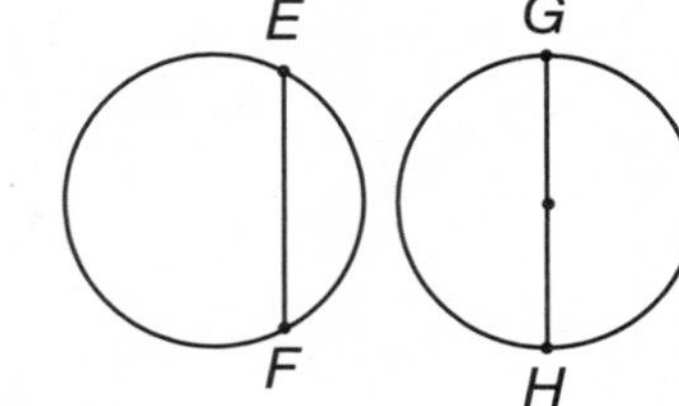

____

6.

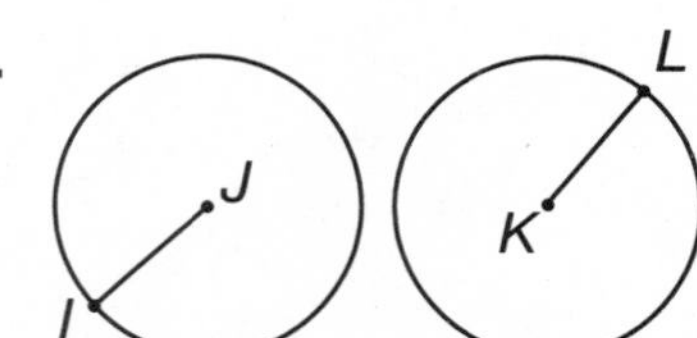

____

STOP

Name ____________________ Date ____________

Mathematics

6A.7

Rotational Symmetry

Use Geometric Methods

DIRECTIONS: Write *yes* beneath each object that has rotational symmetry and *no* beneath objects that do not have rotational symmetry.

> To check if an object has **rotational symmetry,** follow these steps.
> - Trace the object using a small square of tracing paper.
> - Place the traced image on top of the original image. Hold the traced image by a pencil-point in the center of the image.
> - Rotate your tracing paper around the center point. If the traced image matches exactly with the original image before you have rotated the paper in one full circle, then the shape has rotational symmetry.

1. 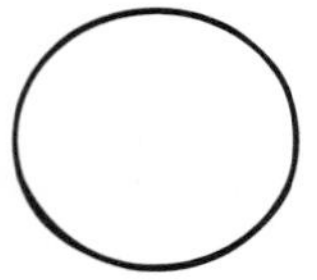

____

2. 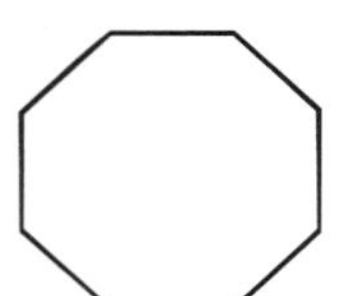

____

3. 

____

4. 

____

5. 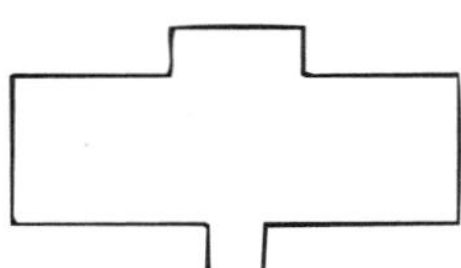

____

6. 

____

7. 

____

8. 

____

9. 

____

10. 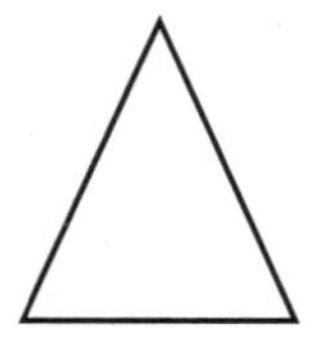

____

11. 

____

12. 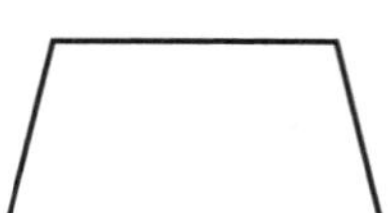

____

STOP

Name ______________________________ Date ______________

Mathematics

6A.8

Constructing Circles

Use Geometric Methods

DIRECTIONS: Use a compass to create the circles described below.

1. **A circle with a radius of 3/4 inch.**

2. **A circle with a radius of 3 1/2 inches.**

GO

Name ______________________________ Date ______________

3. **A circle with a diameter of 2 inches.**

4. **A circle with a diameter of 1 1/4 inches.**

STOP

Name ______________________________ Date ______________

Mathematics

6B.1

Use Geometric Methods

Determining Congruency and Similarity

DIRECTIONS: Classify each pair below as **congruent, similar,** or **neither.**

If two figures are congruent, they have the same size and shape. If two figures are similar, they have the same shape, but different sizes.

1. 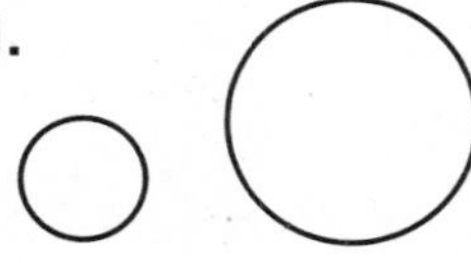

____

2. 

____

3. 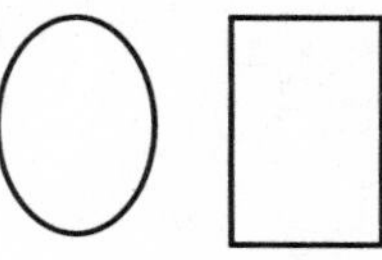

____

4. 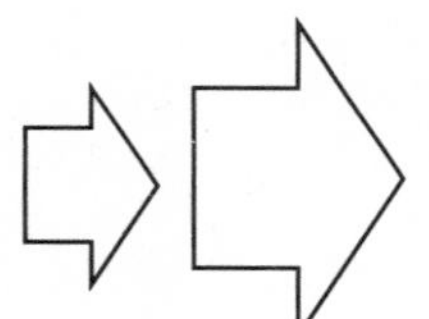

____

5. 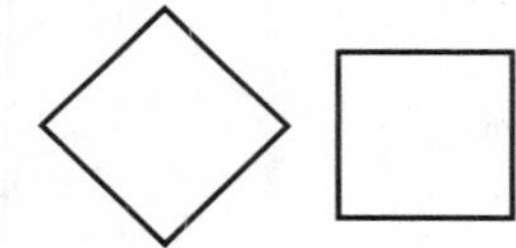

____

6. 

____

DIRECTIONS: Look at each shape below. Draw a shape that is **similar.**

7. 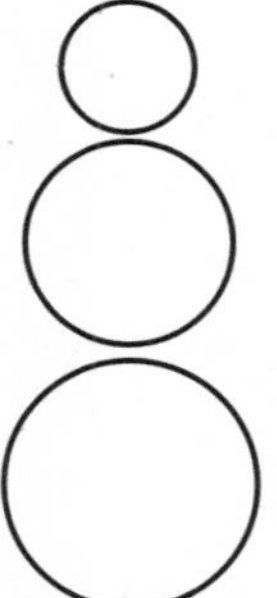

8. 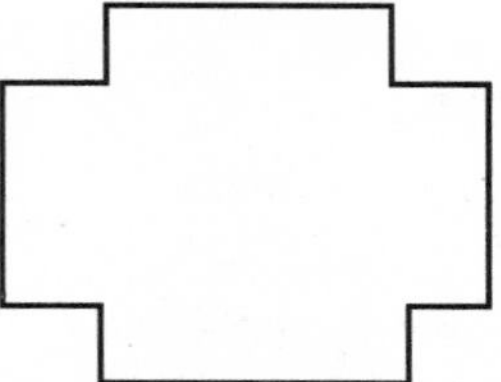

GO

Name ______________________________ Date ______________

DIRECTIONS: Choose the best answer.

9. Which pair of shapes is congruent?

Ⓐ 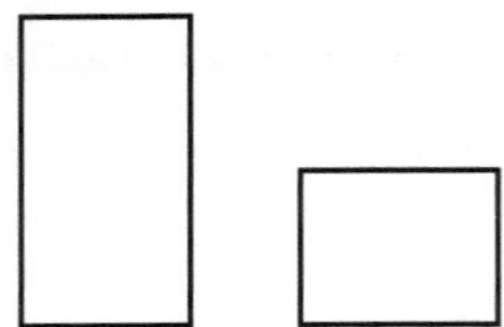

Ⓑ 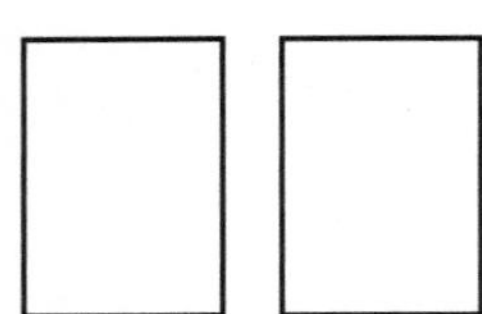

Ⓒ 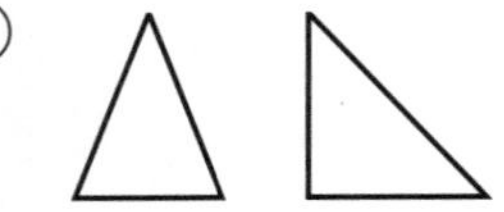

Ⓓ 

10. Which line segment seems to be congruent to $\overline{XY}$?

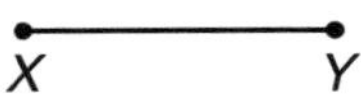

Ⓕ

Ⓖ

Ⓗ

Ⓙ

11. Which pair of shapes is congruent?

Ⓐ 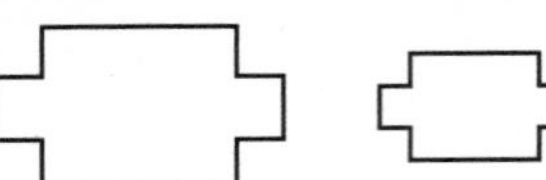

Ⓑ  

Ⓒ  

Ⓓ  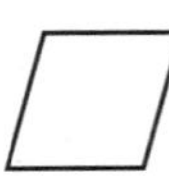

12. Which line segment seems to be congruent to $\overline{AB}$?

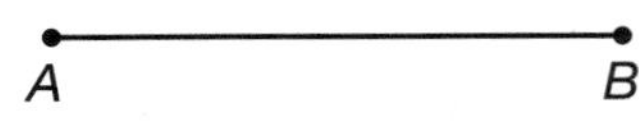

Ⓕ

Ⓖ

Ⓗ

Ⓙ

13. Which pair of shapes is congruent?

Ⓐ 

Ⓑ

Ⓒ 

Ⓓ

STOP

Name ______________________ Date ______________

Mathematics

6B.2

Use Geometric Methods

Identifying Pyramids and Prisms

DIRECTIONS: Next to each shape below, write **prism, pyramid,** or **neither** to show what type of three-dimensional object it is. Be prepared to explain your choices.

Examples:

Pyramids are three-dimensional shapes with the following characteristics:
- one base shaped like a polygon
- triangular faces
- a point on one end

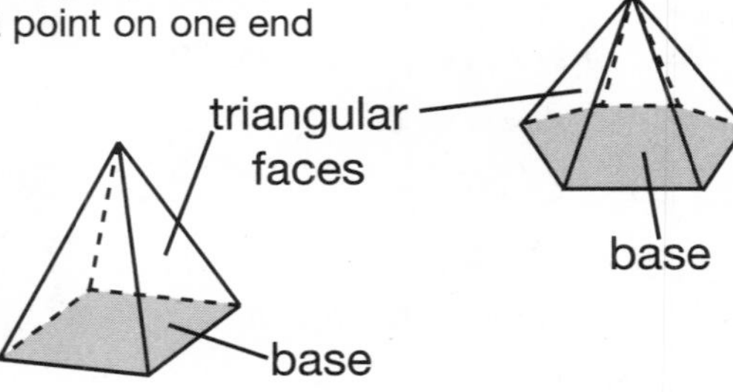

Prisms are three-dimensional shapes with the following characteristics:
- two identical bases shaped like polygons
- rectangular faces

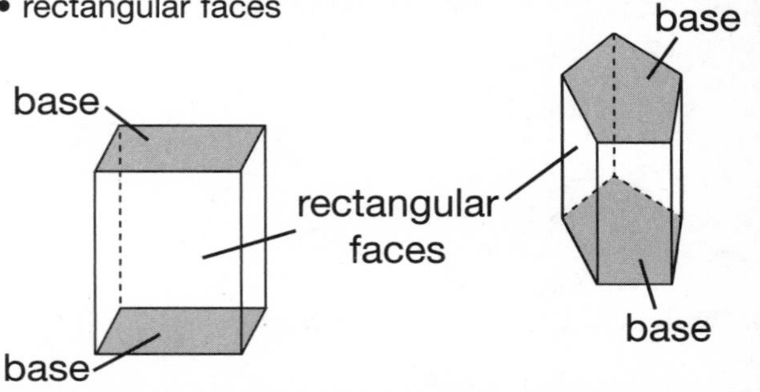

1. 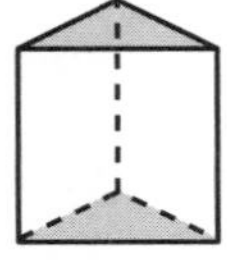
____

2. 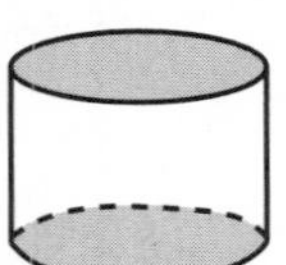
____

3. 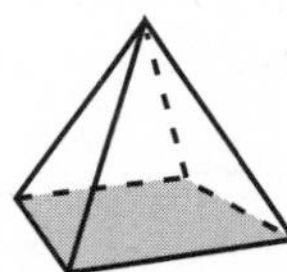
____

4. 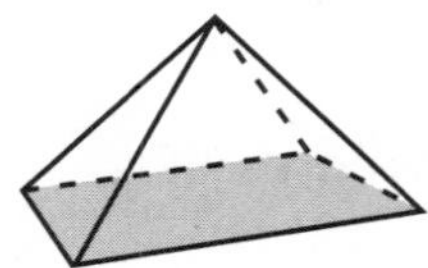
____

5. 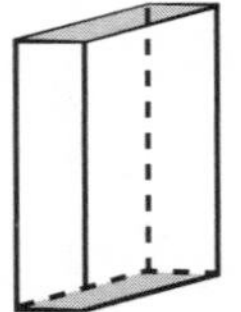
____

6. 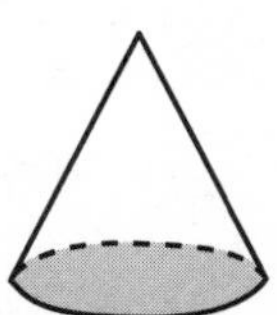
____

7. 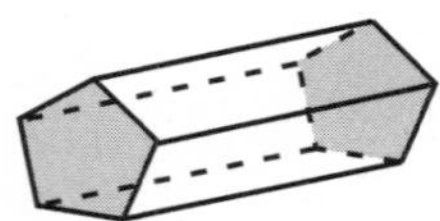
____

8. 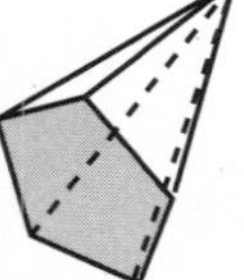
____

9. 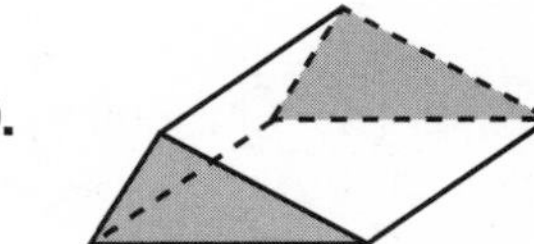
____

STOP

Name ______________________________ Date ____________________

Mathematics

For pages 117–131

Mini-Test 4

Use Geometric Methods

DIRECTIONS: Choose the best answer.

1. These lines are __________ .

Ⓐ parallel
Ⓑ perpendicular
Ⓒ obtuse
Ⓓ None of the above

2. What is the radius of the circle?

Ⓕ 8 m
Ⓖ 4 m
Ⓗ 2 m
Ⓙ 16 m

4 m

3. This is a(n) __________ triangle.

Ⓐ equilateral
Ⓑ isosceles
Ⓒ scalene
Ⓓ None of the above

4. This shape is a(n) __________ .

Ⓕ regular polygon
Ⓖ irregular polygon
Ⓗ regular nonpolygon
Ⓙ irregular nonpolygon

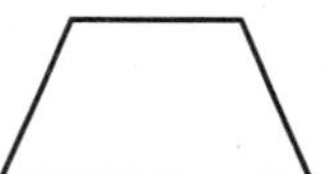

5. A quadrilateral with all sides equal in length is a(n) __________ .

Ⓐ irregular nonpolygon
Ⓑ regular nonpolygon
Ⓒ regular polygon
Ⓓ irregular polygon

6. What type of angle is shown?

Ⓕ acute
Ⓖ right
Ⓗ obtuse
Ⓙ None of the above

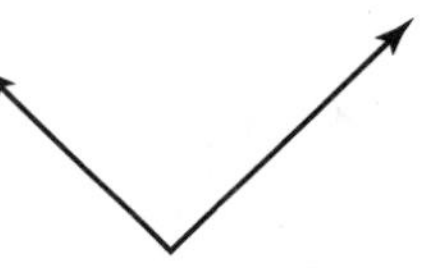

7. This is a(n) __________ triangle.

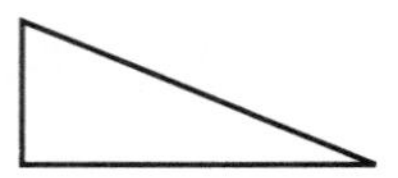

Ⓐ equilateral
Ⓑ isosceles
Ⓒ scalene
Ⓓ None of the above

8. What type of angle is shown?

Ⓕ right
Ⓖ acute
Ⓗ obtuse
Ⓙ None of the above

9. Which line segment seems to be congruent to MN?

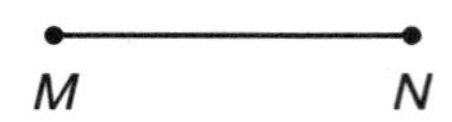

Ⓐ
Ⓑ
Ⓒ
Ⓓ

10. Which two shapes are congruent?

Ⓕ A and B
Ⓖ B and C
Ⓗ B and D
Ⓙ A and C

STOP

Mathematics Standards

Collect, Organize, and Analyze Data

Goal 7: Collect, organize, and analyze data using statistical methods; predict results; and interpret certainty using concepts of probability.

Learning Standard 7A—Students who meet the standard can organize, describe, and make predictions from existing data. *(Data analysis)*

1. Represent data using tables and graphs such as line plots and line graphs. *(See page 134.)*
2. Describe the shape and important features of a set of data and compare related data sets. *(See page 135.)*
3. Arrange given data in order, least to greatest or greatest to least, and determine minimum value, maximum value, range, mode, and median for an odd number of data points. *(See pages 136–137.)*

What it means:
Students should know that the—

- **range** of a set of data is the difference between the greatest value and the lowest value of the set.
- **mode** of a set of data is the one that occurs most often.
- **median** of a set of data is the number in the middle when the numbers are put in order.

4. Compare different representations of the same data and evaluate how well each representation shows important aspects of the data. *(See page 138.)*
5. Propose and justify conclusions and predictions that are based on data. *(See page 139.)*

Learning Standard 7B—Students who meet the standard can formulate questions, design data collection methods, gather and analyze data, and communicate findings. *(Data collection)*

1. Collect data using observations and experiments. *(See page 140.)*
2. Propose a further investigation to verify or refute a prediction. *(See pages 140–141.)*

Learning Standard 7C—Students who meet the standard can determine, describe, and apply the probabilities of events. *(Probability including counting techniques)*

1. List all possible outcomes of a single event and tell whether an outcome is certain, impossible, likely, or unlikely. *(See pages 141–142.)*
2. Describe the probability of an event using terminology such as "5 chances out of 8." *(See page 143.)*

Name ______________________ Date ______________

Mathematics

7A.1

Representing Data

Collect, Organize, and Analyze Data

DIRECTIONS: The data below shows a person's heart rate while jogging. Use the data to make both a line graph and a bar graph and to answer the questions.

Data

Time	Heart Rate
0 min.	80
5 min.	120
10 min.	135
15 min.	147
20 min.	159
25 min.	150

1. **Line Graph**

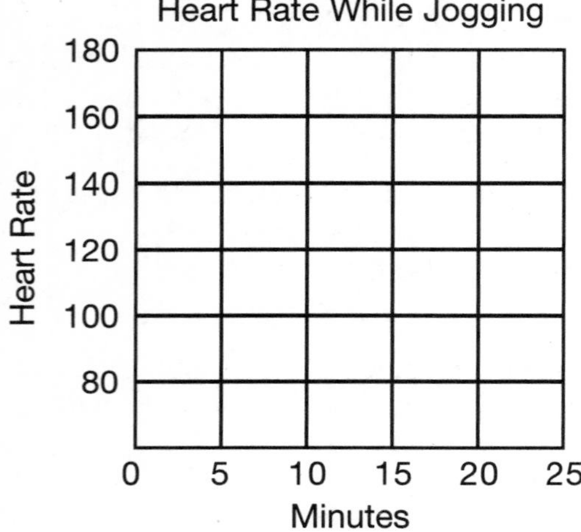

2. **Bar Graph**

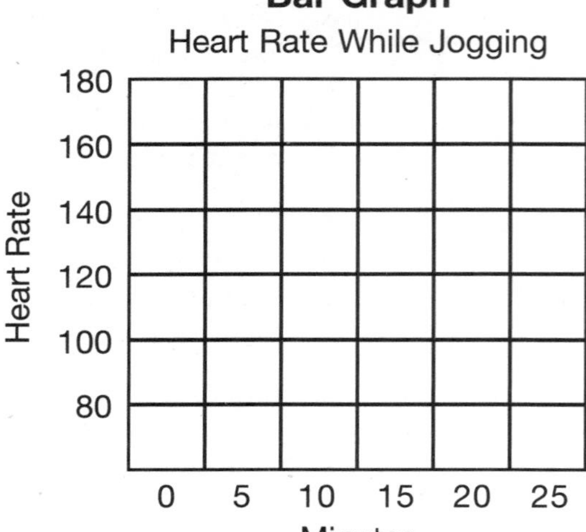

3. **At what time was the jogger's heart rate the highest?________**

4. **During which interval did the jogger's heart rate increase the most?________**

5. **During which interval did the jogger's heart rate increase the least?________**

6. **During which interval did the jogger's heart rate decrease?________**

STOP

Name ______________________ Date ______________

Mathematics

7A.2

Describing and Comparing Data

Collect, Organize, and Analyze Data

DIRECTIONS: The tally chart shows the hair color of some fourth grade students. Choose the best answer.

Brown	Black	Blond	Red

1. Which of these questions could you answer using the information on the tally chart?

Ⓐ How often do the students get their hair cut?

Ⓑ How many students dye their hair?

Ⓒ Which students have long hair?

Ⓓ How many more brown-haired students are there than blond-haired students?

2. Which graph below shows the data on the tally chart?

Ⓕ

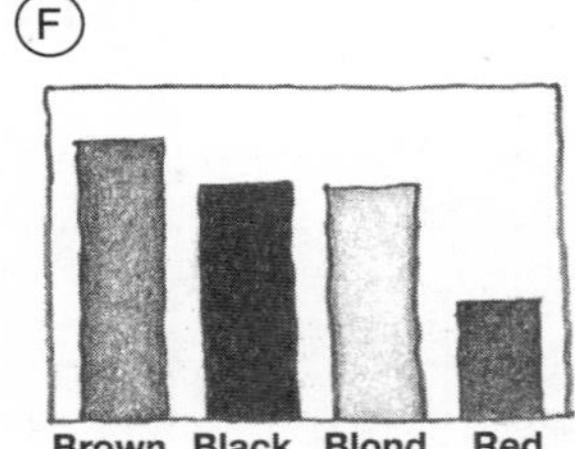

Ⓗ

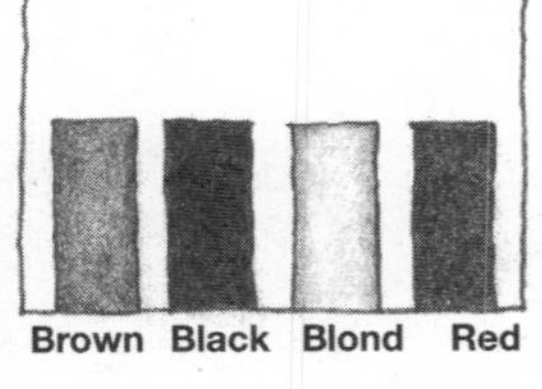

Ⓖ

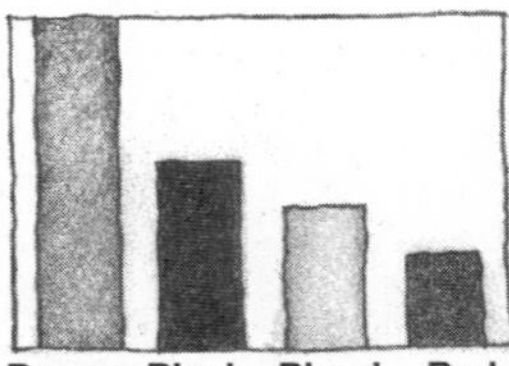

Ⓙ

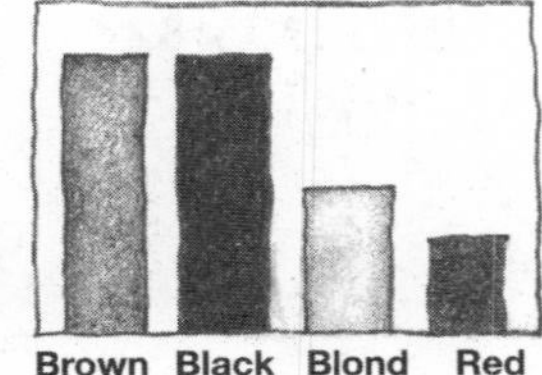

3. Which circle shows the fraction of the students on the tally chart that have black hair?

Ⓐ

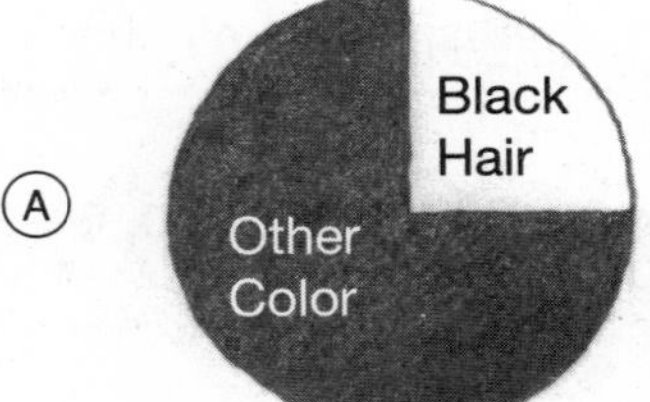

Ⓑ

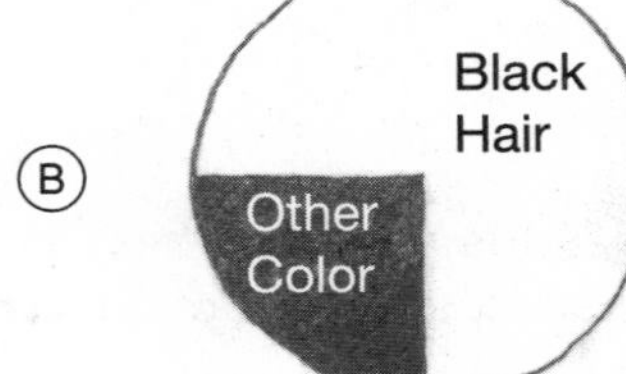

Ⓒ

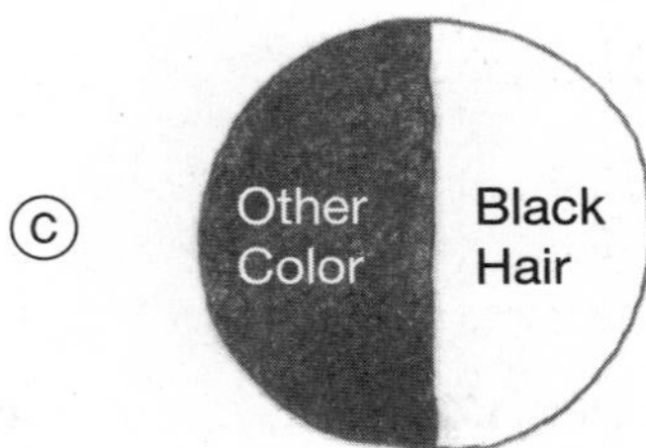

Ⓓ

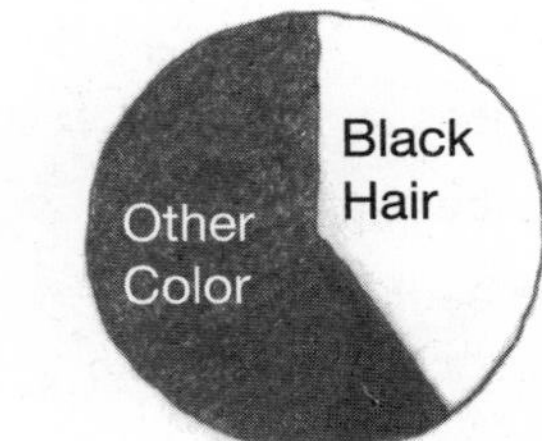

STOP

Name ______________________ Date ______________

Mathematics

7A.3

Determining Range, Median, and Mode

Collect, Organize, and Analyze Data

DIRECTIONS: Choose the best answer.

The **range** of a set of data is the difference between the greatest value and lowest value of the set. The **mode** is the value that occurs most often. The **median** is the number in the middle when the numbers are put in order.

1. What is the mode of this data: 40, 60, 50, 60, 30?

Ⓐ 30
Ⓑ 40
Ⓒ 50
Ⓓ 60

2. Five students heights are 54 inches, 56 inches, 52 inches, 57 inches, and 53 inches. What is the median height?

Ⓕ 53 inches
Ⓖ 54 inches
Ⓗ 56 inches
Ⓙ 54.4 inches

3. Bo's turtles weigh 12 ounces, 10 ounces, and 20 ounces. What is their median weight?

Ⓐ 15 ounces
Ⓑ 11 ounces
Ⓒ 12 ounces
Ⓓ 14 ounces

4. What is the mode of this data: 80, 100, 90, 80, 95, 80?

Ⓕ 80
Ⓖ 90
Ⓗ 95
Ⓙ 100

5. What is the range of this set of data: 40, 42, 65, 39, 43?

Ⓐ 17
Ⓑ 26
Ⓒ 41
Ⓙ 45

6. What is the mode of this data: 21, 34, 44, 21, 36?

Ⓕ 21
Ⓖ 34
Ⓗ 36
Ⓙ 44

7. What is the range of this set of data: 782, 276, 172, 321, 415?

Ⓐ 506
Ⓑ 299
Ⓒ 610
Ⓓ 782

8. What is the mode of this data: 125, 248, 214, 173, 182?

Ⓕ 125
Ⓖ 173
Ⓗ 214
Ⓙ There is no mode.

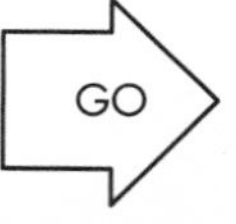

Name ____________________ Date ____________

9. What is the median of this set of data: 52, 56, 23, 53, 46?

Ⓐ 46
Ⓑ 53
Ⓒ 52
Ⓓ 56

10. What is the range of this data: 125, 248, 214, 173, 138?

Ⓕ 190
Ⓖ 193.5
Ⓗ 123
Ⓙ 75

11. What is the range of this data: 75, 100, 100, 100, 95?

Ⓐ 95
Ⓑ 100
Ⓒ 25
Ⓓ 5

12. What is the mode of this data: 75, 100, 100, 100, 95?

Ⓕ 95
Ⓖ 100
Ⓗ 25
Ⓙ 5

13. What is the median of this data: 75, 100, 100, 100, 95?

Ⓐ 75
Ⓑ 95
Ⓒ 100
Ⓓ There is no median.

DIRECTIONS: Sue's grades are shown below. Sue may choose to use the median, mode, or range of these grades for her report card. Answer the questions that follow to determine which will give her the highest grade.

84, 92, 74, 80, 100, 88, 94, 80, 86

14. What is the range?

Ⓕ 18
Ⓖ 26
Ⓗ 74
Ⓙ 75

15. What is the mode?

Ⓐ 26
Ⓑ 74
Ⓒ 100
Ⓓ 80

16. What is the median?

Ⓕ 84
Ⓖ 86
Ⓗ 88
Ⓙ 92

17. Which measure gives Sue the highest grade?

Ⓐ range
Ⓑ mode
Ⓒ median
Ⓓ mean

STOP

Name ______________________________ Date ______________

Mathematics

7A.4

Comparing Different Representations of Data

Collect, Organize, and Analyze Data

DIRECTIONS: The same data can be represented different ways depending on which style of chart is used. Use the information in the following table to fill in the bar graph and circle chart below.

School Election Results			
Grade	Votes for Blue Party	Votes for Red Party	Total Votes by Grade
Third	25	5	30
Fourth	10	16	26
Fifth	15	21	36
Total Votes by Party	50	42	

1\. School Election Results

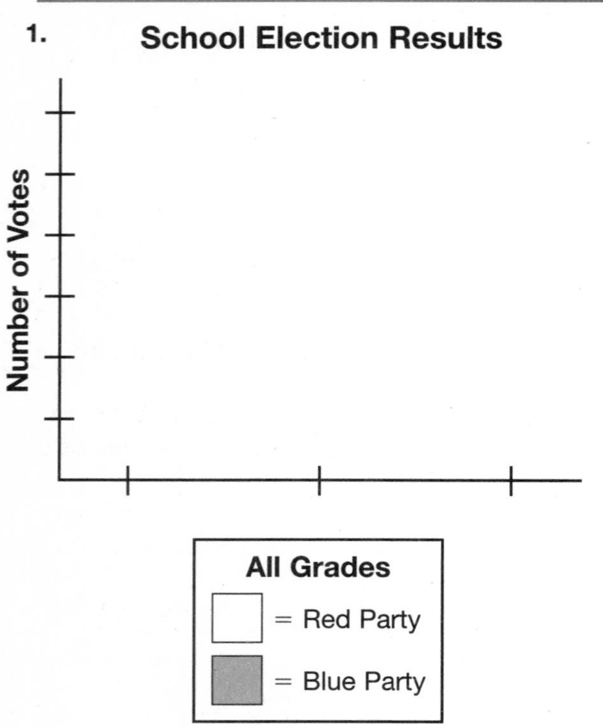

2\. Voters in Each Grade

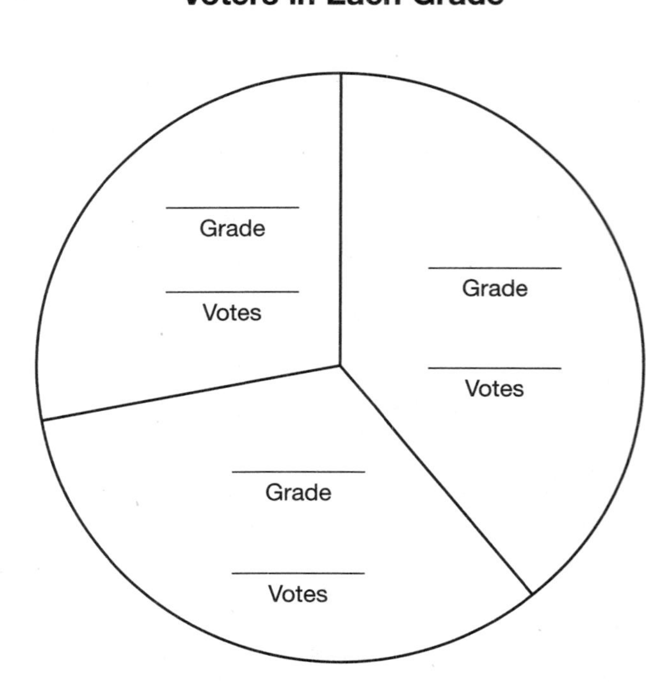

3\. **How well does the bar graph represent the data? the circle graph?**

____

____

____

Name ____________________ Date ____________________

Mathematics

7A.5

Drawing Conclusions Based on Data

Collect, Organize, and Analyze Data

DIRECTIONS: Students in Sari's class had a special game day. Sari went around the room and noted how many students were playing at each game station at a given time. She recorded her findings in a circle graph. Use the circle graph below to answer the questions.

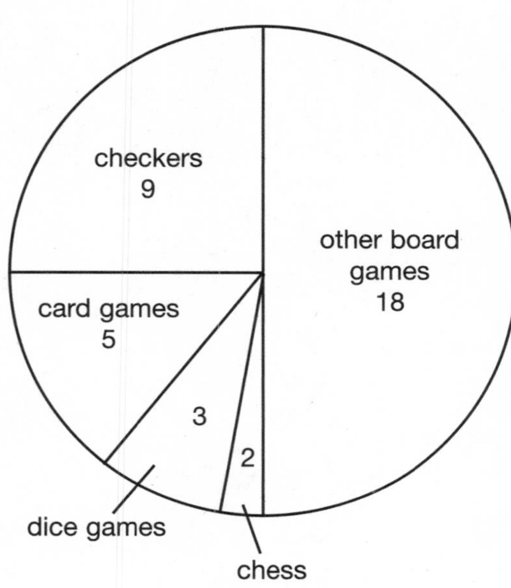

1. **What is the total number of students in Sari's class that played on game day?**

   ____

2. **One game station was very popular, with about half of the students playing there. Which station was it?**

   ____

3. **Which game station had the fewest players?**

   ____

4. **If Sari combined the dice games, card games, and chess stations, would that new group be larger, smaller, or the same size as the checkers group?**

   ____

5. **Half as many students played checkers as played at which game station?**

   ____

6. **Sari's teacher needs to plan for next year's game day. Which game should she consider taking out?**

   ____

7. **Which two stations should she be sure to include?**

   ____

STOP

Name ______________________________ Date ______________

Mathematics

7B.1/7B.2

Collecting Data

Collect, Organize, and Analyze Data

DIRECTIONS: You want to determine the fruit of choice among the students in your class. Conduct an experiment where you have the students choose which of the following fruits is their favorite: an apple, a banana, an orange, strawberries, or watermelon. (You may substitute different fruits for the ones given here.) Use the space below to record your findings in graph form.

1.

DIRECTIONS: What do you think the favorite fruit is in your neighborhood or community? How could you determine this?

2. ______________________________

____

____

____

____

____

____

____

____

Name ______________________ Date ______________

Mathematics

7B.2/7C.1

Determining Possible Outcomes

Collect, Organize, and Analyze Data

DIRECTIONS: Choose the best answer.

Venita is making a sandwich. She has white, wheat, and Italian bread. She can choose from ham, roast beef, and turkey for the meat. Use the following tree diagram to answer questions 1–3.

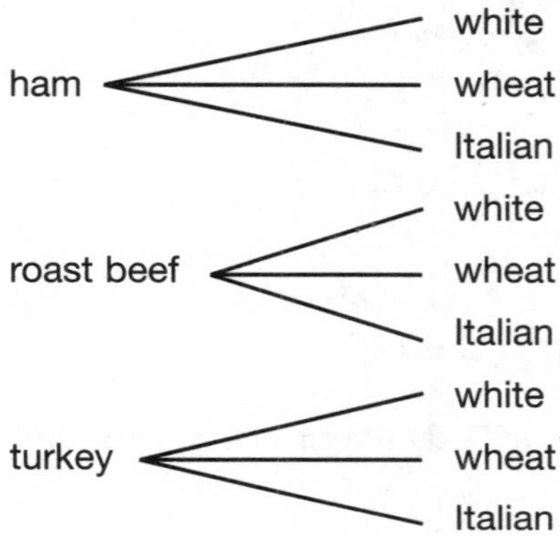

1. How many choices does Venita have?

- Ⓐ 12
- Ⓑ 9
- Ⓒ 3
- Ⓓ 6

2. If Venita decides she doesn't want wheat bread, how many choices does she have?

- Ⓕ 12
- Ⓖ 9
- Ⓗ 3
- Ⓙ 6

3. Which of the following is not an option Venita can choose?

- Ⓐ roast beef on rye
- Ⓑ turkey on Italian
- Ⓒ ham on wheat
- Ⓓ turkey on white

Scott was choosing what to wear one morning. He has jeans or khakis for pants and red, blue, and green shirts. Use the following tree diagram to answer questions 4–6.

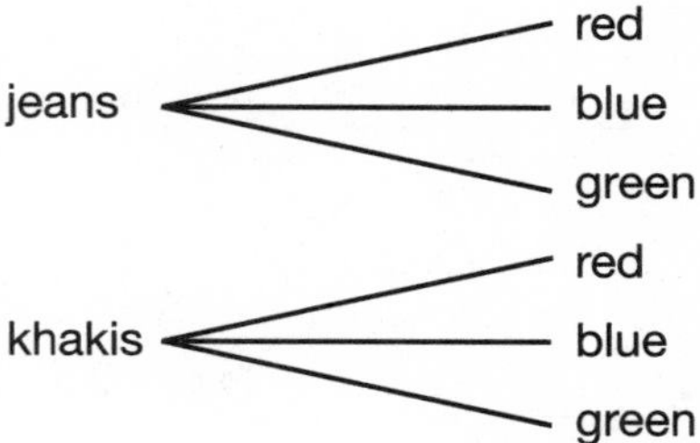

4. How many options does Scott have for outfits?

- Ⓕ 6
- Ⓖ 3
- Ⓗ 8
- Ⓙ 2

5. Which of the following is not an option?

- Ⓐ jeans with red shirt
- Ⓑ khakis with blue shirt
- Ⓒ jeans with yellow shirt
- Ⓓ khakis with green shirt

6. If Scott decides he wants to wear his blue shirt, how many options does he have?

- Ⓕ 6
- Ⓖ 3
- Ⓗ 8
- Ⓙ 2

STOP

Name ______________________________ Date ______________

Mathematics

7C.1

Determining Likelihood of Outcomes

Collect, Organize, and Analyze Data

DIRECTIONS: Look at the spinner. Identify as certain, impossible, likely, or unlikely the probability that the arrow will land on

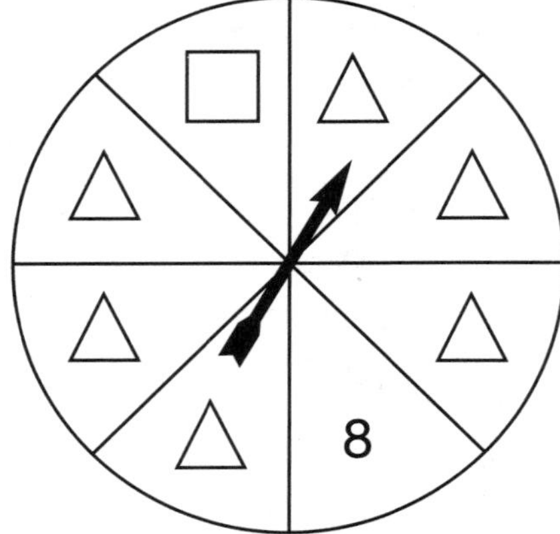

1. **a number.** ______________

2. **an 8.** ______________

3. **a circle.** ______________

4. **a shape.** ______________

5. **a triangle.** ______________

DIRECTIONS: Look at the spinner. Identify as certain, impossible, likely, or unlikely the probability that the arrow will land on

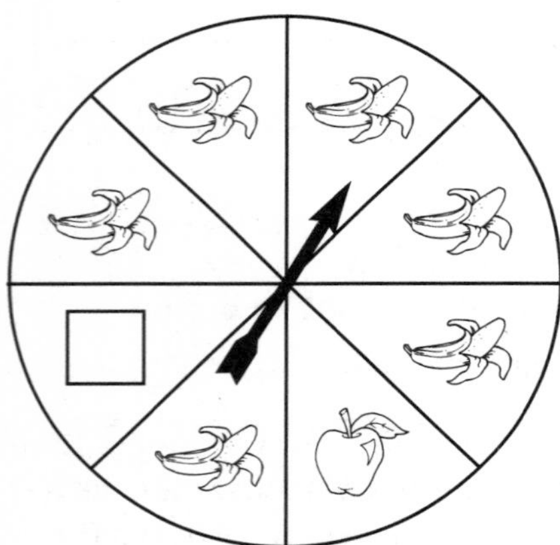

6. **a banana.** ______________

7. **a fruit.** ______________

8. **a star.** ______________

9. **a triangle.** ______________

10. **an apple.** ______________

DIRECTIONS: Look at the spinner. Identify as certain, impossible, likely, or unlikely the probability that the arrow will land on

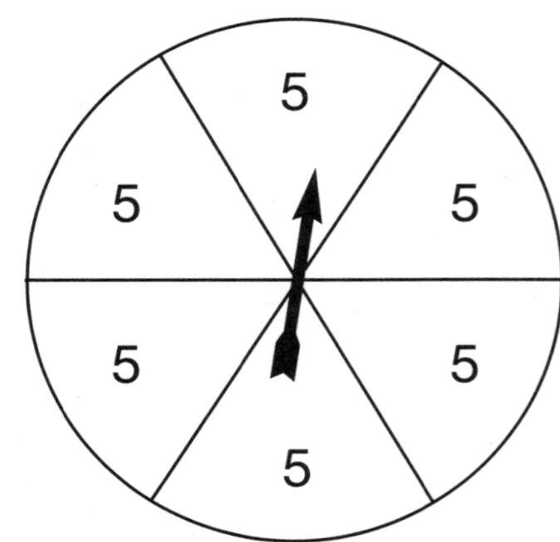

11. **a 5.** ______________

12. **an odd number.** ______________

13. **a triangle.** ______________

14. **a 2.** ______________

STOP

Name ______________________________ Date ______________

Mathematics

7C.2

Describing Probability

Collect, Organize, and Analyze Data

DIRECTIONS: The Room 3 students at Westfield Elementary are bored with their lunches. They decide to hold a surprise lunch day. They put their sandwiches in one pile and their snacks in another. Each student will be blindfolded and then choose one sandwich and one snack from each table. Using the information below, answer the questions.

Sandwich Type	Number
tuna	3
jelly	2
turkey	5
cheese	4
chicken salad	1

Snack Type	Number
cookie	6
carrot sticks	2
chips	3
banana	2
apple	2

1. **If all the snacks are still on the table, what is the probability of a student choosing a cookie as a snack?**

   ____

2. **What is the probability of getting a cookie after 2 cookies have been chosen?**

   ____

3. **If all the sandwiches are still on the table, what is the probability of choosing a turkey sandwich?**

   ____

4. **If all the snacks are still on the table, what is the probability of choosing a fruit?**

   ____

5. **Most of the students have chosen by the time it is Ray's turn. There are 3 sandwiches left—chicken salad, turkey, and tuna. What is the probability that Ray will choose turkey?**

   ____

STOP

Name ______________________ Date ______________

Mathematics

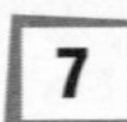

For pages 134–143

Mini-Test 5

Collect, Organize, and Analyze Data

DIRECTIONS: Choose the best answer.

Edison was wrapping a present. He had blue, silver, and gold ribbon and white, red, and black wrapping paper. Use the following tree diagram to answer questions 1–3.

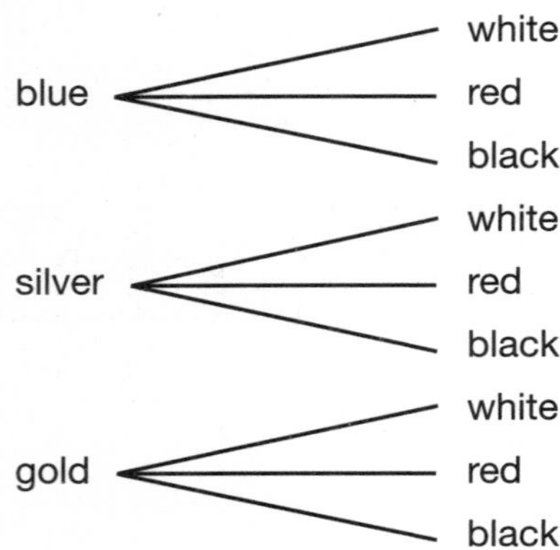

1. **How many wrapping options did Edison have?**
   - Ⓐ 12
   - Ⓑ 3
   - Ⓒ 9
   - Ⓓ 6

2. **Which of the following is not an option?**
   - Ⓕ silver ribbon on white paper
   - Ⓖ blue ribbon on yellow paper
   - Ⓗ blue ribbon on red paper
   - Ⓙ gold ribbon on black paper

3. **If Edison decides not to use the black paper, how many options does he have?**
   - Ⓐ 12
   - Ⓑ 3
   - Ⓒ 9
   - Ⓓ 6

DIRECTIONS: The graph below shows the cost of a ticket to the movies in five different cities. Use the graph for numbers 4–6.

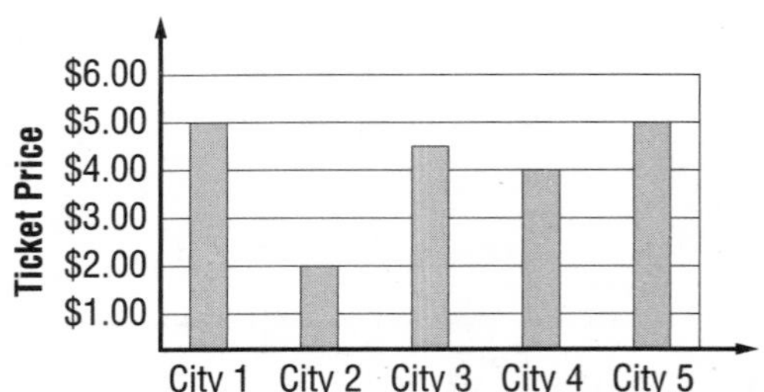

4. **What is the median ticket price?**
   - Ⓕ $5.00
   - Ⓖ $4.00
   - Ⓗ $4.10
   - Ⓙ $4.50

5. **Which ticket price is the mode?**
   - Ⓐ $4.00
   - Ⓑ $10.00
   - Ⓒ $2.00
   - Ⓓ $5.00

6. **What is the range of ticket prices?**
   - Ⓕ $5.00
   - Ⓖ $3.00
   - Ⓗ $2.00
   - Ⓙ $4.00

7. **A bag contains 7 red marbles, 5 green marbles, 3 white marbles, and 2 gold marbles. If you reach into the bag without looking, what is the probability of picking a red marble?**
   - Ⓐ $\frac{7}{10}$
   - Ⓑ $\frac{7}{17}$
   - Ⓒ $\frac{7}{8}$
   - Ⓓ $\frac{7}{9}$

STOP

How Am I Doing?

Mini-Test 1 Page 87 **Number Correct**	**9–10** answers correct	**Great Job!** Move on to the section test on page 147.
	5–8 answers correct	**You're almost there!** But you still need a little practice. Review the practice pages 73–86 before moving on to the section test on page 147.
	0–4 answers correct	**Oops!** Time to review what you have learned and try again. Review the practice section on pages 73–86. Then retake the test on page 87. Now move on to the section test on page 147.
Mini-Test 2 Page 101 **Number Correct**	**7–8** answers correct	**Awesome!** Move on to the section test on page 147.
	5–6 answers correct	**You're almost there!** But you still need a little practice. Review the practice pages 89–100 before moving on to the section test on page 147.
	0–4 answers correct	**Oops!** Time to review what you have learned and try again. Review the practice section on pages 89–100. Then retake the test on page 101. Now move on to the section test on page 147.
Mini-Test 3 Page 115 **Number Correct**	**7** answers correct	**Great Job!** Move on to the section test on page 147.
	4–6 answers correct	**You're almost there!** But you still need a little practice. Review the practice pages 103–114 before moving on to the section test on page 147.
	0–3 answers correct	**Oops!** Time to review what you have learned and try again. Review the practice section on pages 103–114. Then retake the test on page 115. Now move on to the section test on page 147.

How Am I Doing?

Mini-Test 4 Page 132 **Number Correct**	**9–10** answers correct	**Great Job!** Move on to the section test on page 147.
	5–8 answers correct	**You're almost there!** But you still need a little practice. Review the practice pages 117–131 before moving on to the section test on page 147.
	0–4 answers correct	**Oops!** Time to review what you have learned and try again. Review the practice section on pages 117–131. Then retake the test on page 132. Now move on to the section test on page 147.
Mini-Test 5 Page 144 **Number Correct**	**6–7** answers correct	**Awesome!** Move on to the section test on page 147.
	4–5 answers correct	**You're almost there!** But you still need a little practice. Review the practice pages 134–143 before moving on to the section test on page 147.
	0–3 answers correct	**Oops!** Time to review what you have learned and try again. Review the practice section on pages 134–143. Then retake the test on page 144. Now move on to the section test on page 147.

Name ______________________________ Date ______________

Final Mathematics Test

for pages 73–144

DIRECTIONS: Choose the best answer.

1. Which decimal below names the smallest number?

- (A) 0.06
- (B) 0.6
- (C) 0.64
- (D) 6.40

2. What fraction of the shape is shaded?

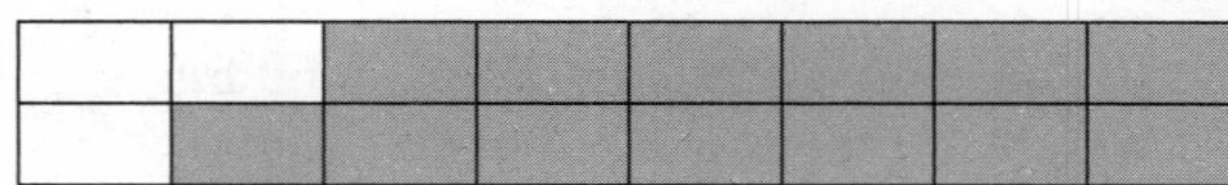

- (F) $\frac{13}{16}$
- (G) $\frac{3}{16}$
- (H) $\frac{3}{8}$
- (J) $\frac{5}{16}$

3. How would you represent owing a friend $4?

- (A) 4
- (B) 0
- (C) − 4
- (D) + 4

4. The temperature was 0° and dropped 10°. What is the new temperature?

- (F) − 10°
- (G) 0°
- (H) 10°
- (J) 20°

5. Find [28 − (4 × 5)] − 4.

- (A) 8
- (B) 4
- (C) 24
- (D) 116

6. Find 3 + (2 × 5).

- (F) 25
- (G) 17
- (H) 13
- (J) 30

7. Find (6 × 4) − 10.

- (A) 24
- (B) 14
- (C) 46
- (D) 0

8. Find 15 ÷ (5 − 2).

- (F) 5
- (G) 1
- (H) 2.5
- (J) 15

9. Find (5 + 2) × (4 + 3).

- (A) 31
- (B) 16
- (C) 49
- (D) 120

GO

Name ______________________________ Date ______________

10. A restaurant served 128 pints of milk in one day. How many quarts of milk was that?

- (F) 64 quarts
- (G) 32 quarts
- (H) 96 quarts
- (J) 16 quarts

11. How many gallons of milk did the restaurant in question 10 serve?

- (A) 64 gallons
- (B) 32 gallons
- (C) 96 gallons
- (D) 16 gallons

12. There are 6 pints of lemonade in a picnic cooler. How many 1-cup containers can be filled using the lemonade in the cooler?

- (F) 3 cups
- (G) 6 cups
- (H) 12 cups
- (J) 15 cups

13. The cooling system on a car holds 16 quarts. How many gallons does it hold?

- (A) 94 gallons
- (B) 32 gallons
- (C) 8 gallons
- (D) 4 gallons

14. Mr. Werner bought a 5-pound roast beef. How many ounces did the roast beef weigh?

- (F) 8 ounces
- (G) 80 ounces
- (H) 10 ounces
- (J) 50 ounces

15. The load limit on a small bridge is 8 tons. What is the load limit in pounds?

- (A) 16,000 pounds
- (B) 1,600 pounds
- (C) 160 pounds
- (D) 8,000 pounds

16. A dime weighs about 2 grams. Find the weight in grams of a roll of 50 dimes.

- (F) 100 grams
- (G) 150 grams
- (H) 200 grams
- (J) 20 grams

17. Kylie ran 5 miles on Tuesday. How many feet did she run?

- (A) 500 feet
- (B) 10,000 feet
- (C) 26,400 feet
- (D) 41,250 feet

GO

Name ______________________________ Date ______________

DIRECTIONS: Choose the best answer for questions 18–21.

18. Find the missing number.

18, 26, 22, _____ , 26, 34, 30, 38

Ⓕ 24
Ⓖ 28
Ⓗ 30
Ⓙ 32

19. Extend the number pattern.

56, 53, 55, 52, 54, 51, 53, _____

Ⓐ 50
Ⓑ 55
Ⓒ 49
Ⓓ 51

20. What is the function rule for the following table?

IN (n)	1	2	3	4	5
OUT (m)	3	5	7	9	11

Ⓕ $m = n + 2$
Ⓖ $m = 2n + 1$
Ⓗ $m = 2n - 1$
Ⓙ $m = 3n$

21. Which of the following expressions is equal to the expression 4(3 + 7)?

Ⓐ $(4 \times 3) + 7$
Ⓑ $4 + 10$
Ⓒ $3 + (4 \times 7)$
Ⓓ $(4 \times 3) + (4 \times 7)$

DIRECTIONS: Use this shape for questions 22 and 23.

4 ft.

16 ft.

22. To change the area of the shape to 96 square feet, what measurement change is needed?

Ⓕ increase length from 16 to 18 ft.
Ⓖ increase width from 4 to 6 ft.
Ⓗ increase length to 17 and width to 5 ft.
Ⓙ increase length from 16 to 19 ft.

23. To change the perimeter of the shape to 20 feet, what measurement change is needed?

Ⓐ decrease width from 4 to 3 ft.
Ⓑ decrease length from 16 to 15 ft.
Ⓒ decrease width from 4 to 1 ft.
Ⓓ decrease length from 16 to 6 ft.

DIRECTIONS: For numbers 24 and 25, let $y = 19 - 2x$.

24. What is y when x is 3?

Ⓕ 25
Ⓖ 13
Ⓗ 17
Ⓙ 10

25. What is y when x is 5?

Ⓐ 9
Ⓑ 17
Ⓒ 24
Ⓓ 26

GO

Name ______________________________ Date ______________

DIRECTIONS: Use the graph below to answer questions 26–28.

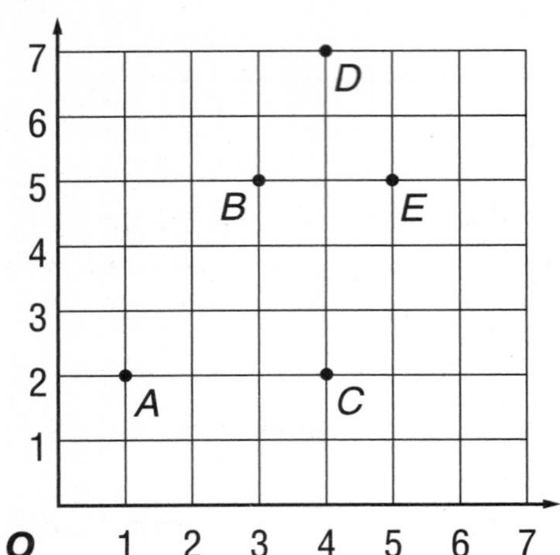

26. What are the coordinates of point A?

- Ⓕ (2, 1)
- Ⓖ (1, 2)
- Ⓗ (1, 1)
- Ⓙ (2, 2)

27. What are the coordinates of point B?

- Ⓐ (4, 2)
- Ⓑ (2, 4)
- Ⓒ (5, 3)
- Ⓓ (3, 5)

28. What are the coordinates of the point that is between B and E?

- Ⓕ (4, 5)
- Ⓖ (5, 4)
- Ⓗ (4, 4)
- Ⓙ (6, 4)

29. What is the diameter of the circle?

- Ⓐ 27 cm
- Ⓑ 18 cm
- Ⓒ 9 cm
- Ⓓ 4.5 cm

30. Which pair of shapes is congruent?

Ⓕ 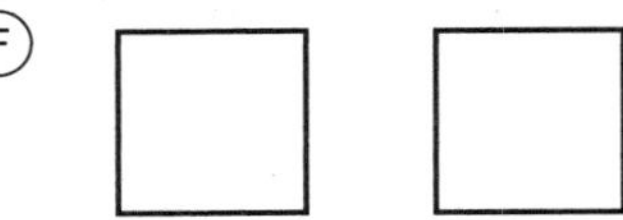

Ⓖ 

Ⓗ 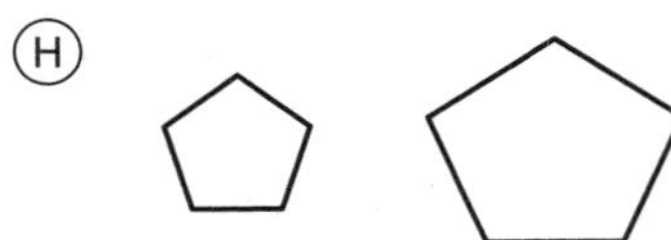

Ⓙ 

31. What type of angle is shown?

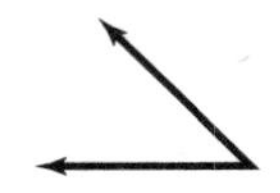

- Ⓐ acute
- Ⓑ right
- Ⓒ obtuse
- Ⓓ None of the above

GO

Name ______________________________ Date ______________

DIRECTIONS: Choose the best answer.

32. What is the mode of this data: 31, 54, 34, 31, 56?

- Ⓕ 31
- Ⓖ 54
- Ⓗ 56
- Ⓙ 34

33. What is the range of this data: 882, 376, 272, 294?

- Ⓐ 376
- Ⓑ 610
- Ⓒ 294
- Ⓓ 484

34. What is the median of this data: 768, 521, 482, 146, 371?

- Ⓕ 521
- Ⓖ 146
- Ⓗ 482
- Ⓙ 371

DIRECTIONS: Use the following tree diagram for numbers 35–37. Adam was dressing to go out and play in the snow. He had a blue coat and a green coat and red, blue, and gray mittens.

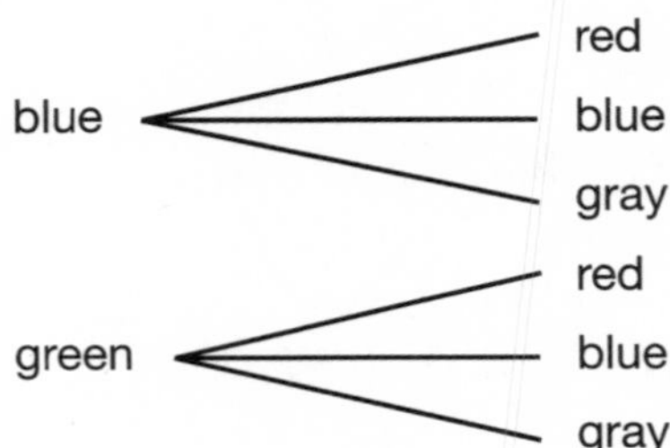

35. How many options does Adam have for outfits?

- Ⓐ 6
- Ⓑ 3
- Ⓒ 8
- Ⓓ 2

36. Which of the following is *not* an option?

- Ⓕ blue coat and gray mittens
- Ⓖ green coat and gray mittens
- Ⓗ blue coat and yellow mittens
- Ⓙ green coat and blue mittens

37. If Adam decides he doesn't want to wear the green coat, how many options does he have?

- Ⓐ 6
- Ⓑ 3
- Ⓒ 8
- Ⓓ 2

DIRECTIONS: Use the following information for numbers 38 and 39. Amanda had 6 green socks, 8 brown socks, and 12 black socks in a basket.

38. If she reaches into the basket without looking and picks out a sock, what is the probability of picking a brown sock?

- Ⓕ 8 out of 13
- Ⓖ 4 out of 13
- Ⓗ 2 out of 3
- Ⓙ 1 out of 2

39. If she reaches into the basket without looking and picks out a sock, what is the probability of picking a green sock?

- Ⓐ 1 out of 2
- Ⓑ 3 out of 4
- Ⓒ 3 out of 13
- Ⓓ 1 out of 3

STOP

Name ______________________________ Date ______________

Final Mathematics Test

Answer Sheet

1 Ⓐ Ⓑ Ⓒ Ⓓ
2 Ⓕ Ⓖ Ⓗ Ⓙ
3 Ⓐ Ⓑ Ⓒ Ⓓ
4 Ⓕ Ⓖ Ⓗ Ⓙ
5 Ⓐ Ⓑ Ⓒ Ⓓ
6 Ⓕ Ⓖ Ⓗ Ⓙ
7 Ⓐ Ⓑ Ⓒ Ⓓ
8 Ⓕ Ⓖ Ⓗ Ⓙ
9 Ⓐ Ⓑ Ⓒ Ⓓ
10 Ⓕ Ⓖ Ⓗ Ⓙ

11 Ⓐ Ⓑ Ⓒ Ⓓ
12 Ⓕ Ⓖ Ⓗ Ⓙ
13 Ⓐ Ⓑ Ⓒ Ⓓ
14 Ⓕ Ⓖ Ⓗ Ⓙ
15 Ⓐ Ⓑ Ⓒ Ⓓ
16 Ⓕ Ⓖ Ⓗ Ⓙ
17 Ⓐ Ⓑ Ⓒ Ⓓ
18 Ⓕ Ⓖ Ⓗ Ⓙ
19 Ⓐ Ⓑ Ⓒ Ⓓ
20 Ⓕ Ⓖ Ⓗ Ⓙ

21 Ⓐ Ⓑ Ⓒ Ⓓ
22 Ⓕ Ⓖ Ⓗ Ⓙ
23 Ⓐ Ⓑ Ⓒ Ⓓ
24 Ⓕ Ⓖ Ⓗ Ⓙ
25 Ⓐ Ⓑ Ⓒ Ⓓ
26 Ⓕ Ⓖ Ⓗ Ⓙ
27 Ⓐ Ⓑ Ⓒ Ⓓ
28 Ⓕ Ⓖ Ⓗ Ⓙ
29 Ⓐ Ⓑ Ⓒ Ⓓ
30 Ⓕ Ⓖ Ⓗ Ⓙ

31 Ⓐ Ⓑ Ⓒ Ⓓ
32 Ⓕ Ⓖ Ⓗ Ⓙ
33 Ⓐ Ⓑ Ⓒ Ⓓ
34 Ⓕ Ⓖ Ⓗ Ⓙ
35 Ⓐ Ⓑ Ⓒ Ⓓ
36 Ⓕ Ⓖ Ⓗ Ⓙ
37 Ⓐ Ⓑ Ⓒ Ⓓ
38 Ⓕ Ⓖ Ⓗ Ⓙ
39 Ⓐ Ⓑ Ⓒ Ⓓ

Illinois Science Content Standards

The science section of the state test measures knowledge in three different areas.

Goal 8: Understand the process of scientific inquiry and technological design to investigate questions, conduct experiments, and solve problems.

Goal 9: Understand the fundamental concepts, principles, and interconnections of the life, physical, and earth/space sciences.

Goal 10: Understand the relationships among science, technology, and society in historical and contemporary contexts.

Illinois Science Table of Contents

Science Standards

Scientific Inquiry and Technological Design

Goal 8: Understand the processes of scientific inquiry and technological design to investigate questions, conduct experiments, and solve problems.

Learning Standard 8A—Know and apply the concepts, principles, and processes of scientific inquiry.

8.A.2a Formulate questions on a specific science topic and choose the steps needed to answer the questions. *(See page 155.)*

8.A.2b Collect data for investigations using scientific process skills including observing, estimating, and measuring. *(See page 156.)*

8.A.2c Construct charts and visualizations to display data. *(See page 157.)*

8.A.2d Use data to produce reasonable explanations. *(See page 158.)*

8.A.2e Report and display the results of individual and group investigations.

Learning Standard 8B—Know and apply the concepts, principles, and processes of technological design.

8.B.2a Identify a design problem and propose possible solutions. *(See page 159.)*

8.B.2b Develop a plan, design, and procedure to address the problem, identifying constraints (e.g., time, materials, technology). *(See page 159.)*

8.B.2c Build a prototype of the design using available tools and materials.

8.B.2d Test the prototype using suitable instruments, techniques, and quantitative measurements to record data.

8.B.2e Assess test results and the effectiveness of the design using given criteria and noting possible sources of error.

8.B.2f Report test design, test process, and test results.

Name ______________________________ Date ______________

Science

8.A.2a

Formulating and Answering Questions

Scientific Inquiry and Technological Design

DIRECTIONS: Read about Ryan's experiment, then answer the questions.

Ryan wanted to find out if people could tell the difference between the taste of cold tap water and cold bottled water. He filled one glass pitcher with tap water and another glass pitcher with bottled water. Then he placed the pitchers in the same refrigerator overnight.

1. **What is the question that Ryan is trying to answer?**

____

____

____

____

____

____

2. **What should be the next step in Ryan's experiment?**

   (A) He should ask several people to taste the tap water.

   (B) He should ask several people to taste the bottled water.

   (C) He should ask several people to taste both types of water and guess which one is tap water and which one is bottled water.

   (D) He should ask several people to taste both types of water and tell which one they like the best.

3. **After he has gathered the data, what should he do with it?**

____

____

____

____

____

____

____

____

4. **How can Ryan best present his findings?**

____

____

____

____

____

____

____

____

____

____

STOP

Name ______________________ Date ______________

Science

8.A.2b

Collecting Data

Scientific Inquiry and Technological Design

DIRECTIONS: Read the graph showing the number of herons on Ash Pond, and then answer the questions.

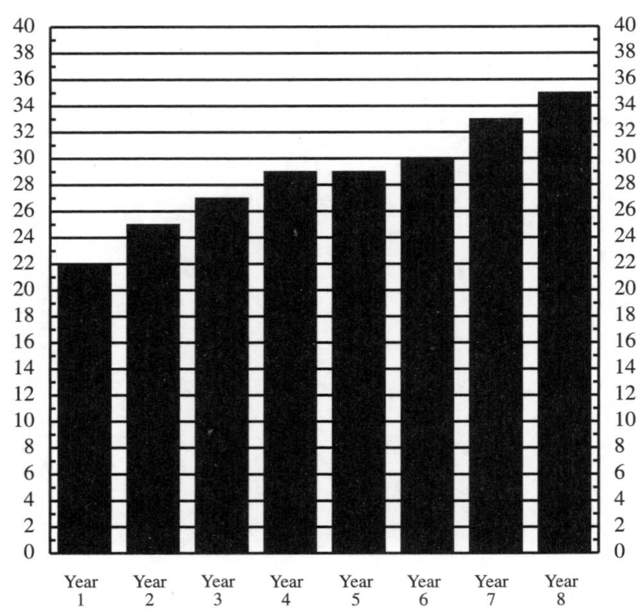

1. In which two years did the number of herons stay the same?

- (A) years 1 and 2
- (B) years 2 and 3
- (C) years 3 and 4
- (D) years 4 and 5

2. Based on the data, how much did the heron population increase between year 1 and year 8?

- (F) by 22
- (G) by 13
- (H) by 12
- (J) by 57

3. What was the average number of herons on Ash Pond over the 8 years?

- (A) 26
- (B) 27
- (C) 28
- (D) 29

4. Based on the data, what could you predict for year 11?

- (F) The number of herons will increase.
- (G) The number of herons will decrease.
- (H) The number of herons will stay the same.
- (J) Herons will become endangered.

Name ______________________ Date ______________

Science **8.A.2c**

Displaying Data

Scientific Inquiry and Technological Design

DIRECTIONS: Ramon and Lila are studying weather. The chart below shows the average daily temperature in Abilene for the past week. In the space below, construct a bar graph to represent the data.

Day	Temperature
Sunday	70°
Monday	72°
Tuesday	69°
Wednesday	74°
Thursday	80°
Friday	91°
Saturday	77°

STOP

Name ______________________ Date ____________

Science

8.A.2d

Scientific Inquiry and Technological Design

Using Data to Produce Reasonable Explanations

DIRECTIONS: Read the passage. Then answer the questions.

Planet Temperatures

Scientists have looked at the other planets in our solar system to see if they would be good places to live. One of the first problems is temperature. Earth's average temperature is about 58°F, which is the temperature on a brisk fall day. Our neighbor Venus is one planet closer to the sun than Earth and much hotter. The average temperature on Venus is 867°F. This is mostly because of Venus's thick atmosphere, which traps the sun's heat so that it cannot escape. The trapping of heat in this way is called the *greenhouse effect.* It is named for the way that hot air is trapped inside a greenhouse and is kept warmer than the air outside. On the other hand, Earth's neighbor Mars is one planet farther away from the sun. It's a little too cold for comfort on Mars. Its average temperature is about –65°F.

1. What is the greenhouse effect?

- (A) air that is trapped by glass and cannot escape
- (B) air that is heated by the sun and then trapped by a planet's thick atmosphere
- (C) air that is heated by the sun and then orbits a planet and keeps it warm
- (D) air that travels from one planet to another

2. Which of these might be an example of the greenhouse effect?

- (F) a car on a summer's day with the air conditioning on
- (G) a parked car on a summer's day with the windows closed
- (H) a car on a summer's day that is traveling down the highway with the windows open
- (J) a parked car on a summer's day with all of the windows open

3. After reading the passage, which of these statements do you think is probably true?

- (A) The average temperature increases the closer a planet is to the sun.
- (B) The average temperature increases the closer a planet is to earth.
- (C) The average temperature decreases the closer a planet is to the sun.
- (D) The average temperature increases the farther a planet is from the sun.

4. After reading the passage, which conclusion can you draw?

- (F) With the proper shelter, it would be possible to live on Mars.
- (G) With the proper shelter, it would be possible to live on Venus.
- (H) Earth's average temperature is colder than Mars' average temperature.
- (J) Earth's average temperature is warmer than Venus's average temperature.

Name ______________________ Date ______________

Science

8.B.2a/8.B.2b

Scientific Inquiry and Technological Design

Identifying and Solving Design Problems

DIRECTIONS: Use the information from the graph to answer the questions.

Anthony constructed three paper airplanes, slanting the wings down on Plane 1, and slanting them up on Plane 2. The wings of Plane 3 were level. The graph shows the average distance each plane flew during a test flight.

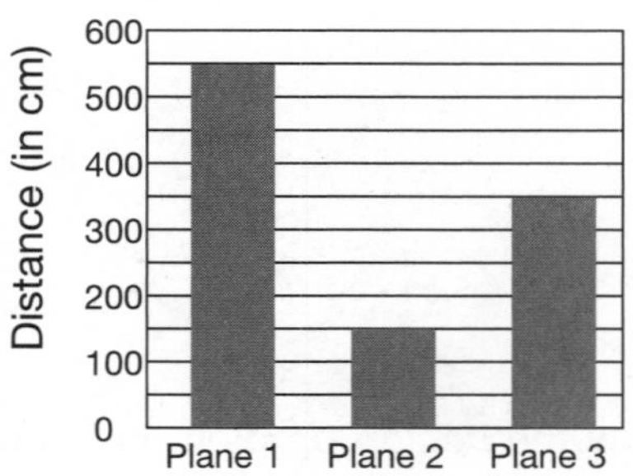

1. Which of the following statements is not true?

Ⓐ Plane 1 flew more than twice as far as Plane 2.

Ⓑ Plane 3 flew half as far as Plane 1.

Ⓒ Plane 2 flew 400 centimeters less than Plane 1.

Ⓓ Plane 2 flew less than half as far as Plane 3.

2. Which of the following conclusions can Anthony draw from the graph?

Ⓕ Paper airplanes fly best with their wings pointed up.

Ⓖ Paper airplanes fly best with level wings.

Ⓗ Paper airplanes fly best with their wings pointed down.

Ⓙ Real airplanes fly best with level wings.

3. Which plane seems to have the most significant design problem? Why do you think so? What is the design problem?

____

____

____

____

____

4. Identify some possible solutions to fix the problem you described in question 3.

____

____

____

____

____

5. How would you go about testing the solutions you described in question 4 to see if they were successful?

____

____

____

____

____

STOP

Name ______________________ Date ______________

Science

8

For pages 155–159

Mini-Test 1

Scientific Inquiry and Technological Design

DIRECTIONS: Choose the best answer.

1. **Fatima went to the library. She looked up the average amount of rain that fell in Jacksonville, Florida, during the month of November for each of the last ten years. What can she predict with this information?**
   - Ⓐ She can predict about how much it will rain in Jacksonville, Florida, next April.
   - Ⓑ She can predict about how much it will rain in Chicago, Illinois, next November.
   - Ⓒ She can predict about how much it will rain in Jacksonville, Florida, next November.
   - Ⓓ She can predict about how much it will rain in Fort Meyers, Florida, next November.

2. **Study the table below. Which month is the most likely to have the most hurricanes?**
   - Ⓕ July
   - Ⓖ August
   - Ⓗ September
   - Ⓙ October

Table of Tropical Storms and Hurricanes (1886–1996)		
Month Formed	**Tropical Storms**	**Hurricanes**
January–April	4	1
May	14	3
June	57	23
July	68	35
August	221	?
September	311	?
October	188	?
November	42	22
December	6	3

3. **Use the information in the table to construct a bar graph that represents the number of tropical storms.**

4. **Identify the design problem in the table pictured below, and propose at least one solution to fix it.**

____

____

____

____

____

____

Science Standards

Life, Physical, and Earth/Space Sciences

Goal 9: Understand the fundamental concepts, principles, and interconnections of the life, physical, and earth/space sciences.

Learning Standard 9A—Know and apply concepts that explain how living things function, adapt, and change.

9.A.2a Describe simple life cycles of plants and animals and the similarities and differences in their offspring. *(See page 162.)*

9.A.2b Categorize features as either inherited or learned (e.g., flower color or eye color is inherited; language is learned). *(See page 163.)*

Learning Standard 9B—Know and apply concepts that describe how living things interact with each other and with their environment.

9.B.2a Describe relationships among various organisms in their environments (e.g., predator/prey, parasite/host, food chains, and food webs). *(See page 164.)*

9.B.2b Identify physical features of plants and animals that help them live in different environments (e.g., specialized teeth for eating certain foods, thorns for protection, insulation for cold temperature). *(See page 165.)*

Learning Standard 9C—Know and apply concepts that describe properties of matter and energy and the interactions between them.

9.C.2a Describe and compare types of energy including light, heat, sound, electrical, and mechanical. *(See page 166.)*

9.C.2b Describe and explain the properties of solids, liquids, and gases. *(See page 167.)*

Learning Standard 9D—Know and apply concepts that describe force and motion and the principles that explain them.

9.D.2a Explain constant, variable, and periodic motions. *(See page 168.)*

9.D.2b Demonstrate and explain ways that forces cause actions and reactions (e.g., magnets attracting and repelling; objects falling, rolling, and bouncing). *(See page 169.)*

Learning Standard 9E—Know and apply concepts that describe the features and processes of the Earth and its resources.

9.E.2a Identify and explain natural cycles of the Earth's land, water, and atmospheric systems (e.g., rock cycle, water cycle, weather patterns). *(See pages 170–171.)*

9.E.2b Describe and explain short-term and long-term interactions of the Earth's components (e.g., earthquakes, types of erosion). *(See pages 170–171.)*

9.E.2c Identify and classify recyclable materials. *(See page 172.)*

Learning Standard 9F—Know and apply concepts that explain the composition and structure of the universe and Earth's place in it.

9.F.2a Identify and explain natural cycles and patterns in the solar system (e.g., order of the planets; moon phases; seasons as related to Earth's tilt, one's latitude, and where Earth is in its yearly orbit around the sun). *(See pages 173–174.)*

9.F.2b Explain the apparent motion of the sun and stars. *(See pages 173–174.)*

9.F.2c Identify easily recognizable star patterns (e.g., the Big Dipper, constellations). *(See page 175.)*

Name ______________________ Date ______________

Science

9.A.2a

Life Cycles of Plants and Animals

Life, Physical, and Earth/Space Sciences

DIRECTIONS: Number each stage of the life cycle in the order it occurs.

1. Moth

_______ larva

_______ adult moth

_______ egg

_______ pupa

2. Oak Tree

_______ tree

_______ acorn

_______ seedling

3. Pig

_______ newborn

_______ piglet

_______ adult pig

4. Human

_______ child

_______ adult

_______ newborn

_______ adolescent

5. Frog

_______ adult frog

_______ tadpole

_______ egg

DIRECTIONS: Choose the best answer.

6. One difference between a lion cub and a flower seedling is that only the _______ .

Ⓐ lion cub needs food

Ⓑ flower seedling needs water

Ⓒ lion cub can move from place to place

Ⓓ flower seedling has parents

7. One similarity between a lion cub and a flower seedling is that _______ .

Ⓕ they both need water to survive

Ⓖ they are both cared for by their parents

Ⓗ they both eat the same kinds of food

Ⓙ all of the above are true

Name ______________________________ Date ______________

Science

9.A.2b

Learned and Inherited Characteristics

Life, Physical, and Earth/Space Sciences

DIRECTIONS: For each of the following, put an **L** in the blank if it is a learned trait. Put an **I** in the blank if it is an inherited trait.

1. __________ **playing tennis**
2. __________ **skin color**
3. __________ **leaves on a tree**
4. __________ **hibernation**
5. __________ **reading**
6. __________ **petal color and flowers**
7. __________ **language**
8. __________ **cheek dimples**
9. __________ **straight or curly hair**
10. __________ **humans building houses**
11. __________ **horses carrying riders**
12. __________ **tadpoles turning into frogs**
13. __________ **bees building hives**
14. __________ **dogs shaking hands**

15. **Describe some learned and inherited characteristics that you have acquired.**

____

____

____

____

____

____

____

____

____

____

____

____

____

____

____

____

STOP

Name ______________________ Date ______________

Science

9.B.2a

Relationships Among Organisms

Life, Physical, and Earth/Space Sciences

DIRECTIONS: Choose the correct word from the parentheses at the end of each sentence to fill in the blanks and complete the definitions.

1. **The place where an organism lives is**

   its ______________________.

   (habitat, community)

2. **All of the living organisms within an area form**

   a ______________________.

   (community, habitat)

3. **The unique role of an organism in the community is**

   its ______________________.

   (habitat, niche)

4. **A biological community and physical environment that interact to form a stable system is called**

   a(n) ______________________.

   (ecosystem, niche)

5. **An organism, usually a green plant, which can make its own food is called**

   a ______________________.

   (consumer, producer)

6. **An organism that lives by feeding on other organisms is called**

   a ______________________.

   (decomposer, consumer)

7. **An organism that feeds on the remains of other organisms is called**

   a ______________________.

   (decomposer, producer)

DIRECTIONS: Answer questions 8 and 9 based on the food chain shown below.

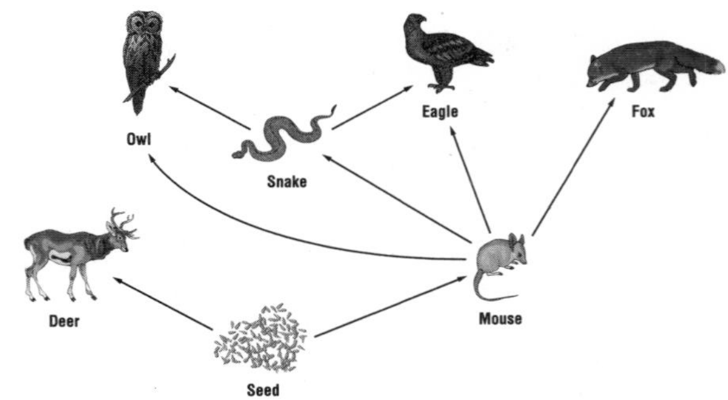

8. **Which of the following statements is true?**
   - (A) Mice eat foxes.
   - (B) Snakes eat mice.
   - (C) Nothing in this food web eats snakes.
   - (D) Owls eat deer.

9. **What would be the most likely result in this ecosystem if all the foxes were removed?**
   - (F) The eagles would begin eating deer.
   - (G) The plants would all die.
   - (H) The deer population would increase.
   - (J) The owls, snakes, and eagles would have more mice to eat.

Name ______________________________ Date ______________________________

Science

9.B.2b

Adaptive Characteristics

Life, Physical, and Earth/Space Sciences

DIRECTIONS: Match the ecosystem of each mystery organism in **Column A** to one or more adaptations that would be most beneficial for its survival in **Column B**.

COLUMN A	COLUMN B
1. __________ in a tree in the rainforest	a. strong legs for climbing
2. __________ underground in the backyard	b. a tail to help it hang from branches
3. __________ on the leaves of a rose bush	c. deep roots to find water
4. __________ in a coral reef	d. the ability to breathe air as well as water
5. __________ on a glacier in Alaska	e. being a color that blends in with leaves
6. __________ on a mountainside	f. strong claws for digging and moving dirt
7. __________ in a polluted stream	g. a thick coat and layer of fat
8. __________ in the desert	h. strong wings to fly and glide
9. __________ on the side of a cliff	i. ability to see in the dark
10. __________ in a cave	j. clear eyelids to keep out sand and dirt
11. __________ in a forest in the midwest	k. hibernating in the winter when food is scarce
12. __________ on the bank of a nearly dry stream	l. ability to completely draw inside a shell

STOP

Name ______________________________ Date ______________

Science

9.C.2a

Types of Energy

Life, Physical, and Earth/Space Sciences

DIRECTIONS: Choose the best answer.

1. **Heat and sound travel in __________ .**
   - (A) beams
   - (B) drops
   - (C) waves
   - (D) currents

2. **When a girl starts running, she is converting stored energy into __________ .**
   - (F) heat energy
   - (G) sound energy
   - (H) kinetic energy
   - (J) light energy

3. **The word *kinetic* relates to __________ .**
   - (A) the amount of matter in an object
   - (B) the energy of motion
   - (C) the attractive force between two objects
   - (D) the measurement of force

4. **What is the name of the energy from the sun?**
   - (F) solar
   - (G) polar
   - (H) ocular
   - (J) lunar

5. **Electric motors transform electrical energy into __________ .**
   - (A) kinetic energy
   - (B) heat energy
   - (C) mechanical energy
   - (D) electrical energy

6. **Emma sees a flash of lightning and then hears the thunder about 5 seconds later. Next, she sees another flash of lightning, and the thunder comes 2 seconds later. What can she conclude?**
   - (F) The light is traveling faster than before.
   - (G) The thunder is getting louder.
   - (H) The lightning is closer than before.
   - (J) The thunder is farther away than before.

7. **How does light travel?**
   - (A) in waves only
   - (B) in particles only
   - (C) in both waves and particles
   - (D) in neither waves nor particles

8. **After a heavy rain, you may see puddles on the road. Eventually, the puddles evaporate due to heat. What is the source of the heat that causes the water to evaporate?**
   - (F) the sun
   - (G) the air
   - (H) the water
   - (J) None of the above

STOP

Name ______________________________ Date ______________

Science

9.C.2b

Properties of Matter

Life, Physical, and Earth/Space Sciences

DIRECTIONS: Choose the best answer.

1. How can you change matter from one state to another?

- (A) by changing its container
- (B) by adding or removing heat
- (C) by dividing it in half
- (D) by changing its volume

2. Ice is water in its __________ state.

- (F) solid
- (G) changing
- (H) liquid
- (J) gas

3. You fill a balloon with steam and then put it in the refrigerator. What do you predict will happen next?

- (A) The balloon will expand.
- (B) The balloon will contract.
- (C) The balloon will pop.
- (D) The balloon will not change.

4. When water freezes, it changes from a __________ .

- (F) gas to a solid
- (G) liquid to a gas
- (H) liquid to a solid
- (J) solid to a gas

5. If matter has a fixed volume but changes its shape to fit its container, it is a __________ .

- (A) solid
- (B) liquid
- (C) gas
- (D) suspension

6. Which of the following cannot be used to classify forms of matter?

- (F) water
- (G) liquid
- (H) gas
- (J) solid

7. Malcom left a cube of ice in a glass on a window sill. In about an hour, the ice changed into a clear substance that took on the shape of the lower part of the glass. Finally, after three days, there appeared to be nothing in the glass at all. What states of matter did the ice cube pass through?

- (A) liquid then gas then solid
- (B) solid then liquid then gas
- (C) gas then liquid then solid
- (D) solid then gas then liquid

STOP

Name ______________________ Date ______________

Science

9.D.2a

Types of Motion

Life, Physical, and Earth/Space Sciences

DIRECTIONS: Read each type of motion described below. If the motion of the object being described is constant, write a **C** in the space provided. If the motion is variable, write a **V** in the space provided. If the motion is periodic, write a **P** in the space provided.

Constant motion means it is a continuous type of motion. **Variable** motion means the motion can change at any time. **Periodic** motion means the motion occurs at regular or predictable intervals.

_____ 1. **The pendulum of a grandfather clock moves back and forth one beat per second.**

_____ 2. **A toy car travels five feet, hits a wall, bounces off it and turns in another direction, then travels another five feet.**

_____ 3. **A bowling ball rolls down the alley.**

_____ 4. **The earth rotates around the sun.**

_____ 5. **A baseball is thrown from the pitcher and caught by the catcher.**

_____ 6. **A baseball is thrown from the pitcher, hit by the batter on the ground to the shortstop, and picked up by the shortstop and thrown to first base.**

_____ 7. **Your heart beats regularly as you sit quietly and read a book.**

_____ 8. **A truck travels on an Interstate highway for 40 miles at 55 miles per hour.**

_____ 9. **A truck travels down Main Street for one block at 25 miles per hour, slows to a stop at a red light, turns left onto Third Avenue, and slowly reaches a speed of 15 miles per hour before stopping again at another red light.**

_____ 10. **The minute hand on your clock moves from 9:01 to 9:02.**

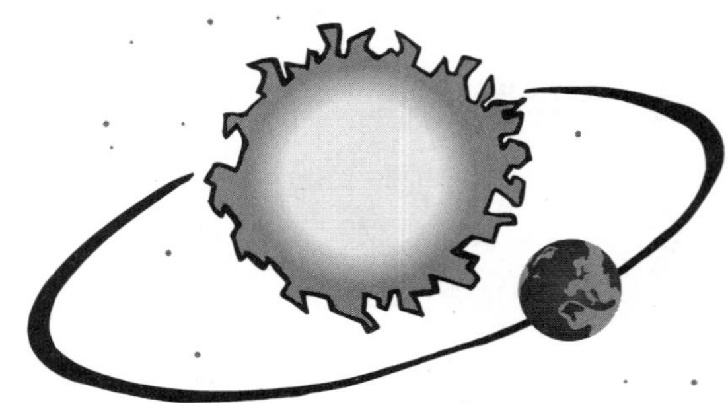

STOP

Name ______________________________ Date ______________

Science

9.D.2b

Forces

Life, Physical, and Earth/Space Sciences

DIRECTIONS: Choose the best answer.

1. **The force that pulls a skydiver back to earth is called ________ .**
   - (A) gravity
   - (B) mass
   - (C) friction
   - (D) inertia

2. **A man standing at the top of the Grand Canyon accidentally knocked some pebbles over the edge. What force will cause them to fall?**
   - (F) gravity
   - (G) magnetism
   - (H) friction
   - (J) solar power

3. **Slippery Sam pours salad oil on the floor because he likes watching people slip when they step on it. Before asking him to oil all the door hinges as punishment, Sam's teacher asks him to explain why oil makes people slip and keeps door hinges from squeaking. If Sam answers correctly, he will say that oil cuts down on __________ .**
   - (A) gravity
   - (B) inertia
   - (C) friction
   - (D) mass

4. **If a marble and a baseball are both dropped 10 feet from the ground at the same time, what will happen?**
   - (F) The marble will hit the ground first.
   - (G) The baseball will hit the ground first.
   - (H) The marble and the baseball will hit the ground at the same time.
   - (J) None of the above

5. **Dot decided to go home and ride in her wagon. She asked her brother Jorge to push her. At first, he pushed her very gently. After a while, he pushed harder. Then Sandra came to visit, and Jorge pushed both of them in the wagon at the same time. Which of the following is true?**
   - (A) Dot went slower when Jorge pushed harder. Dot and Sandra had more gravity than just Dot.
   - (B) Dot went faster when Jorge pushed harder. Dot and Sandra were harder to move than just Dot.
   - (C) Dot went slower when Jorge pushed harder. Dot and Sandra were easier to move than just Dot.
   - (D) Dot went faster when Jorge pushed harder. Dot and Sandra were easier to move than just Dot.

6. **What will happen between these two magnets?**

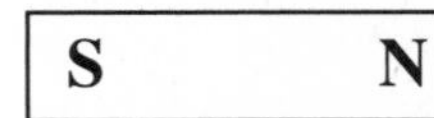

   - (F) attract
   - (G) repel
   - (H) not move
   - (J) None of the above

STOP

Name ______________________________ Date ______________

Science
9.E.2a/9.E.2b

Earth's Processes

Life, Physical, and Earth/Space Sciences

DIRECTIONS: Choose the best answer.

1. **The changes that occurred in the pictures below are probably due to __________ .**

   (A) pollution
   (B) erosion
   (C) tornadoes
   (D) condensation

2. **Christopher was looking at pictures of different mountain ranges in the United States. He was surprised to see that the Appalachian Mountains were smaller and more rounded than the Rocky Mountains. The Appalachian Mountains looked old and worn compared to the Rocky Mountains.**
   (F) The effect of wind and water caused weathering, wearing away the mountains.
   (G) Too many people and animals traveled across the mountains, causing them to wear away.
   (H) All of the snowfall was so heavy that it weighted down the mountains and caused them to shrink.
   (J) The water that used to cover earth wore away parts of the mountains.

3. **During the Ice Age, most of the state of Illinois was covered by a huge glacier that changed the landscape. Which of the following was *not* an effect of the glacier on the landscape of that state?**
   (A) New mountains were made.
   (B) The peaks of hills were scraped off.
   (C) Many deep valleys were filled in.
   (D) Soil was transported miles away from its origin.

4. **What kind of mountains are the Hawaiian Islands?**
   (F) fault-block
   (G) volcanic
   (H) upwarped
   (J) folded

5. **The Adirondack Mountains are upwarped mountains. Today, the rock material that was once present on the tops of these mountains is gone. Why?**
   (A) The rock material was pushed inside earth.
   (B) Sharp peaks and ridges formed over the rock material.
   (C) The rock material became magma.
   (D) The rock material was eroded.

6. **Which of the following is the slowest type of mass movement?**
   (F) abrasion
   (G) creep
   (H) slump
   (J) mudflow

Name ____ Date ____________________

7. What term describes a mass of snow and ice in motion?

Ⓐ loess deposit
Ⓑ glacier
Ⓒ outwash
Ⓓ abrasion

8. Which characteristic is common to all agents of erosion?

Ⓕ They carry sediments when they have enough energy of motion.
Ⓖ They are most likely to erode when sediments are moist.
Ⓗ They create deposits called dunes.
Ⓙ They erode large sediments before they erode small ones.

9. When a puddle of water disappears after the sun comes out, it is called __________ .

Ⓐ displacement
Ⓑ metamorphosis
Ⓒ isolation
Ⓓ evaporation

10. Water vapor forming droplets that form clouds directly involves which process?

Ⓕ condensation
Ⓖ respiration
Ⓗ evaporation
Ⓙ transpiration

11. Most of earth's water is in __________ .

Ⓐ glaciers
Ⓑ lakes
Ⓒ streams
Ⓓ the oceans

12. All the water that is found at earth's surface is the __________ .

Ⓕ carbosphere
Ⓖ hydrosphere
Ⓗ precipitation
Ⓙ pollution

13. 97% of the water on earth is __________ .

Ⓐ salt water
Ⓑ freshwater
Ⓒ rainwater
Ⓓ fog

14. What is a mixture of weathered rock and organic matter called?

Ⓕ soil
Ⓖ limestone
Ⓗ carbon dioxide
Ⓙ clay

15. What is another term for decayed organic matter found in soil?

Ⓐ leaching
Ⓑ humus
Ⓒ soil
Ⓓ sediment

16. What occurs when weathered rock and organic matter are mixed together?

Ⓕ leaching
Ⓖ oxidation
Ⓗ soil erosion
Ⓙ soil formation

17. In the water cycle, how is water returned to the atmosphere?

Ⓐ evaporation
Ⓑ condensation
Ⓒ precipitation
Ⓓ fixation

18. Warm, low-pressure air can hold more water than cold air. As warm air rises, it cools. This causes water vapor to gather together, or condense, into water drops. What kind of weather probably goes along with low air pressure?

Ⓕ clouds and rain
Ⓖ clouds without rain
Ⓗ clear skies
Ⓙ tornadoes

Name ______________________________ Date ______________

Science

9.E.2c

Recyclable Materials

Life, Physical, and Earth/Space Sciences

DIRECTIONS: Study the chart that shows how much one school has helped the environment. Then, answer the questions.

Conservation Efforts at Coe School			
Year	**Pounds of Paper Recycled**	**Pounds of Can Recycled**	**Number of Trees Planted**
2002	550	475	120
2003	620	469	250
2004	685	390	320

1. Which sentence is true about paper recycling at Coe School?

- (A) Students recycled more paper each year.
- (B) Students recycled less paper each year.
- (C) Students never recycled paper.
- (D) Students recycled the same amount of paper each year.

2. Which conservation project did not show better results each year?

- (F) recycling paper
- (G) recycling cans
- (H) planting trees
- (J) They all showed better results each year.

3. Which of the following is the most likely reason for the decrease in can recycling at Coe School?

- (A) Students reduced the amount of canned beverages they were drinking.
- (B) Students found new uses for their cans.
- (C) Students saved their cans.
- (D) Students began recycling their cans at home.

DIRECTIONS: Choose the best answer.

4. When you recycle paper, you help keep the carbon dioxide-oxygen cycle running. Why is this statement true?

- (F) When paper is recycled, the process releases oxygen back into the environment.
- (G) Carbon dioxide is trapped in the paper, and recycling releases it.
- (H) The machinery used to recycle paper releases oxygen.
- (J) Recycling paper saves trees which use carbon dioxide and release oxygen.

5. Which resource could be conserved by recycling a stack of newspapers?

- (A) rocks
- (B) trees
- (C) plastic
- (D) oil

6. Which of the following is an example of recycling to conserve resources?

- (F) walking to the store rather than riding in a car
- (G) taking newspapers to a facility where they will be made into another paper product
- (H) using a glass jelly jar as a pencil holder
- (J) throwing aluminum cans in the trash

Name ______________________________ Date ______________

Science

9.F.2a/9.F.2b

Cycles and Patterns in the Solar System

Life, Physical, and Earth/Space Sciences

DIRECTIONS: Fill in the blanks with the names of planets according to their correct order from the sun.

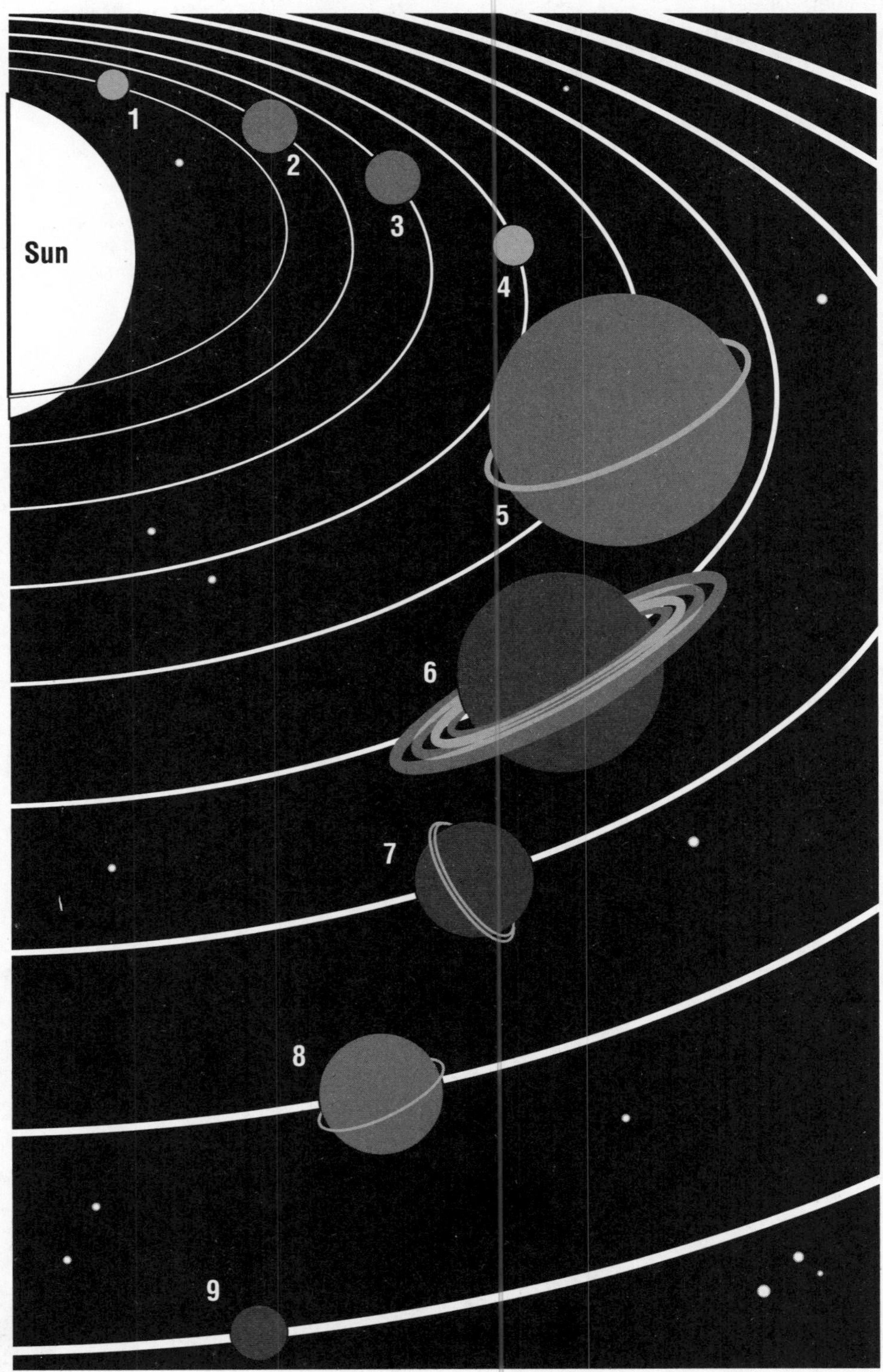

1. ______________

2. ______________

3. ______________

4. ______________

5. ______________

6. ______________

7. ______________

8. ______________

9. ______________

GO

Name ______________________ Date ______________

DIRECTIONS: Read the selection. Choose the best answer.

Why Are There Seasons?

Earth revolves around the sun. It also spins on an invisible axis that runs through its center.

It takes 365 1/4 days, or one year, for earth to revolve once around the sun. Just as the moon moves in an orbit around earth, earth moves around the sun. Earth does not move in a perfect circle. Its orbit is an ellipse, which is a flattened circle, like an oval. As earth revolves around the sun in an elliptical shape, it spins on its invisible axis.

Earth's axis of rotation is not straight up and down, it is tilted. This important feature produces the seasons on earth. No matter where earth is in its rotation around the sun, its axis is tilted in the same direction and at the same angle. So, as earth moves, different parts of it are facing the sun and different parts are facing away. The North Pole is tilting toward the sun in June, so the northern half of earth is enjoying summer. In December, the North Pole is tilted away from the sun, so the northern part of the world experiences winter.

This important relationship between earth and the sun determines how hot and cold we are, when we plants our crops, and whether we have droughts or floods.

10. If North America is having summer, what season would the Australians be enjoying?

- (A) spring
- (B) summer
- (C) winter
- (D) fall

11. What would happen if earth's axis were not tilted, but straight up and down?

- (F) Nothing would change.
- (G) Earth wouldn't change seasons.
- (H) It would always be summer on earth.
- (J) It would always be winter on earth.

DIRECTIONS: Choose the best answer.

12. Picture A shows the moon as it looked on August 1. Picture B shows the moon as it looked on August 14. Which of the following shows how the moon will look on August 28?

A B

- (A)
- (B)
- (C)
- (D)

13. What causes the sun to appear to rise and set?

- (F) Earth's revolution
- (G) the sun's revolution
- (H) Earth's rotation
- (J) Earth's elliptical orbit

STOP

Name ______________________________ Date ______________

Science

9.F.2c

Constellations

Life, Physical, and Earth/Space Sciences

DIRECTIONS: Match the constellations pictured below with their names.

Constellations

A the Big Dipper
B Orion
C Cassiopeia
D Cygnus
E Cepheus

1. __________

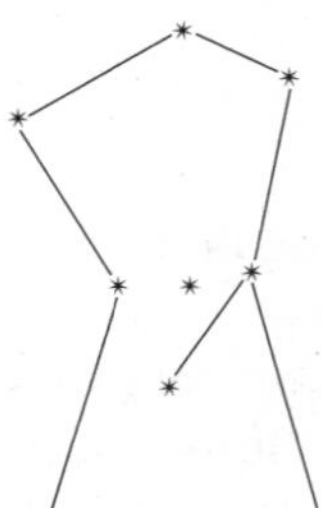

2. __________

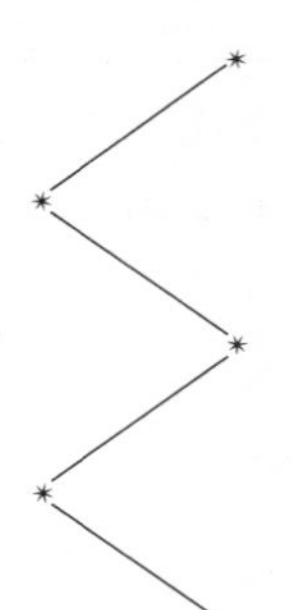

3. __________

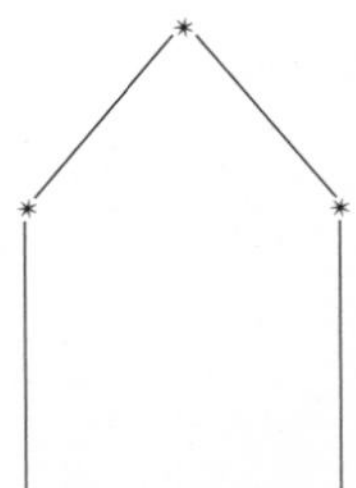

4. __________

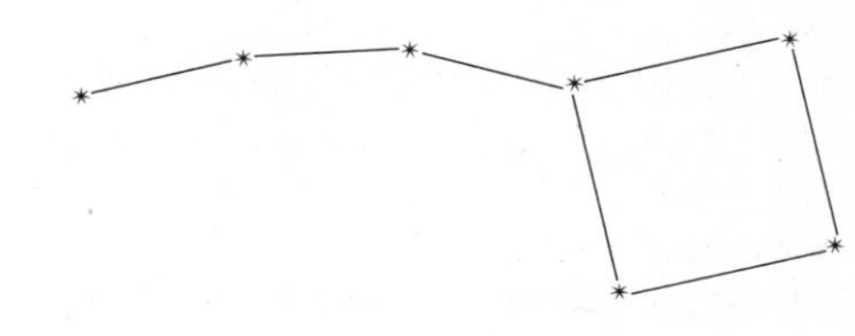

5. __________

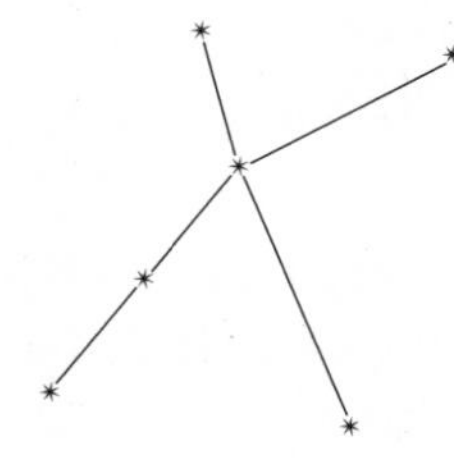

STOP

Name ______________________ Date ______________

Science

For pages 162–175

Mini-Test 2

Life, Physical, and Earth/Space Sciences

DIRECTIONS: Choose the best answer.

1. Which of the following features is inherited?

Ⓐ riding a bike
Ⓑ hair color
Ⓒ counting
Ⓓ talking

2. Instead of making their own food, animals __________ .

Ⓕ eat only plants
Ⓖ eat only other animals
Ⓗ eat plants or other animals
Ⓙ eat only decomposers

3. A tapeworm attaches itself to another animal's intestine. It then absorbs food from that animal. The tapeworm benefits but the other animal is harmed. What kind or organism is a tapeworm?

Ⓐ herbivore
Ⓑ parasite
Ⓒ carnivore
Ⓓ None of the above

4. In a predator-prey relationship, when the prey population increases, the predator population will probably __________ .

Ⓕ increase
Ⓖ decrease
Ⓗ stay the same
Ⓙ not enough information

5. When an object changes its location in space we say it is in __________ .

Ⓐ force
Ⓑ acceleration
Ⓒ motion
Ⓓ velocity

6. Ice, raindrops, and steam are all __________ in different states of matter.

Ⓕ solids
Ⓖ water
Ⓗ liquids
Ⓙ gases

7. What two forces cause erosion?

Ⓐ water and gravity
Ⓑ sun and wind
Ⓒ wind and water
Ⓓ gravity and wind

8. The planet Venus is often called the *morning star.* This is because Venus sometimes rises above the horizon very early in the morning before sunrise. Before sunrise, Venus is often the brightest object in the sky. As the sun rises, Venus becomes fainter and fainter. Predict the day that Venus will rise at 6:00 A.M.

Day	Time That Venus Will Rise
Sunday	6:24 A.M.
Monday	6:20 A.M.
Tuesday	6:16 A.M.
Wednesday	6:12 A.M.
Thursday	6:08 A.M.

Ⓕ Thursday
Ⓖ Friday
Ⓗ Saturday
Ⓙ Sunday

STOP

Science Standards

Relationships Among Science, Technology, and Society

Goal 10: Understand the relationships among science, technology, and society in historical and contemporary contexts.

Learning Standard 10A—Know and apply the accepted practices of science. *(See page 178.)*

10.A.2a Demonstrate ways to avoid injury when conducting science activities (e.g., wearing goggles, fire extinguisher use).
10.A.2b Explain why similar investigations may not produce similar results.
10.A.2c Explain why keeping accurate and detailed records is important.

Learning Standard 10B—Know and apply concepts that describe the interaction between science, technology, and society.

10.B.2a Explain how technology is used in science for a variety of purposes (e.g., sample collection, storage and treatment; measurement; data collection, storage and retrieval; communication of information). *(See page 179.)*
10.B.2b Describe the effects on society of scientific and technological innovation (e.g., antibiotics, steam engine, digital computer). *(See page 180.)*
10.B.2c Identify and explain ways that science and technology influence the lives and careers of people. *(See page 180.)*
10.B.2d Compare the relative effectiveness of reducing, reusing, and recycling in actual situations. *(See page 181.)*
10.B.2e Identify and explain ways that technology changes ecosystems (e.g., dams, highways, buildings, communication networks, power plants). *(See page 181.)*
10.B.2f Analyze how specific personal and societal choices that humans make affect local, regional, and global ecosystems (e.g., lawn and garden care, mass transit). *(See page 181.)*

Name ______________________________ Date ______________

Science

10.A.2a/10.A.2b/10.A.2c

The Practices of Science

Relationships Among Science, Technology, and Society

DIRECTIONS: Read the following story to answer the questions.

Lauren entered the science fair. For her project, she wanted to see which brand of batteries lasts longest: Everglo, Glomore, or Everlasting. She decided to place new batteries into identical new flashlights, turn on the flashlights, then wait for the batteries to run down. She wrote down the following results: Everglo—lasted 19 hours; Glomore—lasted 17 hours; Everlasting—lasted 25 hours.

She then decided to re-do the experiment to confirm the results. For her second experiment, she placed new batteries into the old flashlights that her parents keep in the garage, the kitchen, and their bedroom. She then turned on the flashlights and waited for the batteries to run down. This time she wrote down the following results: Everglo—lasted 13 hours; Glomore—lasted 16 hours; Everlasting—lasted 9 hours.

Lauren was puzzled by the results of her second experiment. Because it was so similar to her first experiment, she thought she would get the same results.

1. What is the best explanation for why Lauren's second experiment had different results than her first experiment?

- (A) Lauren used different brands of batteries in the second experiment.
- (B) The second experiment used old flashlights, while the first experiment used new flashlights.
- (C) The second experiment was too much like the first experiment.
- (D) There is no good explanation; sometimes things just happen.

2. How was Lauren sure that the results of the second experiment were different from the results of the first experiment?

- (F) She read on the side of the battery packages how long each brand would last before it ran down.
- (G) She simply remembered how long it took each brand of battery to run down.
- (H) She recorded exactly how long it took each brand of battery to run down for each experiment.
- (J) She cannot be sure; her experiment was faulty.

3. Tell what Lauren did right in her experiments. Could she have done anything in a better, more scientific way?

____

____

____

____

____

____

4. Which of these is an example of unsafe behavior in a science lab?

- (A) wearing eye goggles
- (B) smelling and tasting unknown chemicals
- (C) avoiding the use of broken or chipped glassware
- (D) tying back long hair when working with flames

Name ______________________________ Date ______________

Science

10.B.2a

Use of Technology in Science

Relationships Among Science, Technology, and Society

DIRECTIONS: Choose the best answer.

1. **Which instrument would a scientist use to look more closely at a leaf?**
   - Ⓐ barometer
   - Ⓑ thermometer
   - Ⓒ microscope
   - Ⓓ beaker

2. **Which instrument would a scientist use to measure air pressure?**
   - Ⓕ odometer
   - Ⓖ kilometer
   - Ⓗ thermometer
   - Ⓙ barometer

3. **Which instrument would a scientist use to measure the speed of a falling object?**
   - Ⓐ a stopwatch
   - Ⓑ a microscope
   - Ⓒ a balance scale
   - Ⓓ a ruler

4. **What tool would a scientist use to measure liquids in a laboratory?**
   - Ⓕ graduated cylinder
   - Ⓖ beaker
   - Ⓗ Petri dish
   - Ⓙ scalpel

5. **Describe one way a scientist may use technology to communicate the findings of an experiment to other scientists.**

____

____

____

____

____

6. **Describe one way technology has made it easier for scientists to help people stay healthy.**

____

____

____

____

____

STOP

Name ______________________________ Date ______________

Science

10.B.2b/10.B.2c

Effects and Influence of Technology

Relationships Among Science, Technology, and Society

DIRECTIONS: Match the need on the right with an example of how humans have used technology to meet that need. Some needs may be used more than once.

_____ **1. development of hunting tools**

_____ **2. building fires**

_____ **3. invention of cars**

_____ **4. development of written language**

_____ **5. building of forts**

_____ **6. invention of the printing press**

_____ **7. irrigation**

_____ **8. development of antibiotics**

_____ **9. invention of the jet engine**

_____ **10. invention of the transistor**

_____ **11. development of coal mining technology**

Ⓐ warmth

Ⓑ food

Ⓒ shelter

Ⓓ communication

Ⓔ transportation

Ⓕ health

12. How do you think the invention of computers has influenced society? How has it influenced you and other people in your family? Give some specific examples.

____

____

____

____

____

____

13. Name at least one technological innovation that you think has been an overall bad influence on society. Explain why you think it has been a bad influence.

____

____

____

____

____

____

STOP

Name ______________________________ Date ______________

Science

10.B.2d/10.B.2e/10.B.2f

Conservation/ Technology and Ecosystems

Relationships Among Science, Technology, and Society

DIRECTIONS: Choose the best answer.

1. **The best example of a way to conserve natural resources is ________ .**
   - (A) regulating toxic emissions from cars
   - (B) the greenhouse effect
   - (C) cutting down on packaging used in consumer goods
   - (D) keeping garbage dumps away from residential areas

2. **Which of the following is not a good soil conservation practice?**
   - (F) planting trees to make a windbreak
   - (G) using strip-cropping on sloping ground
   - (H) planting crops without plowing
   - (J) planting the same crop in a field every year

3. **Which of the following is not a conservation activity?**
   - (A) replace
   - (B) reuse
   - (C) recycle
   - (D) reduce

4. **An example of the opposite of reducing is over-packaging. Which of the following is an example of over-packaging?**
   - (F) filling a cereal box completely
   - (G) putting an item in a cardboard box, then putting that box in another box
   - (H) putting foam packing material around a fragile item
   - (J) packing an item in the smallest possible box

5. **Many power companies burn coal to make electricity. Some power companies burn coal that contains high amounts of an element called *sulfur.* When this coal is burned, the sulfur combines with oxygen to form a poisonous gas called *sulfur dioxide.* When the sulfur dioxide gas is released into the atmosphere, it combines with water to form a powerful chemical called *sulfuric acid.* When it rains, the sulfuric acid returns to earth as acid rain. How does acid rain change the environment?**
   - (A) Acid rain helps clean buildings and roads.
   - (B) Acid rain harms plants and animals.
   - (C) Acid rain returns valuable nutrients to the soil.
   - (D) Acid rain helps clean polluted water.

6. **A renewable resource can be replaced. A nonrenewable resource cannot be replaced. Which of the following is a nonrenewable source of energy?**
   - (F) solar power
   - (G) gas power
   - (H) wind power
   - (J) water power

7. **What can result when poor farming practices occur in areas that receive little rain?**
   - (A) ice wedging
   - (B) oxidation
   - (C) leaching
   - (D) desert formation

8. **What does no-till farming help prevent?**
   - (F) leaching
   - (G) crop rotation
   - (H) overgrazing
   - (J) soil erosion

Name ______________________________ Date ______________

Science

10

For pages 178–181

Mini-Test 3

Relationships Among Science, Technology, and Society

DIRECTIONS: Read the following story to answer questions 1 and 2.

Lily and Corey line one shoebox with white paper and another with black paper. Then they put a thermometer in each shoebox. They place both shoeboxes outside in the sun for one hour. At the start of the experiment, the temperature in both boxes was 72°F. At the end of the hour, the box with the white paper showed a temperature of 85°F, and the box with the black paper showed a temperature of 92°F. Two weeks later, they repeat the experiment with these differences: one shoebox is lined with yellow paper and another with orange paper. On this day, the sky is cloudy and the temperature in both boxes was 65°F at the beginning of the experiment.

1. What will be the most likely outcome of the second experiment?

- (A) The box with the yellow paper will show a temperature of 85°F, and the box with the orange paper will show a temperature of 92°F.
- (B) The box with the orange paper will show a temperature of 85°F, and the box with the yellow paper will show a temperature of 92°F.
- (C) Both boxes will show a temperature of 85°F.
- (D) The temperature inside the box with the orange paper will be a bit higher than the box with the yellow paper, but neither box will show temperatures as high as the boxes in the first experiment.

2. Explain how you arrived at your answer to question 1.

____

____

____

____

DIRECTIONS: Choose the best answer.

3. It is important for scientists to keep accurate and detailed records so __________ .

- (F) they can decide which scientists they want to work with on future projects
- (G) they can decide who is the best scientist
- (H) more scientists can have jobs
- (J) the results of the experiments can be verified

4. Trees are conserved when cardboard and newspapers are __________ .

- (A) hauled to a dump
- (B) burned
- (C) kept in storage
- (D) recycled

5. Walking or riding a bicycle to a store rather than having someone drive you in a car is an example of __________ .

- (F) replacing
- (G) recycling
- (H) reducing
- (J) reusing

6. Which instrument is used to examine the features of the moon?

- (A) hydrometer
- (B) microscope
- (C) thermometer
- (D) telescope

7. A windbreak helps prevent __________ .

- (F) soil depletion
- (G) water erosion
- (H) wind erosion
- (J) None of these

How Am I Doing?

Mini-Test 1 Page 160 **Number Correct**	**4** answers correct	**Great Job!** Move on to the section test on page 184.
	3 answers correct	**You're almost there!** But you still need a little practice. Review the practice pages 155–159 before moving on to the section test on page 184.
	0–2 answers correct	**Oops!** Time to review what you have learned and try again. Review the practice section on pages 155–159. Then retake the test on page 160. Now move on to the section test on page 184.
Mini-Test 2 Page 176 **Number Correct**	**7–8** answers correct	**Awesome!** Move on to the section test on page 184.
	5–6 answers correct	**You're almost there!** But you still need a little practice. Review the practice pages 162–175 before moving on to the section test on page 184.
	0–4 answers correct	**Oops!** Time to review what you have learned and try again. Review the practice section on pages 162–175. Then retake the test on page 176. Now move on to the section test on page 184.
Mini-Test 3 Page 182 **Number Correct**	**7** answers correct	**Great Job!** Move on to the section test on page 184.
	5–6 answers correct	**You're almost there!** But you still need a little practice. Review the practice pages 178–181 before moving on to the section test on page 184.
	0–4 answers correct	**Oops!** Time to review what you have learned and try again. Review the practice section on pages 178–181. Then retake the test on page 182. Now move on to the section test on page 184.

Name ______________________ Date ______________

Final Science Test

for pages 155–182

DIRECTIONS: Read about Zoe's experiment and study her graphs. Then answer the questions.

Zoe wanted to find out how sunlight and water affect a plant's growth. She did an experiment with three different scenarios. Plant A received both water and sunlight. Plant B received water, but no sunlight, and Plant C received sunlight, but no water. Her results are graphed below.

Plant A

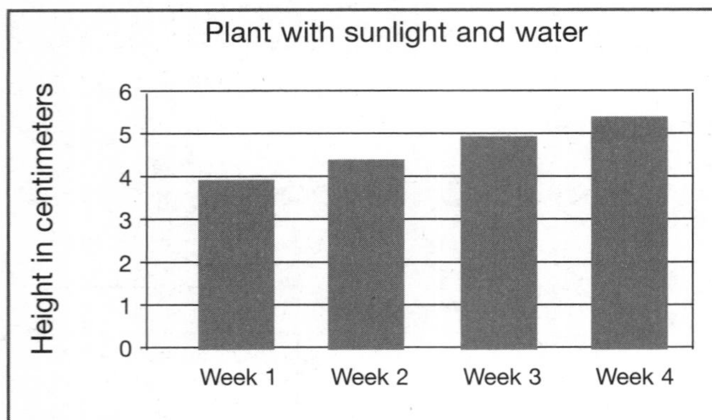

Plant B

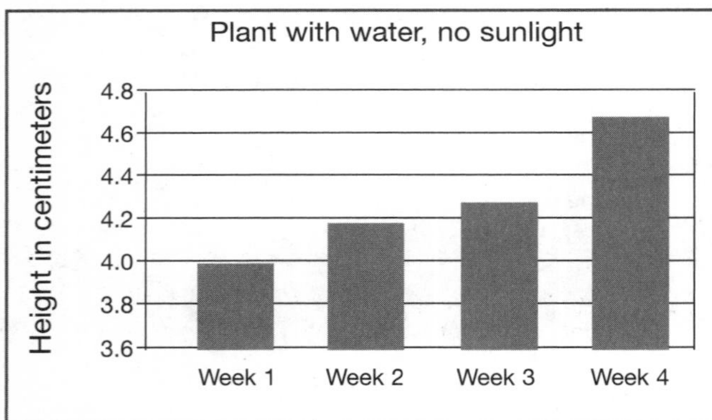

Plant C

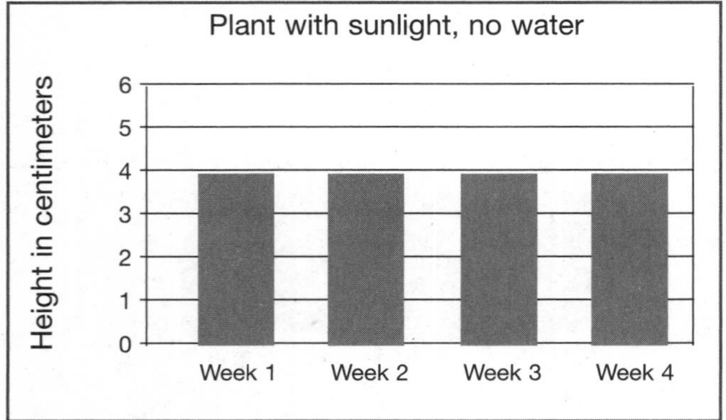

1. **Which of the following was a variable in Zoe's experiment?**
   - (A) type of soil
   - (B) amount of water
   - (C) type of plant
   - (D) duration of experiment

2. **Which plant showed the least growth?**
   - (F) Plant A
   - (G) Plant B
   - (H) Plant C
   - (J) All are equal.

DIRECTIONS: Choose the best answer for each question.

3. **Which of the following statements about plants is not true?**
   - (A) Plant cells have chlorophyll.
   - (B) Plants get food from outside themselves.
   - (C) Plants have limited movement.
   - (D) Plants have the ability to reproduce.

4. **Which of these is an example of camouflage?**
   - (F) The stick insect resembles the twig on which it sits.
   - (G) The young joey grows and develops in its mother's pouch.
   - (H) The anteater has a long, slender snout and a long tongue, which it can thrust into anthills.
   - (J) The porcupine is covered with long sharp quills.

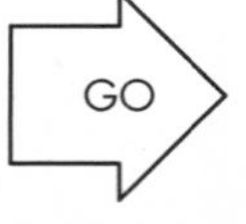

Name ______________________________ Date ______________

5. **Which animal is highest in the food chain?**
   - (A) insect
   - (B) snake
   - (C) rat
   - (D) bear

6. **Which animal would be lowest on a food chain?**
   - (F) frog
   - (G) mosquito
   - (H) duck
   - (J) man

7. **Look at the food chain. Which missing animal might fit in the space?**

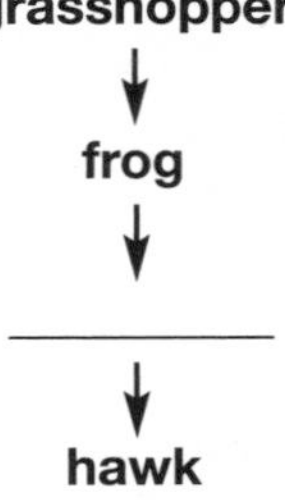

   - (A) shrub
   - (B) grass
   - (C) snake
   - (D) elephant

8. **Which of these would not be found in a desert ecosystem?**
   - (F) cactus
   - (G) lizard
   - (H) otter
   - (J) tortoise

9. **Which animal would not be found in a pond ecosystem?**
   - (A) rabbit
   - (C) insect
   - (B) fish
   - (D) frog

10. **Baseball pitchers use several forces to change the motion of the ball. One force is the strong push from the pitcher's arm that starts the ball moving toward home plate. What force pulls the ball down as it moves?**
   - (F) velocity
   - (G) friction
   - (H) inertia
   - (J) gravity

11. **Study the chart below. What will the moon phase probably be on March 27?**

Date	Moon Phase
December 29	Full moon
January 5	Last quarter
January 11	New moon
January 19	First quarter
January 27	Full moon
February 3	Last quarter
February 10	New moon
February 18	First quarter
February 26	Full moon

   - (A) full moon
   - (B) last quarter
   - (C) new moon
   - (D) first quarter

12. **Renaldo shuffles his feet as he walks across the carpet on a cool, dry day. What will happen when he touches the TV screen?**
   - (F) The TV will turn on.
   - (G) The TV will turn off.
   - (H) A spark will pass between Renaldo and the TV.
   - (J) Nothing will happen.

13. **When water melts from an ice cube, this is an example of a physical change. The water changes from a __________ .**
   - (A) solid to a gas
   - (B) liquid to a vapor
   - (C) solid to a liquid
   - (D) liquid to solid

GO

Name ______________________________ Date ______________

14. **Tuesday afternoon there was a summer shower in Dallas. The next day, Josh noticed the water puddle on the sidewalk in front of his house was becoming smaller and smaller. Which of the following explains what happened to the water?**

    Ⓕ It condensed.
    Ⓖ It evaporated.
    Ⓗ It melted.
    Ⓙ It froze.

15. **Which of the following is not true about glaciers?**

    Ⓐ Most of earth's water is in the form of glaciers.
    Ⓑ Melting glaciers supply water for many people.
    Ⓒ Glacial movements can leave behind valleys.
    Ⓓ Glaciers pick up boulders and sediment as they move.

16. **Study the table below. Predict which season the southern hemisphere will have during the month of September.**

Month	Northern Hemisphere	Southern Hemisphere
December	**Winter**	**Summer**
March	**Spring**	**Autumn**
June	**Summer**	**Winter**
September	**Autumn**	**?**

    Ⓕ autumn
    Ⓖ winter
    Ⓗ summer
    Ⓙ spring

17. **Acid rain forms when water vapor in the atmosphere mixes with __________ .**

    Ⓐ oxygen
    Ⓑ hydrogen
    Ⓒ sulfuric acid
    Ⓓ None of the above

18. **During an equinox, the sun is directly above __________ .**

    Ⓕ the axis
    Ⓖ the South Pole
    Ⓗ the North Pole
    Ⓙ the equator

19. **Which is not part of the water cycle?**

    Ⓐ evaporation
    Ⓑ condensation
    Ⓒ precipitation
    Ⓓ respiration

20. **When water enters a crack in a rock and then freezes, what will possibly happen to the rock?**

    Ⓕ The crack might get larger and split the rock.
    Ⓖ The rock might become stronger due to the ice.
    Ⓗ The rock might melt and change into an igneous rock.
    Ⓙ None of the above

21. **Which of the following are conservation practices?**

    Ⓐ replace, recycle, reuse
    Ⓑ reduce, recycle, reuse
    Ⓒ reduce, recycle, recall
    Ⓓ recycle, replace, recall

Name ______________________________ Date ______________

22. Using old holiday cards in a craft is an example of ________ a resource.

- (F) reusing
- (G) rotating
- (H) replacing
- (J) reducing

23. In a lighted electric lamp, which of the following forms of energy is not present?

- (A) electrical
- (B) solar
- (C) light
- (D) heat

24. What is the name for the energy produced by the sun?

- (F) solar
- (G) electrical
- (H) chemical
- (J) mechanical

DIRECTIONS: Read the passage and use it to answer questions 25 and 26.

Earth is a restless place. Although it may seem perfectly solid to you, the earth below your feet is moving at this very moment! The continents rest on top of the brittle crust of earth, which has broken apart into pieces. These pieces are called *tectonic plates.* They float around on top of the molten interior of earth, much like crackers floating in a bowl of soup. Molten rock, or lava, continues to push up through cracks in the plates. This pushes the plates even farther apart. The continents used to be closer together. Over the years, they have drifted farther apart, at the rate of about 1 inch every year.

25. According to this passage, why do tectonic plates move around?

- (A) They are floating on water.
- (B) Molten rock pushes up through the crack and pushes them apart.
- (C) The continents are drifting apart.
- (D) The crust of the earth is breaking.

26. According to this passage, how long would it take for Europe and North America to move one foot farther apart?

- (F) 6 years
- (G) 8 years
- (H) 10 years
- (J) 12 years

27. The closet planet to the sun is ________ .

- (A) Mars
- (B) Earth
- (C) Venus
- (D) Mercury

28. Which of the following is an inherited trait?

- (F) eye color
- (G) hair color
- (H) skin color
- (J) All of the above

29. Which of the following is a learned characteristic?

- (A) shoe size
- (B) height
- (C) the ability to read
- (D) All of the above

30. Birds fly south for the winter. This is a(n) ________ trait.

- (F) learned
- (G) inherited

31. Cold, dense air sinks. This cold air moving downward creates higher air pressure. As cold air sinks, it warms up. This causes water drops to evaporate. What kind of weather probably goes along with high air pressure?

- (A) clouds and rain
- (B) clouds without rain
- (C) clear skies
- (D) tornadoes

Name ______________________________ Date ______________

Final Science Test

Answer Sheet

1 Ⓐ Ⓑ Ⓒ Ⓓ
2 Ⓕ Ⓖ Ⓗ Ⓙ
3 Ⓐ Ⓑ Ⓒ Ⓓ
4 Ⓕ Ⓖ Ⓗ Ⓙ
5 Ⓐ Ⓑ Ⓒ Ⓓ
6 Ⓕ Ⓖ Ⓗ Ⓙ
7 Ⓐ Ⓑ Ⓒ Ⓓ
8 Ⓕ Ⓖ Ⓗ Ⓙ
9 Ⓐ Ⓑ Ⓒ Ⓓ
10 Ⓕ Ⓖ Ⓗ Ⓙ

11 Ⓐ Ⓑ Ⓒ Ⓓ
12 Ⓕ Ⓖ Ⓗ Ⓙ
13 Ⓐ Ⓑ Ⓒ Ⓓ
14 Ⓕ Ⓖ Ⓗ Ⓙ
15 Ⓐ Ⓑ Ⓒ Ⓓ
16 Ⓕ Ⓖ Ⓗ Ⓙ
17 Ⓐ Ⓑ Ⓒ Ⓓ
18 Ⓕ Ⓖ Ⓗ Ⓙ
19 Ⓐ Ⓑ Ⓒ Ⓓ
20 Ⓕ Ⓖ Ⓗ Ⓙ

21 Ⓐ Ⓑ Ⓒ Ⓓ
22 Ⓕ Ⓖ Ⓗ Ⓙ
23 Ⓐ Ⓑ Ⓒ Ⓓ
24 Ⓕ Ⓖ Ⓗ Ⓙ
25 Ⓐ Ⓑ Ⓒ Ⓓ
26 Ⓕ Ⓖ Ⓗ Ⓙ
27 Ⓐ Ⓑ Ⓒ Ⓓ
28 Ⓕ Ⓖ Ⓗ Ⓙ
29 Ⓐ Ⓑ Ⓒ Ⓓ
30 Ⓕ Ⓖ

31 Ⓐ Ⓑ Ⓒ Ⓓ

Illinois Social Science Content Standards

The social science section of the state test measures knowledge in five different areas.

Goal 11: Understand political systems, with an emphasis on the United States.

Goal 12: Understand economic systems, with an emphasis on the United States.

Goal 13: Understand events, trends, individuals, and movements shaping the history of Illinois, the United States, and other nations.

Goal 14: Understand world geography and the effects of geography on society, with an emphasis on the United States.

Goal 15: Understand social systems, with an emphasis on the United States.

Illinois Social Science Table of Contents

Social Science Standards

Political Systems

Goal 11: Understand political systems, with an emphasis on the United States.

Learning Standard 11A—Understand and explain basic principles of the United States government.

11.A.2 Explain the importance of fundamental concepts expressed and implied in major documents including the Declaration of Independence, the United States Constitution, and the Illinois Constitution. *(See page 191.)*

Learning Standard 11B—Understand the structures and functions of the political systems of Illinois, the United States, and other nations.

11.B.2 Explain what government does at local, state, and national levels. *(See page 192.)*

Learning Standard 11C—Understand election processes and responsibilities of citizens.

11.C.2 Describe and evaluate why rights and responsibilities are important to the individual, family, community, workplace, state, and nation (e.g., voting, protection under the law). *(See page 193.)*

Learning Standard 11D—Understand the roles and influences of individuals and interest groups in the political systems of Illinois, the United States, and other nations.

11.D.2 Explain ways that individuals and groups influence and shape public policy. *(See page 194.)*

Learning Standard 11E—Understand United States foreign policy as it relates to other nations and international issues.

11.E.2 Determine and explain the leadership role of the United States in international settings. *(See page 195.)*

Learning Standard 11F—Understand the development of United States political ideas and traditions.

11.F.2 Identify consistencies and inconsistencies between expressed United States political traditions and ideas and actual practices (e.g., freedom of speech, right to bear arms, slavery, voting rights). *(See page 196.)*

Name ______________________________ Date ______________

Social Sciences

11.A.2

Major Political Documents

Political Systems

DIRECTIONS: Choose the best answer.

1. **Who wrote the Declaration of Independence?**
   - (A) George Washington
   - (B) Thomas Jefferson
   - (C) Abraham Lincoln
   - (D) Ronald Reagan

2. **Which document allows the state of Illinois to send two senators to the U.S. Senate?**
   - (F) the Illinois Constitution
   - (G) the United States Constitution
   - (H) the Gettysburg Address
   - (J) the Declaration of Independence

3. **According to the U.S. Constitution, how old must you be to be a member of the House of Representatives?**
   - (A) there is no age requirement
   - (B) 35
   - (C) 25
   - (D) 18

4. **All of the following are rights guaranteed to all American citizens by the United States Constitution except ______________ .**
   - (F) freedom of religion
   - (G) the right of free speech
   - (H) the right to drive an automobile at age 16
   - (J) the right to vote at age 18

5. **Which of the following documents guarantees the rights of crime victims to be treated "with fairness and respect for their dignity"?**
   - (A) the United States Constitution
   - (B) the Declaration of Independence
   - (C) the Illinois Constitution
   - (D) both A and C but not B

6. **Read the following passage then identify which document it can be found in.**

   We hold these truths to be self-evident, that all men are created equal, that they are endowed by their Creator with certain unalienable Rights, that among these are Life, Liberty and the pursuit of Happiness.

   - (F) the United States Constitution
   - (G) the Illinois Constitution
   - (H) the Gettysburg Address
   - (J) the Declaration of Independence

7. **One reason the Illinois Constitution was established was to______________ .**
   - (A) form a more perfect Union
   - (B) remove all political ties with England
   - (C) eliminate poverty and inequality
   - (D) bring forth upon this continent a new nation

8. **The U.S. Constitution protects American citizens from which of the following actions?**
   - (F) being searched by a police officer for no good reason
   - (G) being put in jail in a foreign country
   - (H) being forced to pay taxes
   - (J) being arrested by a police officer from a state other than the one the person lives in

Name ______________________________ Date ______________

Social Sciences

11.B.2

Political Systems

Local, State, and National Governments

DIRECTIONS: Choose the best answer.

1. **Laws to raise taxes can be passed by ____________ .**
   - Ⓐ local (city) governments
   - Ⓑ state governments
   - Ⓒ the U.S. Congress
   - Ⓓ all of the above

2. **In the United States, all of the following can be carried out only by the national government except ____________ .**
   - Ⓕ to declare war
   - Ⓖ to put criminals in prison
   - Ⓗ to establish post offices
   - Ⓙ to impeach a president

3. **Anna lives in Springfield. Her purse was stolen. She should probably contact ____________ .**
   - Ⓐ the U.S. Army
   - Ⓑ the Illinois National Guard
   - Ⓒ the Springfield police department
   - Ⓓ none of the above since government is not responsible for police protection

4. **Which of the following levels of government makes laws regulating how old you must be before you can get married?**
   - Ⓕ the national government
   - Ⓖ the state government
   - Ⓗ the country government
   - Ⓙ the city government

5. **A tornado caused a great deal of damage in southwestern Illinois. The people of southwestern Illinois are least likely to receive financial assistance to rebuild their homes from ____________ .**
   - Ⓐ the U.S. government
   - Ⓑ the Illinois government
   - Ⓒ the Chicago city council
   - Ⓓ none of the above are likely to help

6. **Foreign policy is generally the responsibility of the ____________ .**
   - Ⓕ state government
   - Ⓖ county government
   - Ⓗ city government
   - Ⓙ national government

7. **Curriculum standards for Illinois schools are generally established by ____________ .**
   - Ⓐ the state of Illinois
   - Ⓑ the governor of Illinois
   - Ⓒ each individual school
   - Ⓓ local school boards throughout the state

8. **If you let your yard become overgrown with weeds, you could be fined by the ____________ .**
   - Ⓕ U.S. government
   - Ⓖ state government
   - Ⓗ city government
   - Ⓙ none of the above since government cannot force people to keep their yards clean and mowed

Name ______________________________ Date ______________

Social Sciences

11.C.2

Political Systems

Rights and Responsibilities of Citizens

DIRECTIONS: Choose the best answer.

1. Every right has a responsibility that goes with it. For example, as Americans, we have the right to free speech. But this right means that we must also be sure ____________ .

- (A) never to criticize the government
- (B) to write to the president at least once every year
- (C) that the things we say are accurate and truthful
- (D) to silence any viewpoint we disagree with

2. To be a responsible citizen, all Americans should ____________ .

- (F) obey the law
- (G) stay informed about current events
- (H) vote
- (J) all of the above

3. In the United States, every citizen over the age of 18 has the right to vote. What are some responsibilities citizens have when it comes to voting? Explain your answer.

____

____

____

____

____

____

4. In the United States, if you are accused of a crime and cannot afford to hire a lawyer, the government will provide a lawyer for you. How does this benefit the accused person?

____

____

____

____

____

____

5. The U.S. Constitution guarantees the following rights to all U.S. citizens. Place a 1 beside the right you think is most important, a 2 beside the right you think is next important, and so on. Then briefly explain your rankings.

_____ The right to keep and bear arms

_____ The right to a speedy and public trial

_____ The right of to vote

_____ The right to practice their religion

____

____

____

____

____

____

STOP

Name ______________________________ Date ______________

Social Sciences

11.D.2

The Shaping of Public Policy

Political Systems

DIRECTIONS: Read the passage and answer questions 1 and 2.

In 1955, an African-American woman named Rosa Parks refused to give her seat on a city bus in Montgomery, Alabama, to a white passenger. At that time, her action was against the law. She was arrested. Many African-Americans in Montgomery then boycotted, or refused to ride, city buses any longer. Two-thirds of city bus riders were African-American. As a result, the bus company lost most of its business. After more than a year, the law was changed and African-Americans no longer had to give their seats to other bus passengers.

1. In 1955, many African-Americans in Montgomery, Alabama, __________ the city bus company.

- (A) lobbied
- (B) boycotted
- (C) petitioned
- (D) banned

2. How did the actions of the African-American community in Montgomery influence public policy?

- (F) An unfair, discriminatory law was changed.
- (G) Bus fare for all riders was lowered.
- (H) White bus riders had to give up their seats to African-American passengers.
- (J) Public policy was not influenced by their actions.

DIRECTIONS: Choose the best answer.

3. Special interest groups hire people to influence public officials for or against a specific cause. This person is called a ____________ .

- (A) boycotter
- (B) protester
- (C) lobbyist
- (D) candidate

4. Which of the following is not a special interest group that tries to influence the way Congress votes on important issues?

- (F) National Rifle Association
- (G) World Wildlife Federation
- (H) National Organization for Women
- (J) All of these groups try to influence the way Congress votes.

5. Sometimes individuals or groups do not like how the government or a company is handling something. They can show their disapproval by holding a demonstration. Some people demonstrate by picketing, or carrying signs that state their point of view. Some people demonstrate by sitting in front of a building of the company or government office with which they do not agree. This makes it difficult for other people to enter the building. People involved in these types of demonstrations are also called __________ .

- (A) petitioners
- (B) protesters
- (C) lobbyists
- (D) candidates

Name ______________________________ Date ______________________

Social Sciences

11.E.2

Political Systems

The United States and Foreign Policy

DIRECTIONS: Choose the best answer.

1. **In which of the following ways does the United States become involved in the affairs of other nations?**
   - (A) providing money to help build schools
   - (B) sending food to countries unable to produce enough for their own people
   - (C) supplying military support
   - (D) all of the above

2. **In the United States, the ____________ have the power to make treaties with foreign nations.**
   - (F) president and all 50 state governors
   - (G) president and the Senate
   - (H) mayors of the 25 largest American cities
   - (J) House of Representatives and the Supreme Court

3. **In 1960, about 3 percent of the total amount of money spent by the U.S. government went toward helping other countries. In 2000, that percent changed to about ____________ .**
   - (A) 0.5 percent
   - (B) 5 percent
   - (C) 15 percent
   - (D) 50 percent

4. **The term "foreign policy" means ____________ .**
   - (F) the amount of money one nation sends to another
   - (G) the political policy of one nation in its relations with other nations
   - (H) one country wants to take over another country
   - (J) restricting the number of immigrants that come into a nation

5. **The United States has an official foreign policy regarding ____________ .**
   - (A) Bolivia
   - (B) China
   - (C) Nigeria
   - (D) all of the above

6. **The United States sends officials called __________ to other nations. These are officials who usually live in the foreign nation and represent the United States in its dealings with the nation.**
   - (F) generals
   - (G) senators
   - (H) ambassadors
   - (J) attorneys

STOP

Name ______________________________ Date ______________

Social Sciences

11.F.2

Political Ideals in the United States

Political Systems

DIRECTIONS: One of the most cherished ideals in America is that all people are created equal. Read the scenarios below and write a **C** in the space provided if you think it is consistent with this ideal. Write an **I** if you think it is inconsistent with this ideal.

_____ **1. The practice of slavery**

_____ **2. Women gain the right to vote**

_____ **3. All accused criminals are entitled to legal representation**

_____ **4. Charging a poll tax before allowing an individual to vote**

_____ **5. Freedom of religion**

_____ **6. Separate schools for white and black children are abolished**

DIRECTIONS: Read the passage and then answer the questions.

William was a U.S. citizen. William, however, did not like many things the president and Congress were doing. He thought their actions were wrong and immoral. So, William used his computer to make a booklet that told how much he disliked the U.S. government. He printed many copies of the booklet. Then, he went downtown and gave the booklets to people he passed on the street. He was not doing this in an angry way. If someone did not want the booklet, William simply moved on to the next person. He did not start any fights with anyone.

One woman did not like what William wrote in the booklet. She asked a police officer, who was patrolling nearby, to stop William from passing out his booklets. The police officer grabbed the box of booklets William was carrying and read one of them. Then, he took the booklets away from William and arrested him.

7. Were any of William's constitutional rights violated in this incident?

- Ⓐ No, William did not have the right to say bad things about the government.
- Ⓑ Yes, but William should have been arrested anyway because what he was doing was wrong.
- Ⓒ Yes, William's right to free speech was violated.
- Ⓓ Yes, William's right to freedom of religion was violated.

8. William claimed that the police officer had no right to take his booklets away from him. Which constitutional right does William probably think the officer violated?

- Ⓕ the thirteenth amendment, which made slavery illegal
- Ⓖ the fourth amendment, which limits the government's right to search or take personal belongings
- Ⓗ the third amendment, which prohibits the government from forcing citizens to house soldiers in their homes
- Ⓙ the second amendment, which gives citizens the right to own guns so that states can maintain militias

Name ______________________ Date ______________

Social Sciences

11

For pages 191–196

Mini-Test 1

Political Systems

DIRECTIONS: Choose the best answer.

1. **Which of the following documents was written by the Pilgrims to establish a government in the New World?**
   - Ⓐ the Illinois Constitution
   - Ⓑ the Declaration of Independence
   - Ⓒ the Mayflower Compact
   - Ⓓ the United States Constitution

2. **Brittany lives in Peoria. She wants to open a hair salon in her home. Which level of government can tell her if it is legal to operate a business out of her house?**
   - Ⓕ the Peoria city government
   - Ⓖ the Illinois state senate
   - Ⓗ the U.S. House of Representatives
   - Ⓙ the U.S. Senate

3. **All Americans have a constitutional right to ____________ .**
   - Ⓐ three meals per day
   - Ⓑ express their political opinions
   - Ⓒ live in a nice house
   - Ⓓ free health care

4. **Which of the following is not an acceptable way to influence public policy?**
   - Ⓕ join a peaceful protest march
   - Ⓖ threaten to stop buying a company's products if it continues practices you do not like
   - Ⓗ offer to buy the mayor a new car if she votes the way you want her to on an important issue
   - Ⓙ write a letter to the editor of the local newspaper expressing your opinion

5. **The following table shows the five countries that received the most financial aid from the United States in 2000. What can we conclude from the table?**

Country	Amount of U.S. Foreign Aid Received in 2000
Israel	$4.069 billion
Egypt	$2.054 billion
Colombia	$0.902 billion
West Bank/Gaza	$0.485 billion
Jordan	$0.427 billion

   - Ⓐ The U.S. government should stop spending money in other countries.
   - Ⓑ The U.S. government is very interested in affairs in Israel and Egypt.
   - Ⓒ The U.S. government does not help other countries.
   - Ⓓ The U.S. government does not take good enough care of its own citizens.

6. **The United States stands for many ideals, such as freedom. Which of the following is an example of an inconsistency between what the United States is supposed to stand for and actual events?**
   - Ⓕ allowing restaurants to refuse to serve people because of their race
   - Ⓖ putting people in jail for acts of treason
   - Ⓗ allowing people to say unpopular things
   - Ⓙ stopping factories from polluting rivers and streams

STOP

Social Science Standards

Economic Systems

Goal 12: Understand economic systems, with an emphasis on the United States.

Learning Standard 12A—Understand how different economic systems operate in the exchange, production, distribution, and consumption of goods and services.

12.A.2a Explain how economic systems decide what goods and services are produced, how they are produced, and who consumes them. *(See page 199.)*

12.A.2b Describe how incomes reflect choices made about education and careers. *(See page 200.)*

12.A.2c Describe unemployment. *(See page 201.)*

Learning Standard 12B—Understand that scarcity necessitates choices by consumers.

12.B.2a Identify factors that affect how consumers make their choices. *(See page 202.)*

12.B.2b Explain the relationship between the quantity of goods/services purchased and their price. *(See page 203.)*

12.B.2c Explain that when a choice is made, something else is given up. *(See page 204.)*

Learning Standard 12C—Understand that scarcity necessitates choices by producers.

12.C.2a Describe the relationship between price and quantity supplied of a good or service. *(See page 203.)*

12.C.2b Identify and explain examples of competition in the economy. *(See page 205.)*

12.C.2c Describe how entrepreneurs take risks in order to produce goods or services. *(See page 206.)*

Learning Standard 12D—Understand trade as an exchange of goods or services.

12.D.2a Explain why people and countries voluntarily exchange goods and services. *(See page 207.)*

12.D.2b Describe the relationships among specialization, division of labor, productivity of workers, and interdependence among producers and consumers. *(See page 208.)*

Learning Standard 12E—Understand the impact of government policies and decisions on production and consumption in the economy.

12E.2a Explain how and why public goods and services are provided. *(See page 209.)*

12.E.2b Identify which public goods and services are provided by differing levels of government. *(See page 209.)*

Name ______________________________ Date ______________

Social Sciences

12.A.2a

Types of Economic Systems

Economic Systems

DIRECTIONS: Choose the best answer.

1. **Suppose you want a new CD player. If you live in the United States, you would probably need to ____________ .**
   - (A) ask the government to give you one
   - (B) go to the store and buy one
   - (C) ask the government for permission, then go to the store and buy one
   - (D) buy one from the government

2. **The kind of economic system where individuals own most of the stores, farms, and factories is called a ____________ economy.**
   - (F) socialist
   - (G) command
   - (H) market
   - (J) developing

3. **The kind of economic system where the government controls most of the stores, farms, and factories is called a ____________ economy.**
   - (A) socialist
   - (B) command
   - (C) market
   - (D) developing

4. **In a market economy, the price of a pound of hamburger ____________ .**
   - (F) never changes
   - (G) rises a little bit every year
   - (H) is set by the government
   - (J) depends on how much hamburger is available and how many people want to buy it

5. **In the United States, who is allowed to buy a house?**
   - (A) whoever the government allows to buy one
   - (B) college graduates only
   - (C) anyone who can afford to buy one
   - (D) only top government officials

6. **Marcus manages an automobile factory. If he lives in a country that has a command economy, ____________ .**
   - (F) the government will probably tell him how many cars to build this month
   - (G) he will decide all by himself how many cars to build this month
   - (H) the employees of the factory will tell him how many cars they feel like making this month
   - (J) he will probably examine sales figures before deciding how many cars to build this month

STOP

Name ______________________________ Date ______________

Social Sciences

12.A.2b

Economic Systems

Education, Career Choice, and Income

DIRECTIONS: Look at the following types of jobs. If you think the job pays a high salary, place an **H** in the space provided. If you think the job pays a medium salary, place an **M** in the space provided. If you think the job pays a low salary, place an **L** in the space provided.

_____ **1. Surgeon**

_____ **2. Auto mechanic**

_____ **3. Stockbroker**

_____ **4. Dishwasher**

_____ **5. Trash collector**

_____ **6. Flight engineer**

_____ **7. Carpenter**

_____ **8. Cashier**

_____ **9. Lawyer**

DIRECTIONS: Look at the following types of jobs. If you think the job requires a lot of education, place an **E+** in the space provided. If you think the job requires a medium amount of education, place an **E** in the space provided. If you think the job does not require much education at all, place an **E–** in the space provided.

_____ **10. Surgeon**

_____ **11. Auto mechanic**

_____ **12. Stockbroker**

_____ **13. Dishwasher**

_____ **14. Trash collector**

_____ **15. Flight engineer**

_____ **16. Carpenter**

_____ **17. Cashier**

_____ **18. Lawyer**

DIRECTIONS: Compare your answers to questions 1-9 to your answers to questions 10-18. How do you think income and education are related?

19. ____

____

____

____

____

____

____

____

____

____

____

STOP

Name ______________________________ Date ______________

Social Sciences

12.A.2c

Unemployment

Economic Systems

DIRECTIONS: Choose the best answer.

1. **The unemployment rate measures the number of people in an economy who ____________ .**
   - Ⓐ do not have a job
   - Ⓑ are not working, but who have been looking for a job
   - Ⓒ are retired
   - Ⓓ are lazy

2. **When the economy is strong and growing, the unemployment rate usually ____________ .**
   - Ⓕ goes down
   - Ⓖ goes up
   - Ⓗ stays the same
   - Ⓙ rises and falls with no clear pattern

3. **Which of the following are unemployed?**
   - Ⓐ a fourth grader who goes to school all day
   - Ⓑ a grandma and grandpa who stay at home all day caring for their grandchildren
   - Ⓒ a factory worker who was fired last week but has applied for three new jobs today
   - Ⓓ all of them are unemployed

4. **Which of the following events is most likely to increase unemployment?**
   - Ⓕ a factory receives a new order for machine parts
   - Ⓖ most of the printers a company has built this year do not work right
   - Ⓗ a new video game comes out and everyone wants it
   - Ⓙ the weather has been very good, and farmers have a big harvest this year

DIRECTIONS: Read the short news article. Then, answer the questions.

The unemployment rate in the United States dropped this month to 5.9 percent. Last month, the unemployment rate was 6.1 percent. This month about 250,000 people applied for unemployment benefits for the first time. Last month, the number of people who applied was 325,000. The good economic news pleased the president and Congress.

5. **After reading the article, we can conclude that ____________ .**
   - Ⓐ 250,000 people are unemployed this month
   - Ⓑ 325,000 people found new jobs last month
   - Ⓒ more people are working this month as compared to last month
   - Ⓓ fewer people are working this month as compared to last month

6. **The events described in the article probably happened because ____________ .**
   - Ⓕ the president and Congress ordered businesses to hire more workers
   - Ⓖ several businesses decided that it was not nice to fire employees, so they rehired them
   - Ⓗ unemployed workers picketed factories until they were rehired
   - Ⓙ the economy got a little bit better this month

Name ______________________ Date ______________

Social Sciences

12.B.2a

Economic Systems

Factors Affecting Consumer Choice

DIRECTIONS: Choose the best answer.

1. **Suppose this week the price of hamburger goes down and the price of steak goes up. Customers visiting Fred's Meat Market today will probably ___________ .**
   - (A) buy more steak and less hamburger
   - (B) buy the same amount of steak and more hamburger
   - (C) buy less steak and more hamburger
   - (D) buy less steak and less hamburger

2. **Consumers decide what to buy because of ___________ .**
   - (F) the quality of a product
   - (G) the availability of a product
   - (H) the price of a product
   - (J) all of the above

DIRECTIONS: Read the story and then answer the questions.

On Rick's 18th birthday, he decided to buy a car. He read about all of the latest models to find the very best. After doing his research, Rick decided that he wanted a Euro 220E. The Euro 220E had lots of great features. It came with a 10-year warranty. It even had a computer and DVD player as standard equipment! This was the car for Rick. So, he hurried down to the nearest Euro dealer. He was happy to see dozens of brand-new 220Es sitting in the lot. He asked to test drive one. The salesman looked at Rick and smiled. "The basic Euro 220E costs $125,000, son. Are you sure you can afford the payments?" Rick didn't say a word as he left the car lot. When he got home, he picked up the newspaper and began comparing used car prices.

3. **Why did Rick decide not to buy the car?**
   - (A) He decided at the last minute that he could find a better car.
   - (B) There were not enough Euro 220Es available for everyone who wanted to buy one.
   - (C) He realized that he could not afford it.
   - (D) He decided it was not the right color.

4. **Economic decisions can be hard to make because we cannot have everything we want. This is called *scarcity.* Scarcity forces consumers to make choices. Which scarce resource limited Rick's choice?**
   - (F) money
   - (G) the number of used cars available
   - (H) the number of new Euro 220Es available
   - (J) all of the above

5. **Suppose one year from now Rick won $500,000 in the lottery. Would he finally be able to have his dream of owning a brand-new 220E?**
   - (A) Yes, he would then have enough money to buy one.
   - (B) Yes, he could afford to buy one but only if the dealership still had them on hand.
   - (C) No, the salesman would remember Rick from earlier and refuse to sell it to him.
   - (D) No, the salesman could not legally sell the car to Rick after refusing to sell it to him once before.

Name ______________________________ Date ______________

Social Sciences

12.B.2b/12.C.2a

Economic Systems

Supply, Demand, and Price

DIRECTIONS: Choose the best answer.

1. **Suppose you ran a thing-a-ma-bob factory. As the producer, at what price would you be most likely to produce the greatest number of them?**
   - (A) $1.00
   - (B) $2.50
   - (C) $5.00
   - (D) the same number will be sold no matter the price

2. **Explain your answer to question 1.**

   ____

   ____

   ____

   ____

3. **Suppose you needed some thing-a-ma-bobs. At what price would you be most likely to purchase the greatest number of them?**
   - (F) $1.00
   - (G) $2.50
   - (H) $5.00
   - (J) the same number will be purchased no matter the price

4. **When the price of something goes up, the number of people who want to buy the item usually ______________ .**
   - (A) goes up also
   - (B) goes down
   - (C) stays the same
   - (D) drops to zero

5. **This fall, Danny decided to charge neighbors $5 per hour to rake leaves. He got a few customers, but not as many as he thought he would. What would most likely happen if Danny lowered his price to $3 per hour?**
   - (F) More people would decide to let Danny rake their leaves.
   - (G) Danny would make a lot less money.
   - (H) Danny would lose most of his customers.
   - (J) His friend Alison would start raking leaves too at $5 per hour.

6. **What happens when supply of a product goes down but demand goes up?**
   - (A) The price of the product stays the same.
   - (B) The price of the product goes down.
   - (C) Producers will no longer want to make the product.
   - (D) The price of the product goes up.

7. **A big winter storm knocked out power to a community for several days. A local store kept several generators in stock. The generators provided a source of electricity. However, the store did not usually sell very many because they were expensive. When the storm hit the community, the store ran out of generators and had to order more. Why do you think people wanted to purchase the generators even though they were still expensive?**

   ____

   ____

   ____

   ____

STOP

Name ______________________________ Date ______________

Social Sciences

12.B.2c

Opportunity Cost

Economic Systems

DIRECTIONS: Read the story and then answer the questions.

Jenny has $20 to spend. She would like to have the latest Biggie Boys CD, which costs $17. She'd also like to go out for pizza and a movie with her friends Maria and Chantel. She figures that would cost about $15. Then again, her brother's birthday is next week. Jenny knows he's a fan of those Wally Wizard books. She could surprise him with the newest book for $19.50. Of course, she really should repay her dad for that $10 she borrowed a few days ago. And for just $7.50, she could refill her secret supply of Choco-Nut bars she keeps hidden in her room. All the way home from school, Jenny thought and thought about what to do with that money.

Opportunity cost is the next best alternative that is given up when a choice is made.

1. After reading the story, we can conclude that ___________ .

- (A) Jenny does not know how to manage her money wisely
- (B) Jenny likes to spend money only on herself
- (C) the $20 will not buy Jenny everything she wants
- (D) all of the above are true

2. Suppose Jenny decides to repay the $10 she borrowed from her dad. In that case, she will have to give up ___________ .

- (F) going out for pizza and a movie with her friends
- (G) refilling her secret supply of Choco-Nut bars
- (H) buying the Biggie Boys CD
- (J) both F and H

3. After thinking it over, Jenny decides to rank her choices: her first choice is buying a Wally Wizard book for her brother, second is buying the Biggie Boys CD, third is repaying her dad, fourth is going out for pizza and a movie with her friends, and fifth is refilling her secret supply of Choco-Nut bars. Her opportunity cost is the item that is ranked second on her list. In this case, Jenny's opportunity cost is ___________ .

- (A) buying the Biggie Boys CD
- (B) repaying her dad and refilling her supply of Choco-Nut bars
- (C) buying the Wally Wizard book
- (D) all of the other choices are Jenny's opportunity cost

4. Which of the following actions could Jenny take to get rid of her opportunity cost?

- (F) She could buy the Biggie Boys CD after all.
- (G) She could go out with her friends but buy their pizza for them.
- (H) She could put the money in the bank instead of spending it.
- (J) None of the above. In each case, Jenny is giving something up.

Name ______________________________ Date ______________

Social Sciences

12.C.2b

Competition

Economic Systems

DIRECTIONS: Choose the best answer.

Businesses face **direct competition** from other businesses that sell the same or similar products. Businesses face **indirect competition** from companies that sell products that can act as a substitute.

1. Ryan operates Ryan's Bakery. Which of the following stores is a direct competitor of Ryan's?

- (A) Sparkle Dry Cleaners
- (B) Tasty Pastry and Donut Shop
- (C) Billy's Fruits and Vegetables
- (D) Mr. Speedy Office Supplies

2. Which of the following is an indirect competitor of Ryan's Bakery?

- (F) The Hairport Hair Salon
- (G) Patty's Pants Shack
- (H) Frizzle's Ice Cream Palace
- (J) The Book Nook

3. All of the following are indirect competitors of Bellywhopper's Hamburgers except ________.

- (A) Stereo City
- (B) Pickin' Fried Chicken
- (C) The Ribs King
- (D) Taco Castle

4. La Chi Chi is a fancy Mexican restaurant where most meals cost at least $50. Which of the following is the closest competitor to La Chi Chi?

- (F) Bellywhopper's Hamburgers, where you can get a meal for $1.99
- (G) Bella Roma, an elegant Italian restaurant with a strict dress code for all customers
- (H) Pickin' Fried Chicken, where nothing on the menu costs more than $5.00
- (J) All of the above are restaurants, so they are all close competitors to La Chi Chi.

5. Which of the following is a direct competitor to Cactus Cola?

- (A) Yummy Cola
- (B) Clear Spring bottled water
- (C) Flavorade sports drink
- (D) all of the above

6. Which of the following is an indirect competitor to Cactus Cola?

- (F) Yummy Cola
- (G) Clear Spring bottled water
- (H) both F and G
- (J) neither F nor G

7. For years, Phil's Service Station was the only gas station in Smallville. There was no other place to buy gasoline within 30 miles of Phil's. But last week, Biggie Oil Company opened a brand-new gas station about $\frac{1}{4}$ mile from Phil's Service Station. Now that Phil's has a direct competitor, what do you think will happen to the price of gas at Phil's?

- (A) It will go down.
- (B) It will go up.
- (C) It will stay the same.
- (D) None of the above. Phil's will be out of business within a few days.

STOP

Name ______________________________ Date ______________

Social Sciences

12.C.2c

Entrepreneurship

Economic Systems

DIRECTIONS: Read the story and then answer the questions.

Ten years ago, Wally Anderson opened his own business: Wally's Computer Repair. Wally's business fixes broken computers and printers. Wally used $25,000 of his own money to buy equipment and rent office space. The bank also loaned him $75,000 to help his business get off the ground. (Of course, Wally had to pay the loan back to the bank.)

When Wally first started his store, he was the only employee. He often worked more than 14 hours every day. But over the years, he has hired others to help him with the work. He hired Marcia Fitzgerald to manage the business's finances. Darius Jackson is the lead repair person. Nine other people also work at Wally's store. Wally is very proud of his employees. He is also proud to own his own business. He hopes one day to own and operate another computer repair shop in another town.

An **entrepreneur** is someone who starts, runs, and assumes the risk for a business.

1. In the above story, who is the entrepreneur?

- (A) Darius Jackson
- (B) Marcia Fitzgerald
- (C) Wally Anderson
- (D) all of the employees of Wally's Computer Repair

2. Entrepreneurs _______________ .

- (F) always make every decision about a business, no matter how small
- (G) must sometimes borrow money to get their businesses started
- (H) never hire people to help with their business
- (J) can own only one business at a time

3. Wally took some risks when he began his store ten years ago. Probably the greatest risk he took was that _______________ .

- (A) he should not have worked 14-hour days
- (B) he would have lost a lot of money if his business had failed
- (C) no one should ever try to operate a business alone
- (D) he did not know how to fix computers

4. Which of the following statements is not true?

- (F) Wally invested a lot of time and money to start his business.
- (G) Because of Wally, several people have jobs.
- (H) Ten years ago, Wally did not know for sure if his business would succeed.
- (J) Now that Wally's business has been around for ten years, Wally no longer has any risk in running his store.

Name ______________________________ Date ______________

Social Sciences

12.D.2a

Trading Goods and Services

Economic Systems

DIRECTIONS: Select the best answer.

1. **Trading goods and services with people for other goods and services or money is called ____________ .**
   - (A) division of labor
   - (B) extortion
   - (C) exchange
   - (D) scarcity

2. **When two people or countries trade voluntarily, ____________ .**
   - (F) they each have something the other one wants
   - (G) they should both think they are better off after the trade than before the trade
   - (H) no one forces them to make the trade
   - (J) all of the above

DIRECTIONS: Examine the table below and then answer the questions.

Name of Country	Resources it has available to trade	Resources it needs from other countries
Erehwon	bananas, coffee, coal	wheat
Utopia	coal	rice
Mythos	wheat, rice	oil
Freedonia	wheat, coffee, rice	bananas

3. **Based on the information in the table, which country is Freedonia most likely to trade with?**
   - (A) Erehwon
   - (B) Utopia
   - (C) Mythos
   - (D) Freedonia is not likely to trade with any of the other countries.

4. **Based on the information in the table, which country is Utopia least likely to trade with?**
   - (F) Erehwon
   - (G) Freedonia
   - (H) Mythos
   - (J) Utopia is likely to trade with all of the other countries.

5. **Mythos might be unwilling to trade with any of the other countries listed because ____________ .**
   - (A) Mythos has all the resources it needs
   - (B) none of them want the resources Mythos has to offer
   - (C) none of them have the oil Mythos needs
   - (D) no one in Mythos likes bananas

6. **One way for Erehwon to get the resources it needs would be to ____________ .**
   - (F) buy it from Mythos
   - (G) trade bananas with Freedonia for it
   - (H) buy it from Freedonia
   - (J) all of the above

STOP

Name ______________________________ Date ______________

Social Sciences

12.D.2b

Specialization and Productivity

Economic Systems

DIRECTIONS: Select the best answer.

1. **When the production of a good is broken down into several separate tasks, with different workers performing each task, it is called ___________ .**
   - Ⓐ productivity
   - Ⓑ division of labor
   - Ⓒ entrepreneurship
   - Ⓓ unemployment

2. **Building a car is a complicated job. The fastest way to build a car is ___________ .**
   - Ⓕ for many people to do one part of the job and become very good at it
   - Ⓖ for one person to build the car all alone
   - Ⓗ both F and G would be equally fast
   - Ⓙ F would be faster at first, but after a while G would be faster

DIRECTIONS: When workers are specialized, they have particular skills that they use to do their jobs. Specialization on the job has both good points and bad points. Write a **B** beside each condition if you think it is a benefit of specialization. Write a **D** if you think it is a disadvantage of specialization.

_____ 3. **Over time, specialized workers become very good at what they do.**

_____ 4. **Production can slow down if a specialized worker is out sick.**

_____ 5. **Specialized workers make fewer mistakes.**

_____ 6. **Specialized workers may become bored performing the same task every day.**

_____ 7. **It takes less time to train a worker to do one or two tasks than to do many tasks.**

8. **At the Well-Built Bicycle Company, each bicycle is built completely by one person. At the Speedy Bicycle Company, a team of 15 specialized employees builds each bicycle. Each member of the team does a little bit of the work. Which company do you think builds more bicycles in a typical week? Explain your answer.**

____

____

____

____

____

Name ______________________________ Date ______________

Social Sciences

12.E.2a/12.E.2b

Economic Systems

Public Goods and Services

DIRECTIONS: Choose the best answer.

1. **Which of the following is *not* a reason why government provides public goods and services?**
   - (A) to promote public safety
   - (B) politicians love spending as much of the public's money as they can
   - (C) to keep people healthy
   - (D) to educate citizens

2. **Public goods and services are paid for by ____________ .**
   - (F) taxes
   - (G) library fees
   - (H) the entrance fee to a city park
   - (J) all of the above

3. **A type of tax where you pay an amount based on the value of your home is called a(n) ____________ .**
   - (A) value-added tax
   - (B) property tax
   - (C) income tax
   - (D) sales tax

4. **A type of tax where you pay an extra amount based on the total price of items you purchase is called a(n) ____________ .**
   - (F) value-added tax
   - (G) property tax
   - (H) income tax
   - (J) sales tax

5. **Which of the following is *not* a public service provided by your local government?**
   - (A) snow removal
   - (B) lawn care
   - (C) street repair
   - (D) police protection

DIRECTIONS: For each of the following public goods and services, write an **L** if it is provided by your local (city) government, write an **S** if it is provided by the Illinois state government, or write an **N** if it is provided by the U.S. (national) government.

_____ 6. **Post office**

_____ 7. **Illinois State patrol**

_____ 8. **Fire department**

_____ 9. **Armed forces**

_____ 10. **City parks**

_____ 11. **Sidewalk repair**

_____ 12. **Driver's license registration**

STOP

Name ______________________________ Date ______________

Social Sciences

12

For pages 199–209

Mini-Test 2

Economic Systems

DIRECTIONS: Choose the best answer.

1. **Identify the person who will probably earn the highest income.**
   - (A) a high-school dropout who delivers pizza
   - (B) a plumber who attended vocational school
   - (C) a nuclear engineer with an advanced college degree
   - (D) a salesman with an associate's degree in marketing

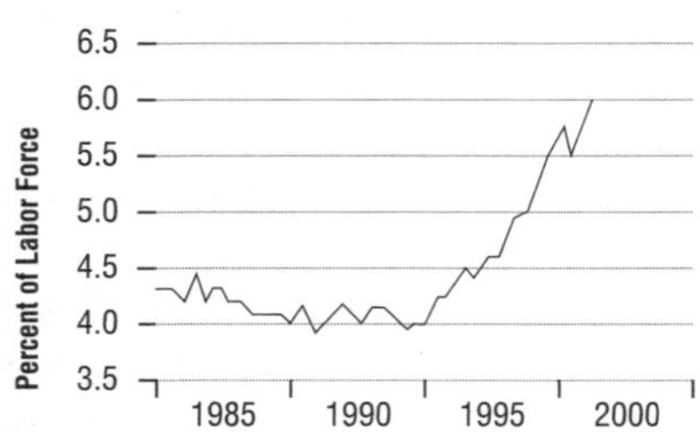

2. **The chart above shows the unemployment rate for Tinytown over a period of twenty years. Examine the chart and then select which response is most likely to be true.**
   - (F) The economy was better in 1990 than in 2000.
   - (G) The economy was better in 2000 than in 1990.
   - (H) The unemployment rate has been falling since 1985.
   - (J) Tinytown's economy would be hurt if unemployment fell below 4 percent.

3. **Rudy has enough money to buy one of the following: a DVD, a book, a new shirt, or a new game. He ranks his choices as follows: game, DVD, shirt, book. What is his opportunity cost?**
   - (A) the game
   - (B) the DVD
   - (C) the DVD, shirt, and book
   - (D) There is no opportunity cost in this situation.

DIRECTIONS: Read the story and then answer question 4.

Last holiday season, Ziffle's Department Store had 100 Dancing Danny dolls in stock. Dancing Danny dolls were in high demand last year. Ziffle's was able to charge customers $50 each for the dolls and sold them out in one day. This holiday season, Ziffle's ordered 500 of the dolls. Sadly, the Dancing Danny fad has passed. Very few people want the dolls this year.

4. **Which of the following will Ziffle's most likely charge for Dancing Danny dolls this year?**
   - (F) $100
   - (G) $75
   - (H) $50
   - (J) $25

5. **Francine owns and operates Francine's Corner Deli. Because she runs her own business, we would call her a(n) __________ .**
   - (A) indirect competitor
   - (B) entrepreneur
   - (C) socialist
   - (D) unemployed person

6. **Not much coffee is grown in the United States. Both Colombia and Brazil grow coffee. One way for the United States to get coffee would be to ____________ .**
   - (F) buy it from Colombia and Brazil
   - (G) trade another product with Brazil for coffee
   - (H) trade another product with Colombia for coffee
   - (J) all of the above

7. **A type of tax where you pay an extra amount based on what you earn is called a(n) ____________ .**
   - (A) unemployment tax
   - (B) property tax
   - (C) income tax
   - (D) sales tax

Social Science Standards

History

Goal 13: Understand events, trends, individuals, and movements shaping the history of Illinois, the United States, and other nations.

Learning Standard 13A—Apply the skills of historical analysis and interpretation.

13.A.2a Read historical stories and determine events which influenced their writing. *(See page 213.)*

13.A.2b Compare different stories about a historical figure or event and analyze differences in the portrayals and perspectives they present. *(See page 214.)*

13.A.2c Ask questions and seek answers by collecting and analyzing data from historic documents, images, and other literary and nonliterary sources.

Learning Standard 13B—Understand the development of significant political events.

13.B.2a (US) Describe how the European colonies in North America developed politically. *(See page 215.)*

13.B.2b (US) Identify major causes of the American Revolution and describe the consequences of the Revolution through the early national period, including the roles of George Washington, Thomas Jefferson, and Benjamin Franklin. *(See page 216.)*

13.B.2c (US) Identify presidential elections that were pivotal in the formation of modern political parties. *(See page 217.)*

13.B.2d (US) Identify major political events and leaders within the United States historical eras since the adoption of the Constitution, including the westward expansion, Louisiana Purchase, Civil War, and twentieth-century wars as well as the roles of Thomas Jefferson, Abraham Lincoln, Woodrow Wilson, and Franklin D. Roosevelt. *(See page 218.)*

13.B.2a (W) Describe the historical development of monarchies, oligarchies, and city-states in ancient civilizations. *(See page 219.)*

13.B.2b (W) Describe the origins of Western political ideas and institutions (e.g. Greek democracy, Roman republic, Magna Carta, Common Law, the Enlightenment). *(See page 220.)*

Learning Standard 13C—Understand the development of economic systems.

13.C.2a (US) Describe how slavery and indentured servitude influenced the early economy of the United States. *(See page 221.)*

13.C.2b (US) Explain how individuals, including John Deere, Thomas Edison, Robert McCormack, George Washington Carver, and Henry Ford, contributed to economic change through ideas, inventions, and entrepreneurship. *(See page 222.)*

13.C.2c (US) Describe significant economic events, including industrialization, immigration, the Great Depression, the shift to a service economy, and the rise of technology, that influenced history from the industrial development era to the present. *(See page 223.)*

13.C.2a (W) Describe the economic consequences of the first agricultural revolution, 4000 B.C.–1000 B.C. *(See page 224.)*

13.C.2b (W) Describe the basic economic systems of the world's great civilizations, including Mesopotamia, Egypt, Aegean/Mediterranean, and Asian civilizations, 1000 B.C.–500 B.C. *(See page 225.)*

13.C.2c (W) Describe basic economic changes that led to and resulted from the manorial agricultural system, the industrial revolution, the rise of the capitalism, and the information/communication revolution. *(See page 226.)*

Learning Standard 13D—Understand Illinois, United States, and world social history.

13.D.2a (US) Describe the various individual motives for settling in colonial America. *(See page 227.)*

13.D.2b (US) Describe the ways in which participation in the westward movement affected families and communities. *(See page 228.)*

13.D.2c (US) Describe the influence of key individuals and groups, including Susan B. Anthony/suffrage and Martin Luther King, Jr./civil rights, in the historical eras of Illinois and the United States. *(See page 229.)*

13.D.2 (W) Describe the various roles of men, women, and children in the family, at work, and in the community in various time periods and places (e.g., ancient Rome, Medieval Europe, ancient China, Sub-Saharan Africa). *(See page 230.)*

Learning Standard 13E—Understand Illinois, United States, and world environmental history.

13.E.2a (US) Identify environmental factors that drew settlers to the state and region. *(See page 231.)*

13.E.2b (US) Identify individuals and events in the development of the conservation movement including John Muir, Theodore Roosevelt, and the creation of the National Park System. *(See page 232.)*

13.E.2c (US) Describe environmental factors that influenced the development of transportation and trade in Illinois. *(See page 231.)*

13.E.2a (W) Describe how people in hunting and gathering and early pastoral societies adapted to their respective environments. *(See page 233.)*

13.E.2b (W) Identify individuals and their inventions (e.g., Watt/steam engine, Nobel/TNT, Edison/electric light) which influenced world environmental history. *(See page 234.)*

Name ______________________________ Date ______________

Social Sciences **History**

13.A.2a

Matching Events to Historical Stories

DIRECTIONS: The following passages were written about actual events in American history. Match the selection with the correct event.

A I am tired of fighting. Our chiefs are killed. Looking Glass is dead. Toohulhulsote is dead. The old men are all dead. It is the young men who say yes or no. . . . Hear me, my chiefs. I am tired. My heart is sick and sad. From where the sun now stands I will fight no more forever.

B Listen, my children, and you shall hear
Of the midnight ride of Paul Revere,
On the eighteenth of April, in Seventy-five;
Hardly a man is now alive
Who remembers that famous day and year.

C I then shouted into M [the mouthpiece] the following sentence: "Mr. Watson—Come here—I want to see you." To my delight he came and declared that he had heard and understood what I said.

D Close behind the first gang come the [other workers] and a lively time they make of it. It is a grand Anvil Chorus that these sturdy sledges [hammers] are laying across the Plains; it is in triple time, three strokes to a spike. There are ten spikes to a rail, four hundred rails to a mile, eighteen hundred miles to San Francisco.

E But O heart! heart! heart!
O the bleeding drops of red,
Where on the deck my Captain lies,
Fallen cold and dead.

F I was really aware, visually aware, that the moon was in fact a sphere, not a disk. It seemed almost as if it were showing us its roundness, its similarity in shape to our earth, in a sort of welcome. I was sure then that it would be a hospitable host. It had been awaiting its first visitors for a long time.

_____ **1. Workers build the transcontinental railroad that links the east and west coasts of the United States.**

_____ **2. The British march on Concord, Massachusetts at the beginning of the American Revolution.**

_____ **3. Neil Armstrong prepares to land on the moon.**

_____ **4. Chief Joseph of the Nez Perce Indian nation surrenders to the U.S. Army.**

_____ **5. Abraham Lincoln is assassinated.**

_____ **6. Alexander Graham Bell invents the telephone.**

Name ______________________________ Date ______________

Social Sciences | History

13.A.2b

Different Perspectives on Historical Events

DIRECTIONS: Read the passages. Then, answer the questions.

The British government had no right to tax the colonies. American colonists had no elected representatives in the British Parliament. As a result, the colonists had no vote in British elections. In 1765, the British required the colonists to pay a tax stamp. This was a tax paid on documents, newspapers, and other printed papers. The colonists strongly disagreed with the Stamp Act, and they were right to do so. Colonists should not have been taxed without having someone to represent them in Parliament.

As man can be in but one place, at once, he cannot have the advantages of multiplied residence. He that will enjoy the brightness of sunshine, must quit the coolness of the shade. He who goes voluntarily to America, cannot complain of losing what he leaves in Europe. He, perhaps, had a right to vote for a knight or burgess; by crossing the Atlantick [sic], he has not nullified [done away with] his right; but he has made its exertion no longer possible. By his own choice he has left a country, where he had a vote and little property, for another, where he has great property, but no vote.

1. The main point of the first passage is that ___________ .

Ⓐ colonists should not have to pay any taxes of any kind

Ⓑ colonists should not be taxed by the British because they had no vote in British elections

Ⓒ the British had every right to tax their colonies

Ⓓ all taxes are unlawful

2. The main point of the second passage is that ___________ .

Ⓕ whatever the colonists want is acceptable

Ⓖ the colonists should not be taxed

Ⓗ the colonists have no right to complain about losing their vote in British elections

Ⓙ the British Army should arrest all colonists who refuse to pay their taxes

3. Which writer do you think probably approved of the Stamp Act?

Ⓐ the writer of the first passage

Ⓑ the writer of the second passage

Ⓒ neither probably approved of it

Ⓓ cannot tell from the content of the passages

4. Which writer was more sympathetic toward the colonists?

Ⓕ the writer of the first passage

Ⓖ the writer of the second passage

Ⓗ they both would have been sympathetic to the Revolution

Ⓙ cannot tell from the content of the passages

Name ______________________ Date ______________

Social Sciences History

13.B.2a (US)

Development of European Colonies in North America

DIRECTIONS: Choose the best answer.

1. **The first English colony in North America was founded in ___________ .**
   - (A) California
   - (B) Massachusetts
   - (C) Virginia
   - (D) Florida

2. **Place names such as Santa Cruz and San Diego are common in the southwestern part of North America. This gives a clue that this area was first colonized by settlers from ___________ .**
   - (F) Ireland
   - (G) Spain
   - (H) France
   - (J) England

3. **Which of the following countries did not have a strong colonial presence in North America?**
   - (A) India
   - (B) England
   - (C) France
   - (D) Spain

4. **This state was named after French king Louis XIV. The influence of the French colonists and legal system can still be felt today in ___________ .**
   - (F) Maryland
   - (G) Louisiana
   - (H) Wyoming
   - (J) Hawaii

5. **Which religion had a strong influence in the development of the New England colonies, particularly Massachusetts?**
   - (A) Catholicism
   - (B) Buddhism
   - (C) ancestor worship
   - (D) Puritanism, which was practiced by the Pilgrims

6. **Many colonists came to North America with ___________ .**
   - (F) the hope of making money
   - (G) the desire for religious freedom
   - (H) a desire for adventure
   - (J) all of the above

7. **When William Penn wanted to encourage people to come to his new colonies in North America, he emphasized all of the following except ___________ .**
   - (A) a government where the people would be represented
   - (B) religious freedom for all
   - (C) harsh, restrictive laws
   - (D) low taxes

STOP

Name ______________________ Date ______________

Social Sciences | History

13.B.2b (US)

Causes of the American Revolution

DIRECTIONS: Read the passage. Then, answer the questions.

In the mid-1700s, Great Britain defeated France in the French and Indian War. As a result, it won vast new lands in North America. Unfortunately, the war was very expensive. Great Britain tried to make up some of the money it spent fighting the war by taxing the colonists.

Though the tax angered colonists, the way Great Britain created the tax angered them even more. Normally, the assembly elected by a colony decided the money matters for that colony. But this time, no assembly had been allowed to help decide. The British Parliament made this decision. Angry assembly members said the tax was unfair since they had no hand in it. The British took back this tax, but later passed another tax. This angered the colonists even more. They became outraged when British soldiers shot several protesting colonists in what was named the Boston Massacre. Many colonists began to fear the British soldiers. They considered them to be the enemy.

1. One way the French and Indian War contributed to American independence was that ____________ .

Ⓐ it cost Great Britain a lot of money, which it tried to make up by taxing the colonists

Ⓑ all traces of French influence were removed from North America

Ⓒ British soldiers left North America and the colonists took control

Ⓓ all of the above

2. Which of the following was *not* a major cause of the American Revolution?

Ⓕ Colonists were feeling much more independent because the French were no longer in North America.

Ⓖ Great Britain tried to ban all but one religion in the colonies

Ⓗ Colonists feared the British soldiers in North America might turn against them.

Ⓙ Many colonists resented being taxed by the British without having any representation in the British Parliament.

3. What happened when the colonists protested the taxing by the British?

Ⓐ The British Parliament decided to remove the tax.

Ⓑ The French and Indian War started.

Ⓒ The British decided to tax the colonies even more.

Ⓓ British soldiers shot several of the protesters.

4. Which of the following men played an important role as a soldier during the American Revolution and also became the first president of the United States?

Ⓕ Andrew Jackson

Ⓖ Abraham Lincoln

Ⓗ George Washington

Ⓙ Samuel Adams

Name ____________________ Date ____________

Social Sciences

History

13.B.2c (US)

Presidential Elections and Political Parties

DIRECTIONS: Read the passage. Then, answer the questions.

After the American Revolution, the main political party was the Federalist Party. They were in favor of a strong national government. Thomas Jefferson thought that the states should have a major role in the new U.S. government. He formed a political party called the Democratic-Republicans. This party was in favor of states' rights.

During the 1820s, the Democratic-Republicans split into two parts. Those from the east supported a strong national government and a national bank. They called themselves the Democratic Party. The leader of this party was Andrew Jackson. He was elected president in 1828 and 1832.

By 1836, a new party called the *Whigs* was formed. This party disagreed with President Jackson. Candidates from the Whig Party were elected president in 1840 and 1848.

By the 1850s, most Whigs in the southern states became Democrats. They supported slavery. Northern Whigs and some Democrats in the north formed the Republican Party. They did not support slavery. The Republican candidate for president in 1860 was Abraham Lincoln. He won the election and helped bring an end to slavery. Except for brief periods, Republicans controlled the national government for more than 70 years. Both the Republican and Democratic parties still exist today.

1. Two major political parties in the years following the American Revolution were the ____________ parties.

- (A) Republican and Democrat
- (B) Democratic-Republican and Whig
- (C) Whig and Federalist
- (D) Federalist and Democratic-Republican

2. The election of which U.S. president strengthened the Democratic Party?

- (F) George Washington
- (G) Thomas Jefferson
- (H) Andrew Jackson
- (J) Abraham Lincoln

3. The main issue that caused the Republican Party to be formed was ____________ .

- (A) taxes
- (B) slavery
- (C) the formation of a national bank
- (D) foreign policy

4. The election of Abraham Lincoln to president in 1860 ____________ .

- (F) began a long period of Republican control of the U.S. government
- (G) brought about the end of the Democratic Party
- (H) made the Republican Party grow in the southern United States
- (J) caused the Federalist Party to split into two groups

5. Until the 1930s, most African-Americans tended to be Republicans. This was largely because ____________ .

- (A) Democrats wanted to raise taxes and Republicans wanted to lower taxes
- (B) the Democratic Party would not campaign in areas where African-Americans lived
- (C) a Republican president helped end slavery in the United States
- (D) it was illegal for African-Americans to vote

STOP

Name ______________________________ Date ______________

Social Sciences

13.B.2d (US)

History

Major U.S. Events and Leaders

DIRECTIONS: Choose the best answer.

1. **At the request of President Thomas Jefferson, these two men explored the western territory that the United States bought in the Louisiana Purchase.**
   - (A) Henry Hudson and John Cabot
   - (B) Paul Revere and John Paul Jones
   - (C) John Smith and Pocahontas
   - (D) Meriwether Lewis and William Clark

2. **In the mid-1800s, many Americans came to believe that it was their right to claim the land and spread across the entire continent. This became known as "manifest [obvious] destiny." Which of the following events in American history is *not* an example of the American belief in Manifest Destiny?**
   - (F) Texas becomes a state in 1845.
   - (G) The first Thanksgiving takes place between the Pilgrims and Native Americans.
   - (H) Settlers begin moving into the Great Plains states.
   - (J) Settlers travel to California with the hopes of finding gold. This results in the Gold Rush of 1849.

3. **Who was the president of the United States during the American Civil War?**
   - (A) Theodore Roosevelt
   - (B) Andrew Jackson
   - (C) Abraham Lincoln
   - (D) Andrew Johnson

4. **American women were first allowed to vote in a presidential election in __________ .**
   - (F) 1776
   - (G) 1920
   - (H) 1976
   - (J) none of the above; American women have always been able to vote in presidential elections

5. **The main enemy of the United States during World War I was __________ .**
   - (A) Germany
   - (B) Canada
   - (C) England
   - (D) Mexico

6. **This president began bringing U.S. troops home from Vietnam. He also was forced to resign because of his illegal actions during the 1972 election campaign. Which president was this?**
   - (F) Jimmy Carter
   - (G) Bill Clinton
   - (H) George W. Bush
   - (J) Richard Nixon

7. **Which of the following individuals is known for his role in leading the Civil Rights movement of the 1960s?**
   - (A) Martin Luther King, Jr.
   - (B) John F. Kennedy
   - (C) Bill Clinton
   - (D) Richard Nixon

Name ______________________________ Date ______________

Social Sciences

History

13.B.2a (W)

Political Power in Ancient Civilizations

A **democracy** is a way of governing where all citizens take charge of their own affairs. A **monarchy** is a government that is ruled by a king or queen. In an **oligarchy,** the majority of the people are governed by only a few people (such as a powerful family or small group of important people).

DIRECTIONS: Choose the best answer.

1. **The first Greek city-states were ruled by kings. They were known as ___________ .**

   Ⓐ monarchies
   Ⓑ democracies
   Ⓒ republics
   Ⓓ oligarchies

2. **In Greece, rule by kings gave way in time to government by the leading families. These would be known as ___________ .**

   Ⓕ direct democracies
   Ⓖ oligarchies
   Ⓗ representative democracies
   Ⓙ anarchies

City-states were independent communities. They were the first attempts of people to create governments where they ruled themselves. They consisted of a small city surrounded by rural farmland. Most important, they were not governed by a higher authority such as an empire or nation.

3. **The passage above describes a(n) ___________ .**

   Ⓐ metropolis
   Ⓑ city-state
   Ⓒ suburb
   Ⓓ oligarchy

4. **Which of the following was a city-state in ancient Greece?**

   Ⓕ New York
   Ⓖ London
   Ⓗ Sparta
   Ⓙ Paris

5. **In the fifth century B.C., the city-state of Athens was a republic led by a man named Pericles. Some people could vote. The majority of people, however, were not recognized as citizens and could not vote. For that reason, ___________ .**

   Ⓐ The people of Athens had more freedom that we do in the United States today.
   Ⓑ Athens was really a monarchy.
   Ⓒ Athens was not a true democracy.
   Ⓓ All of the above are true.

STOP

Name ______________________________ Date ______________

Social Sciences

History

13.B.2b (W)

Origins of Western Political Ideas

DIRECTIONS: Study the table of key events that helped form western political ideas. Then, answer the questions.

Time and Place	Event
5th century B.C., Greece	Idea of democracy is born.
5th century B.C., Rome	Tribunes (or committees) can veto or reject the act of any judge that is unjust to any citizen.
1st century B.C., Rome	Rome is now ruled by a king and is no longer a republic.
Middle Ages, Europe	People who live in the cities want peaceful trade, not wars. They demand contracts from the kings to guarantee their business rights.
1215, England	The Magna Carta is signed.
Mid-1300s, England	The British Parliament is made up of two bodies—the House of Lords (noblemen) and the House of Commons (middle-class).
1642-1651, England	Civil war breaks out in England. Some groups demand that the House of Commons should have all of the political power. They don't want the power to rest with the House of Lords and any future king.
late 1600s, England	John Locke argues that natural law guarantees men the rights to life, liberty, and property.
mid 1700s, France	Writer Jean-Jacques Rousseau calls for political democracy.

1. A democracy is a way of governing in which the whole body of citizens takes charge of its own affairs. The concept of democracy was invented by the ___________ .

- (A) English
- (B) ancient Romans
- (C) ancient Greeks
- (D) Celts

2. In ancient Rome, a tribune ___________ .

- (F) belonged to the lower order of citizens and could not vote
- (G) was a group of people who wanted peaceful trade
- (H) was ruled by a king
- (J) could reject the act of any judge that was unjust to any citizen

3. This document states the rights that are guaranteed to the English people. English barons and churchmen wrote this document. King John placed his seal on it on June 15, 1215. Which document was this?

- (A) the Magna Carta
- (B) the Domesday book
- (C) the Declaration of Independence
- (D) the Book of Runes

4. During what period of time did some people in England begin to argue that the House of Lords and the king should not have any political power?

- (F) in 1215
- (G) during the mid-1700s
- (H) during the English Civil War
- (J) in the Middle Ages

Name ______________________________ Date ______________

Social Sciences

History

13.C.2a (US)

Influence of Slavery on the American Economy

DIRECTIONS: Read the passage and then choose the best answer.

For a long time in this country, slavery was accepted. George Washington, this nation's first president, owned over 200 slaves. In fact, eight of the first twelve presidents were slave owners.

From the beginning, some Americans thought slavery was wrong. Most of the people who opposed slavery lived in the northern half of the nation. Many people in the South supported slavery. In the South, a plantation's success or failure might depend on the slaves who worked there.

The rocky soil of New England did not encourage great big farms. So, New England farmers could, with the help of their families, farm their own fields. They had little use for slaves. In addition, many mills and factories were being built in the North. That meant fewer northerners were making their living by farming.

In the South, giant plantations grew up. Some of the crops grown on a plantation needed a great deal of care. Tobacco especially took a lot of work. The southern farmer needed help farming his many acres of crops. The least expensive year-round help he could get was a slave.

1. **Based on the passage, which of the following statements is *not* true?**
   - (A) Slavery was accepted in this country for many years.
   - (B) Several presidents were slave owners.
   - (C) There were a lot of plantations in the North that required the use of slaves to care for the crops.
   - (D) Most people who opposed slavery lived in the northern half of the nation.

2. **From this passage you can predict that slavery became most important to the ____________ economy in the United States.**
   - (F) Western
   - (G) Southern
   - (H) Northern
   - (J) Midwestern

DIRECTIONS: Read the following facts about the early U.S. economy. If it tended to encourage slavery, write an **S+** in the space provided. If it tended to discourage slavery, write an **S–**.

______ **3. Rocky New England soil did not encourage large farms, so New England families could usually farm their own fields.**

______ **4. The growing of tobacco required a great deal of care and labor.**

______ **5. Many mills and factories were built in the North.**

______ **6. Fertile southern soil encouraged very large farms, and the warmer southern climate had a longer growing season. Farmers could not operate such large farms by themselves.**

______ **7. Slaves were the least-expensive year-round help an employer could get.**

Name ______________________________ Date ______________

Social Sciences | History

13.C.2b (US)

American Inventors

DIRECTIONS: Study the list of inventors and inventions/innovations below. Then, answer the questions.

Name	Invention or Innovation
Alexander Graham Bell	Telephone
John Deere	Steel plowshare
Henry Ford	Automobile assembly line
Bill Gates	Computer software
Joseph F. Glidden	Barbed wire
Thomas Edison	Electric lightbulb
John Kellogg	Cereal flakes
Samuel Morse	Telegraph
Cyrus Hall McCormick	Mechanical reaper
Isaac Singer	Improved sewing machine

1. Which individual is incorrectly matched with his invention or innovation?

- (A) John Deere—steel plowshare
- (B) Joseph F. Glidden—barbed wire
- (C) John Kellogg—telegraph
- (D) Isaac Singer—sewing machine

2. Whose invention was most responsible for freeing farmers from hours of heavy labor?

- (F) Cyrus Hall McCormick
- (G) Alexander Graham Bell
- (H) Bill Gates
- (J) Henry Ford

3. Which inventor created something that allowed people to talk to each other over distances?

- (A) Joseph Glidden
- (B) Alexander Graham Bell
- (C) Bill Gates
- (D) Charles Goodyear

4. How did the invention of the electric lightbulb contribute to economic change in the United States?

- (F) Automobile factories appeared in every American city, creating jobs for millions of Americans.
- (G) It allowed travelers to move from the East Coast to the West Coast in a matter of hours, not days.
- (H) Businesses could more easily operate at night.
- (J) All of the above.

5. Henry Ford knew that he could make lots of money selling cars if he could make them cheaply. That way, many people would be able to afford to buy them. What do you think was his solution for building cars without raising their cost?

- (A) He paid his workers only pennies a day.
- (B) He hired only illegal aliens and forced them to work long hours.
- (C) He put the people who built his cars in a line along a conveyor belt.
- (D) He built his cars with inferior quality parts.

6. Eli Whitney invented the cotton gin, which separated cotton from its seed. This caused the demand for cotton to rise greatly. To meet the demand, southern farmers began to devote their whole plantations to cotton growing. How do you think his invention encouraged slavery?

____

____

____

STOP

Name ______________________________ Date ______________

Social Sciences

History

13.C.2c (US)

U.S. Economic History

DIRECTIONS: Read the passage. Then, answer the questions.

By the mid-1800s, the Industrial Revolution was in full swing in the United States. During this time, work that was usually done by hand began to be done by machines. Many large factories began to be built. By the late 1800s, little open land remained for farming, but the rapidly growing cities offered jobs in factories. These jobs were very attractive to the many immigrants who came to the United States looking for a better life.

American stores became larger to sell the many new products being invented and produced. Before, people had to go to several small shops to find what they wanted. Now, they could find much of what they needed under one roof.

Larger and larger companies were creating the products people bought. Many of these companies joined together in a new kind of business organization called a *trust.* In a trust, a board of directors lowers the competition among its companies and sets the prices. When one organization sells nearly all of the available supply for one product, it is called a *monopoly.* A monopoly can be dangerous because it can keep the prices for its goods high. The organization does not worry about another business selling the same thing for less because it is the main one selling that product. The U.S. government eventually passed laws to stop trusts. This allowed other companies to compete for business and helped to keep prices lower.

1. Before the Industrial Revolution, __________ .

- (A) stores were stocked with only a few necessary items
- (B) most work was done by hand rather than by machines
- (C) there were few factories to produce products
- (D) all of the above

2. In the late 1800s and early 1900s, greater industrialization in the United States __________ .

- (F) increased the number of the nation's farmers
- (G) created more factory jobs
- (H) meant more products were made by hand
- (J) completely ruined the American economy

3. Which of the following statements about immigration to the United States is *not* true?

- (A) Many immigrants to the United States in the late 1800s took jobs at factories.
- (B) The United States is a nation of immigrants.
- (C) A century ago, immigrants were important to the American economy, but they contribute nothing today.
- (D) Immigrants came to the United States in search of a better life.

4. The late 1800s saw the rise of many large monopolies in American business. A monopoly exists when __________ .

- (F) only one person makes all the decisions about a company
- (G) a business sells only one item
- (H) a company operates in only a few locations
- (J) one organization sells nearly all of the available supply of one product

STOP

Name ______________________________ Date ______________

Social Sciences

History

13.C.2a (W)

The First Agricultural Revolution

DIRECTIONS: Read the passage. Then, answer the questions.

Before agriculture became widely used, people had to spend most of their time looking for food. They gathered plants, hunted, or fished for food. About 10,000 years ago, though, people in the Middle East began to learn how to care for herds and flocks of animals. They also began to grow plants for food, medicine, and other uses.

Early farmers used hand tools such as digging sticks and stone sickles. By 4000 B.C., plows replaced the digging sticks. By about 3000 B.C., Egyptian farmers were using plows attached to oxen. Plow animals helped farmers plant and grow more crops. They also saved farmers from doing the heaviest work.

Since about 5000 B.C., Farmers in Egypt and Mesopotamia used irrigation. Irrigation is a method of supplying water to farmland. Irrigation techniques were also used in ancient Asian and Native American societies.

As farmers were able to grow more and more food, people began to do other things besides tend crops and care for livestock. People took up a variety of occupations. They made goods that they could trade with farmers for food. Towns and cities began to develop. Different types of people—all doing different things—learned the advantages of living together. The division of labor, an important economic rule, had begun.

1. Agriculture involves all of the following except ___________ .

- (A) harvesting crops
- (B) digging for coal
- (C) planting seeds
- (D) raising livestock

2. Prehistoric people spent most of their time ___________ .

- (F) making items for trade with farmers
- (G) plowing fields and irrigating crops
- (H) looking for food
- (J) building cities

3. The development of the plow ___________ .

- (A) increased the amount of food that farmers could grow
- (B) caused more people to become hunters and gatherers
- (C) slowed the development of cities and towns
- (D) all of the above

4. As better agricultural techniques were invented, ___________ .

- (F) people lived shorter and shorter lives
- (G) towns became smaller and smaller
- (H) people had more time to devote to other tasks besides getting food
- (J) more people wanted to become farmers

5. Which of the following is an example of division of labor?

- (A) A farmer who keeps livestock begins growing crops as well.
- (B) All members of a society spend most of their time hunting and gathering food.
- (C) A farmer grows many different types of crops, not just one or two.
- (D) A tailor makes a garment and trades it to a farmer for a bushel of wheat.

Name ______________________________ Date ______________

Social Sciences

History

13.C.2b (W)

Economies of the World's Great Civilizations

DIRECTIONS: Economic aspects of some of the world's great civilizations are briefly explained below. Read each of the descriptions and then answer the questions.

Mesopotamia: Mesopotamia was located between the Tigris and Euphrates rivers. It was made up of city-states. The leaders who ruled the city-states also controlled the local irrigation systems. This civilization had excellent agricultural techniques. In this economy, metalworking and pottery-making businesses grew. Great cities and some of the world's first libraries were built here.

Indus Valley: The economy depended on livestock and crops, such as wheat, rice, dates, melons, and cotton. There were large places to store grain. A textile, or fabric, industry developed because of the cotton crops. Raw cotton was brought to the cities. Here it was spun, woven, and dyed. Fabrics were probably traded with Mesopotamia, Afghanistan, and southern India.

Chou Dynasty (China): The Chou people used both hunting and agriculture to make a living. This dynasty saw the rise of a middle class. Iron was also introduced during this time.

Aegean: This was the earliest civilization in Europe. It appeared on the coasts and islands of the Aegean Sea. Sea travel and trade, especially with the Middle East and with Egypt, were important to its economy. There were landowners, tenant farmers, servants and slaves, priests and priestesses in this civilization. It also had many trades and professions.

1. The leaders of the city-states in ancient Mesopotamia also controlled the __________ .

- (A) local irrigation systems
- (B) metalworking businesses
- (C) libraries
- (D) pottery making businesses

2. How did fabric-making become important in the Indus Valley economy?

- (F) Few animals lived in the region, so there were not enough animal hides from which to make clothes.
- (G) The religion of the Indus Valley people taught that fabric making was important.
- (H) Cotton was a main crop grown there.
- (J) People of the Indus Valley liked to wear nice clothes.

3. Agriculture was important in __________ .

- (A) China during the Chou Dynasty
- (B) Mesopotamia
- (C) the Indus Valley society
- (D) all of the above

4. The ancient Aegeans lived in __________ .

- (F) Africa
- (G) Asia
- (H) Europe
- (J) South America

5. Some of the earliest libraries were built in __________ .

- (A) the Indus Valley
- (B) Mesopotamia
- (C) Aegean society
- (D) none of the above

Name ______________________________ Date ______________

Social Sciences

History

13.C.2c (W)

Manorial Systems and the Economy

DIRECTIONS: Read the passage and then answer the questions.

In feudalistic societies, peasants worked on large estates, called *manors.* Peasants were the lowest class in this society. They lived in nearby villages and were bound to the lord of the manor. The lord usually lived in a castle or other strong building on the manor grounds. The peasants had rights to farm part of the manor land, but they had to work on the lord's land as well. The peasants also had to give the lord part of what they grew on their own land. The peasants could graze their livestock in the meadow, but only the lord could use the nearby woods, ponds, and streams for hunting and fishing.

A manor could almost completely support itself. Mills, bakeries, and breweries supplied the needs of the lord as well as the peasants. Women generally spun thread, wove fabrics, and sewed. Salt and iron were the main goods that needed to be brought into the manor. Little commerce, or trade, was necessary.

1. What type of society is described in this passage?

Ⓐ democratic
Ⓑ capitalistic
Ⓒ feudalistic
Ⓓ socialistic

2. In feudalistic societies, people of the lowest rank were the __________ .

Ⓕ peasants
Ⓖ lords
Ⓗ knights
Ⓙ noblemen

3. Which of the following statements about manors is *not* true?

Ⓐ Manors were large estates.
Ⓑ Peasants were the main workers.
Ⓒ Peasants had to travel to other cities to get the supplies that they needed.
Ⓓ A manor could almost completely support itself.

4. Which of the following describes the relationship between the peasants and the lord of the manor?

Ⓕ Peasants had to farm part of the lord's land.
Ⓖ Peasants were not allowed to use the lord's land for hunting and fishing.
Ⓗ The manor provided for the needs of both the lord and the peasants.
Ⓙ All of the above.

5. By the thirteenth century, many small towns had spread across Europe. The townspeople were not self-sufficient like the small groups of peasants on the manors were. How do you think this changed the economy of Europe?

Ⓐ People fled Europe in great numbers looking for a better life elsewhere.
Ⓑ Townspeople developed lifestyles based on the idea of trade.
Ⓒ Townspeople begged to be taken care of by the lords again.
Ⓓ Agriculture died out in Europe within a century.

Name ______________________ Date ______________________

Social Sciences **History**

13.D.2a (US)

Reasons for Settling in Colonial America

DIRECTIONS: Read the passage. Then, answer the questions.

European settlers began arriving in North America in the early 1600s. They came for many reasons. The English settlers who established Jamestown, Virginia, wanted their own land. They also thought they would find gold. Later, colonists sought wealth through farming and trade. Supporters of Charles II came to the Carolinas for land to raise crops. Many Dutch settled in New York and New Jersey. They hoped to establish large estates. Hard-working Swedes were among the early settlers in Delaware. English debtors, or people who owed money to others, came to Georgia to start a new life.

Puritan colonists from England settled in Massachusetts to escape certain laws and rules. They wanted to worship in their own way. In England, their religion was not popular. English Catholics settled in Maryland in search of religious freedom.

The first German immigrants to North America arrived in the 1680s. They were attracted to Pennsylvania, where William Penn promised complete religious freedom to all settlers to his colony. Penn also said settlers could take part in their own government. Other Germans, especially Lutherans and Mennonites, came to North America to escape being forced into European armies. They were hard-working farmers who produced grains, beef, hams, and hides.

1. Religious freedom was the main reason for coming to North America for __________ .

- (A) early settlers in Georgia
- (B) many colonists in Pennsylvania
- (C) Virginia colonists
- (D) the Dutch who came to New York

2. English Catholics settled in __________ .

- (F) Maryland
- (G) Massachusetts
- (H) Georgia
- (J) the Carolinas

3. Europeans started to settle in North America in the __________ .

- (A) 1600s
- (B) 1700s
- (C) 1800s
- (D) 1900s

4. Colonists from which European country were trying to avoid military service?

- (F) England
- (G) Germany
- (H) Sweden
- (J) Holland

5. Early settlers to New York mainly wanted to __________ .

- (A) gain great wealth
- (B) convert Native Americans to Christianity
- (C) worship in their own way
- (D) escape creditors back in Europe

6. Delaware was the destination for many colonists from __________ .

- (F) Norway
- (G) Germany
- (H) Sweden
- (J) France

STOP

Name ______________________________ Date ______________

Social Sciences

History

13.D.2b (US)

Effects of Westward Expansion

DIRECTIONS: Choose the best answer.

1. **In 1803, the United States purchased a large portion of land from France. The land was west of the Mississippi River and went all the way to the Rocky Mountains. This became known as the Louisiana Purchase. After the Louisiana Purchase, many Americans started moving westward. Settlers first moved west __________ .**
   - (A) across the Missouri River toward the Appalachian Mountains, then farther west to the Rocky Mountains and the Mississippi River
   - (B) over the Rocky Mountains toward the Missouri River, then farther west to the Mississippi River and the Appalachian Mountains
   - (C) beyond the Appalachian Mountains toward the Mississippi River, then farther west to the Missouri River and the Rocky Mountains
   - (D) across the Mississippi and Missouri Rivers, then farther west over the Appalachian and then the Rocky Mountains

2. **As white settlers moved west across North America, most Native American communities __________ .**
   - (F) lived easily with the settlers
   - (G) were squeezed out so the settlers could take their land
   - (H) were protected from the settlers by acts of Congress
   - (J) grew right alongside the settlers' communities

3. **This law allowed any head of a household over the age of 21 to claim 160 acres of land in the Great Plains for only a small fee. In return, the settlers had to agree to spend five years living there and improving the land. The law was called the __________ .**
   - (A) Homestead Act
   - (B) Endangered Species Act
   - (C) Federal Communications Act
   - (D) Fugitive Slave Act

4. **Many ranchers disliked the farmers who moved into the prairie states in the middle of the nineteenth century. Which of the following do you think is a reason why the ranchers disliked the farmers?**
   - (F) Farmers often fenced their property with barbed wire. This prevented the ranchers' cattle from roaming freely.
   - (G) Farmers competed with ranchers for scarce water supplies.
   - (H) Farmers plowed up the grassy plains that was used by the livestock for food.
   - (J) All of the above.

5. **Which of the following was not a hardship faced by farm families living on the Great Plains during the mid-1800s?**
   - (A) harsh weather
   - (B) loneliness
   - (C) pollution from nearby factories
   - (D) lack of water

6. **In 1849, gold was discovered in California. Which of the following communities grew the most because of that discovery?**
   - (F) Chicago
   - (G) Wichita
   - (H) San Francisco
   - (J) Cincinnati

Name ______________________________ Date ______________

Social Sciences

History

13.D.2c (US)

Key Individuals and Groups in U.S. Social History

DIRECTIONS: Study the table below and use it to help you answer the questions.

Name	Accomplishment
Ralph Abernathy	Civil rights leader
Jane Addams	Social worker who did much to help the poor
Susan B. Anthony	Fought to get women the right to vote
Mary McLeod Bethune	Established a school for young black women
Cesar Chavez	Labor union leader who fought for farm workers' rights
Betty Friedan	Challenged traditional roles for women
Anne Hutchinson	New England colonist who stood up for her own beliefs
Jesse Jackson	Civil rights leader
Mother Jones	Labor union leader, miners' rights supporter
Martin Luther King	Civil rights leader, Nobel Peace Prize winner
Sandra Day O'Conner	First woman to serve on the U.S. Supreme Court
Rosa Parks	Civil rights supporter, sparked famous boycott that helped start the U.S. civil rights movement
Harriet Tubman	Worked with the Underground Railroad to free slaves
Malcolm X	Civil rights leader

1. She was one of the first New England colonists to question the religious authority of the Puritan leaders. She preferred to follow her sense of right and wrong. Her protests helped to establish the principle of freedom of religion. Who is she?

- (A) Jane Addams
- (B) Mother Jones
- (C) Anne Hutchinson
- (D) Betty Friedan

2. Which of the following people helped American women gain the right to vote?

- (F) Sandra Day O'Connor
- (G) Susan B. Anthony
- (H) Martin Luther King
- (J) Harriet Tubman

3. She helped make life better for America's poor. She established Hull House, a center in Chicago where poor immigrants could get help. She also helped end child labor in Illinois and helped create the first public playground in Chicago. Who is she?

- (A) Sandra Day O'Connor
- (B) Rosa Parks
- (C) Anne Hutchinson
- (D) Jane Addams

4. Cesar Chavez is best known for ____________ .

- (F) establishing the Peace Corps
- (G) helping migrant farm workers live better lives
- (H) saving our nation's forests
- (J) ending Jim Crow laws that favored white Americans over African Americans

Name ______________________________ Date ______________

Social Sciences

History

13.D.2 (W) Women, Men, and Children

DIRECTIONS: Choose the best answer.

1. **Which of the following statements is true?**
   - (A) Under English common law of England almost all of a married woman's property came under her husband's control.
   - (B) Early Roman law described women as children, lower in importance and position to men.
   - (C) In the Muslim societies of the Middle East, women have traditionally owned and managed their own property.
   - (D) All of the above statements are true.

2. **In most ancient civilizations, women usually did work associated with the home. Which of these jobs were they usually *not* most responsible for?**
   - (F) raising children
   - (G) cooking
   - (H) hunting
   - (J) washing clothes

3. **In most societies throughout history, wealth passes from the parents to the sons. Usually their wealth goes to the oldest son. Some New Guinea societies were very different from most throughout history because ___________ .**
   - (A) wealth passed from parents to daughters, not to sons
   - (B) religion was an important part of everyday life
   - (C) soldiers were almost always men
   - (D) a woman was allowed to marry only one man at a time

4. **Before the Industrial Revolution in the 1800s, ___________ .**
   - (F) most families made education their first priority
   - (G) only children of the wealthy and powerful did not have to do physical labor
   - (H) most families had only one child
   - (J) it was very uncommon for any child to work in or outside the home

DIRECTIONS: Read the passage and then answer the questions.

Ancient African societies were often organized into small groups. Each group identified itself with an important ancestor. Special respect was given to older members of the community. These tribal elders were thought of as wise and experienced. They were responsible for managing the community. They tried to be as fair to everyone as possible. Their main goal was to help the community remain peaceful and prosperous. Under this system everyone in the community shared in the wealth as well as the hardships of their common life.

5. **Who would probably be the most respected member of an ancient African society?**
   - (A) a newborn baby
   - (B) a 20-year old shepherd
   - (C) a 35-year-old pottery maker
   - (D) a 50-year-old tribal elder

6. **Based on the passage, most people in an ancient African community were probably ___________ .**
   - (F) very poor, though a few were quite wealthy
   - (G) very wealthy, though a few were poor
   - (H) no better or worse off than their neighbors
   - (J) hostile to each other most of the time

Name ______________________________ Date ______________

Social Sciences | History

13.E.2a/13.E.2c (US)

Environmental Factors That Shaped Illinois

DIRECTIONS: Read the passage. Then, answer the questions.

Native Americans used to hunt deer and bear that roamed in Illinois. The first white men to cross the Illinois prairies were French. They were Father Jacques Marquette and Louis Joliet. They used the Mississippi, Illinois, Des Plaines, and Chicago rivers on their travels. Beginning in 1680, another French explorer, La Salle, claimed the region for France. By 1750, the region contained about 2,000 French people and a few black slaves.

Shortly before the Revolutionary War, Chicago was settled on Lake Michigan. Settlement in the state was mainly in the southern third of the area, though, until the early 1800s.

Early pioneers traveled into Illinois from the east. Here, they got their first look at the great prairie of the Midwest. This is the main feature of the land. Settlers were drawn to Illinois mainly for farming. The state also has other resources such as coal, oil, and timber.

Many entered the region by means of the Cumberland Road, which ended at present-day Vandalia. By the time Illinois became a state in 1818, about 40,000 people lived there. Most of the people lived along the Mississippi, Wabash, and Ohio rivers. After the Civil War, farming was growing in the state, but manufacturing was growing even faster. The state's central location makes Illinois a center for business and travel.

1. Most of the first Europeans who entered modern-day Illinois were ____________ .

Ⓐ French trappers and hunters

Ⓑ English factory workers

Ⓒ German farmers

Ⓓ Irish railroad workers

2. This important trail was a leading factor in settling the Midwest. It led as far west as Vandalia, Illinois.

Ⓕ the Oregon Trail

Ⓖ the Appian Way

Ⓗ the Cumberland Road

Ⓙ the Santa Fe Trail

3. Most of Illinois is ____________ .

Ⓐ rocky, hilly, and barren

Ⓑ covered with tall trees

Ⓒ fertile farmland

Ⓓ covered with lakes

4. Which of the following natural resources did *not* draw people into Illinois?

Ⓕ coal

Ⓖ oil

Ⓗ diamonds

Ⓙ timber

5. All of the following are important transportation routes in Illinois except ____________ .

Ⓐ the Mississippi River

Ⓑ the Rio Grande

Ⓒ the Ohio River

Ⓓ the Great Lakes

6. The development of trade in Illinois has been helped because the state ____________ .

Ⓕ has useful natural resources

Ⓖ is centrally located

Ⓗ is close to major rivers

Ⓙ all of the above

Name ______________________________ Date ______________

Social Sciences

History

13.E.2b (US)

The U.S. Conservation Movement

DIRECTIONS: Choose the best answer.

1. At the beginning of the twentieth century, this U.S. president worked hard to create national forests and parks.

Ⓐ George Washington
Ⓑ Ronald Reagan
Ⓒ Theodore Roosevelt
Ⓓ George H. Bush

2. This U.S. conservationist was largely responsible for the establishment of the Sequoia and Yosemite National Parks in 1890.

Ⓕ Al Gore
Ⓖ Robert E. Lee
Ⓗ Bill Gates
Ⓙ John Muir

3. The U.S. National Park System includes ___________ .

Ⓐ recreation areas
Ⓑ monuments, memorials, and cemeteries
Ⓒ seashores, lakeshores, and scenic riverways
Ⓓ all of the above

4. Her book, *Silent Spring,* warned of the dangers of pesticides such as DDT.

Ⓕ Rachel Carson
Ⓖ Hillary Clinton
Ⓗ Dolly Madison
Ⓙ Rosa Parks

5. The Endangered Species Act ___________ .

Ⓐ made it illegal to hunt some animals that are close to extinction
Ⓑ allowed forests to be inspected to help find and remove diseases in the trees
Ⓒ allowed private individuals to mine coal on government land
Ⓓ required U.S. citizens to recycle newspapers and cans

6. Which U.S. government agency enforces laws that help keep the environment clean?

Ⓕ Better Business Bureau
Ⓖ Environmental Protection Agency
Ⓗ Federal Bureau of Investigation
Ⓙ Secret Service

7. The first U.S. National Park was ___________ .

Ⓐ Addo Elephant National Park
Ⓑ Mount Fuji National Park
Ⓒ Yellowstone National Park
Ⓓ the Bavarian Forest

Name ______________________________ Date ______________

Social Sciences **History**

13.E.2a (W)

Adaptation of Native Peoples to Their Environment

DIRECTIONS: Different Native American cultures lived in different environments. Read about some of them below. Then, answer the questions.

Native Americans of the Eastern Forests: This environment had plenty of rain. The summers were especially warm and rainy. It had large, lush forests and many lakes and streams that were home to abundant fish and game. They planted corn, pumpkin, squash, beans, tobacco, and gourds. They did not need to search for wild food.

Native Americans of the Plains: This environment had rolling, grassy prairie lands but few trees. The trees grew mainly beside rivers. Large herds of animals such as elk, deer, antelope, and buffalo grazed on the prairie. The tribes followed the herds across the plains.

Native Americans of the Southwest: This environment was high and dry. Most of the rain fell in the summer when it could help plants grow. Winter snow from the mountains supplied water for streams, springs, and water holes. The Pueblos developed irrigation and were able to grow their food.

Native Americans of the Desert: The Seed Gatherers lived in the driest parts of California and other western desert regions. There were few game animals. They gathered berries, nuts, seeds, and roots for food. They ground the seeds into flour for gruel.

Native Americans of the Northwest: This environment had heavy rainfall along the northern Pacific coast. The ocean and the rivers were full of fish. It had tall, dense forests. They gathered bulbs, berries, and seeds.

Native Americans of the Far North: This environment was frozen under ice and snow for at least half of the year. Most vegetables would not grow here, and there were very few trees.

1. Which of the following do you think was the main source of food for Native Americans of the Far North?

- (A) snow and ice
- (B) cows, pigs, and chickens
- (C) fish and Arctic sea and land animals
- (D) wheat and fruit

2. Native Americans of the Plains were less likely to settle into permanent villages because ____________ .

- (F) their main food source was always on the move
- (G) they did not like to farm
- (H) they did not like to eat vegetables and fruits
- (J) they were unable to build their own dwellings

3. Which of the following do you think were least likely to be expert fishers?

- (A) Native Americans of the Northwest
- (B) Native Americans of the Desert
- (C) Native Americans of the Far North
- (D) Native Americans of the Eastern Forests

4. Native Americans of the Eastern Forests did not gather much of their food. Why not?

- (F) Other Native American societies brought food to them.
- (G) They were lazy.
- (H) Their environment was harsh and most vegetable foods did not flourish there.
- (J) They knew how to grow their own food.

Name ______________________________ Date ______________

Social Sciences

History

13.E.2b (W)

Important Inventions in Environmental History

DIRECTIONS: Match the inventor in Column A with the invention in Column B. A clue is provided beside each inventor's name.

Column A	Column B
______ 1. **Thomas Edison *(bright idea)***	**A. dynamite**
______ 2. **James Watt *(s-s-see it go!)***	**B. early electric furnace**
______ 3. **Alfred Nobel *(boom boom)***	**C. electric lightbulb**
______ 4. **Karl Benz *(as in Mercedes)***	**D. first mechanical refrigeration system**
______ 5. **William Siemens *(hot stuff)***	**E. steam engine**
______ 6. **John Gorrie *(he was cool)***	**F. early automobile**
______ 7. **John Deere *(farm boy)***	**G. first steel plow**

8. Explain the impact you think the electric lightbulb has had on the environment.

____

____

____

____

____

____

Name ______________________________ Date ______________

Social Sciences

13

For pages 213–234

History

Mini-Test 3

DIRECTIONS: Choose the best answer.

1. Which of the following do you think would have most likely agreed that "taxation without representation" was unfair?

- Ⓐ the king of England
- Ⓑ a British soldier
- Ⓒ an American colonist
- Ⓓ a member of the British Parliament

2. Before 1880, most immigrants to the United States came from ___________ .

- Ⓕ Europe
- Ⓖ China
- Ⓗ India
- Ⓙ South America

3. Which of the following constitutional rights was a direct result of the colonists' struggle with Great Britain?

- Ⓐ Slavery was made illegal.
- Ⓑ Citizens had the right to refuse having soldiers lodged in their homes.
- Ⓒ Citizens gained rights that were not listed in the United States Constitution.
- Ⓓ Women gained the right to vote.

4. Which of the following events had the most impact on the formation of the main political parties in today's United States?

- Ⓕ the Louisiana Purchase
- Ⓖ the discovery of gold in California
- Ⓗ the Civil War
- Ⓙ the September 11, 2001, terrorist attack on the United States

5. The belief that it was the right of Americans to spread across the entire continent and claim the land is known as ___________ .

- Ⓐ the Louisiana Purchase
- Ⓑ Manifest Destiny
- Ⓒ the Magna Carta
- Ⓓ the Declaration of Independence

6. The plow was developed ___________ .

- Ⓕ by 4000 B.C.
- Ⓖ by 2000 B.C.
- Ⓗ in the Middle Ages
- Ⓙ by John Deere in the mid-nineteenth century

7. A monarchy is ___________ .

- Ⓐ a way of governing where all citizens take charge of their own affairs
- Ⓑ a government that is ruled by a king or queen
- Ⓒ a government where the majority of the people are governed by only a few people
- Ⓓ an independent community

8. Early settlers to Virginia ___________ .

- Ⓕ sought religious freedom
- Ⓖ hoped to get rich
- Ⓗ were escaping military service in Europe
- Ⓙ were eager to start their own country

9. Westward movement across America was spurred by ___________ .

- Ⓐ farmers
- Ⓑ miners
- Ⓒ ranchers
- Ⓓ all of the above

STOP

Social Science Standards

Geography

Goal 14: Understand world geography and the effects of geography on society, with an emphasis on the United States.

Learning Standard 14A—Locate, describe, and explain places, regions, and features on the earth.

14.A.2a Compare the physical characteristics of places including soils, land forms, vegetation, wildlife, climate, natural hazards. *(See page 237.)*

14.A.2b Use maps and other geographic representations and instruments to gather information about people, places and environments. *(See page 237.)*

Learning Standard 14B—Analyze and explain characteristics and interactions on the earth's physical systems.

14.B.2a Describe how physical and human processes shape spatial patterns including erosion, agriculture, and settlement. *(See page 238.)*

14.B.2b Explain how physical and living components interact in a variety of ecosystems including desert, prairie, flood plain, forest, tundra. *(See page 239.)*

Learning Standard 14C—Understand relationships between geographic factors and society.

14.C.2a Describe how natural events in the physical environment affect human activities. *(See page 240.)*

14.C.2b Describe the relationships among location of resources, population distribution, and economic activities (e.g., transportation, trade, communications). *(See page 241.)*

14.C.2c Explain how human activity affects the environment. *(See page 242.)*

Learning Standard 14D—Understand the historical significance of geography.

14.D.2a Describe how physical characteristics of places influence people's perceptions and their roles in the world over time.

14.D.2b Identify different settlement patterns in Illinois and the United States and relate them to physical features and resources. *(See page 243.)*

Name ______________________________ Date ______________

Social Sciences **Geography**

14.A.2a/14.A.2b

Geographic Regions of Earth

DIRECTIONS: Use the map below to select the best answer.

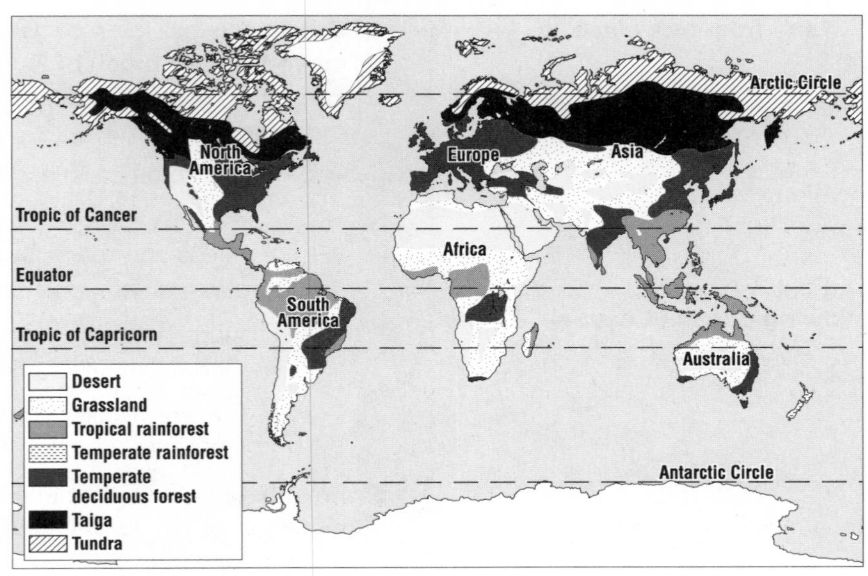

1. Based on the map above, we can conclude that organisms living in the southeastern part of North America probably are most like organisms in ____________ .

(A) the northern parts of Asia
(B) most of Africa
(C) southwestern North America
(D) western Europe

2. Thin, rocky, or sandy soil covers most ____________ .

(F) grasslands
(G) deserts
(H) temperate deciduous forests
(J) temperate rainforests

3. The Inuit are native peoples who live in the far north. Which types of environments do the Inuit mostly live in?

(A) taiga and tundra
(B) desert and grassland
(C) taiga and temperate deciduous forest
(D) tundra and tropical rainforest

4. Except for Antarctica, which continent on earth does not have any deserts?

(F) Australia
(G) South America
(H) Europe
(J) Africa

5. Which types of environments runs north to south in the middle section of North America?

(A) desert
(B) grassland
(C) taiga
(D) tropical rainforest

Name ______________________________ Date ______________

Social Sciences

Geography

14.B.2a

Effect of Physical Processes on the Earth

DIRECTIONS: Select the best answer.

1. **The movement of soil from one place to another is called ___________ .**
   - (A) evaporation
   - (B) erosion
   - (C) condensation
   - (D) pollution

2. **Which of the following does not cause erosion?**
   - (F) wind
   - (G) rain
   - (H) a farmer plowing a field
   - (J) all of the above cause erosion

3. **Coral reefs such as the one shown in the figure above are formed ___________ .**
   - (A) over long periods of time from the shells deposited by animals
   - (B) by humans who pour concrete into the water and wait for it to harden
   - (C) by the gravitational pull of the sun and moon on the earth
   - (D) quickly when low places in the land fill with rainwater

4. **During the last Ice Age, large ice sheets moved across much of Northern Europe, Asia, and North America. One result of this movement was that ___________ .**
   - (F) all life on earth ended and had to start again
   - (G) cities and towns throughout the world were destroyed
   - (H) huge amounts of material were crushed and eventually turned into soil
   - (J) the earth's first oceans were created

5. **Scientists believe that one reason the elevation of the Appalachian Mountains is much lower than the elevation of the Rocky Mountains is because ___________ .**
   - (A) volcanoes continually blow the tops off of the Appalachians
   - (B) miners chipped away most of the Appalachians when they were searching for coal
   - (C) the Appalachians are much older than the Rockies, and erosion from rain has had a greater effect there
   - (D) much of the Appalachians have been damaged due to overgrazing by livestock

6. **The Grand Canyon was largely formed by the effects of the ___________ .**
   - (F) Mississippi River
   - (G) Colorado River
   - (H) Ohio River
   - (J) Pacific Ocean

Name ______________________________ Date ______________

Social Sciences | Geography

14.B.2b

Interactions in an Ecosystem

DIRECTIONS: Choose the best answer.

1. **All the organisms that live in an area and the nonliving elements of an environment are called a(n) ___________ .**
   - (A) food chain
   - (B) ecosystem
   - (C) biome
   - (D) population

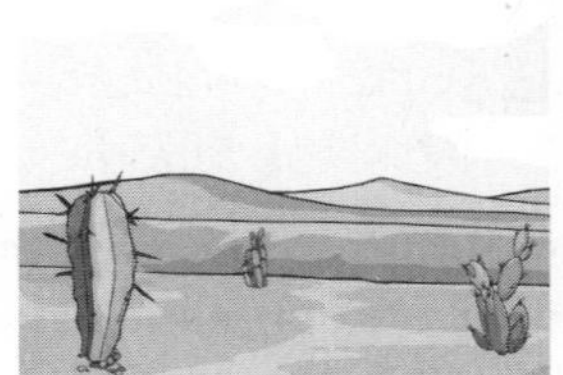

2. **Organisms depend on nonliving elements of their ecosystems as well as living elements. How do the above figures best illustrate this fact?**
   - (F) Environments that have plenty of water usually support more and different organisms than environments with little water.
   - (G) Most organisms need oxygen for breathing.
   - (H) Nonliving elements in an ecosystem do not affect the type of organisms that live there.
   - (J) Ecosystems change over time.

3. **Which of the following is the least important environmental factor for species that live in a water habitat?**
   - (A) the temperature of the water
   - (B) the amount of sunlight present
   - (C) the amount of dissolved oxygen in the water
   - (D) wind

4. **The climate of a land ecosystem greatly affects the types of life that can be supported by the ecosystem. *Climate* refers to ___________ .**
   - (F) the average weather pattern in an area over a long period of time
   - (G) the motions in the atmosphere that create air currents
   - (H) an area's distance above sea level
   - (J) the living organisms in a certain area

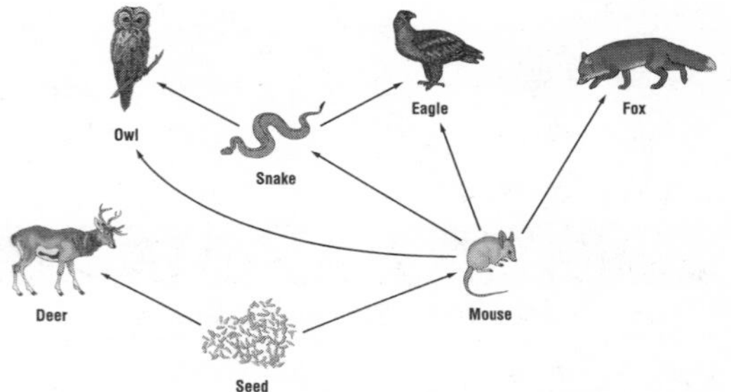

5. **In the figure above, why do you think the foxes would suffer if all the mice were removed from the ecosystem?**
   - (A) Fewer plants would grow in the ecosystem. This would decrease the number of places the foxes could live.
   - (B) The foxes would need to compete with the owl for snakes.
   - (C) Mice are the only source of food for the foxes in this ecosystem.
   - (D) The deer would begin to eat the foxes.

6. **The type of soil present in an ecosystem has the most influence on ___________ .**
   - (F) the amount of rainfall the ecosystem receives
   - (G) the climate in the ecosystem
   - (H) the kinds of plant life that grow in the ecosystem
   - (J) the water cycle in the ecosystem

STOP

Name ______________________ Date ______________

Social Sciences **Geography**

14.C.2a

Effect of Natural Events on Human Activities

DIRECTIONS: Choose the best answer.

1. **This spring, your neighbor's yard was full of dandelions; your yard had none. Next spring, you will find that you need to start weeding dandelions from your yard too. Which of the following is probably most responsible for this situation?**
   - (A) the amount of rain that falls in your area next spring
   - (B) the type of soil that is in your yard
   - (C) the average temperature next spring
   - (D) the wind carrying dandelion seeds to other areas

Characteristics of the Tundra
There is less than 25 cm annual rainfall
The winters are six to nine months long
The average temperature is −12°C
Only the top portion of the soil thaws during the short, cold summer
The soil is not fertile and does not support many plants

2. **The physical environment of the tundra** __________.
   - (F) guarantees that almost no farming will occur there
   - (G) makes it impossible for people to live there at all
   - (H) would make it a poor spot to go ice fishing
   - (J) all of the above are true

3. **How does the physical environment of the tundra affect the clothes worn by the people who live there?**
   - (A) The temperature requires people to dress very warmly.
   - (B) Lack of plant life means that animal skins are used extensively for clothing.
   - (C) Both A and B.
   - (D) Neither A nor B.

4. **Earthen dams are sometimes covered with plants to provide stability and prevent them from washing away. Which types of plants should be used in such situations?**
   - (F) a variety of plants that grow well in that particular environment
   - (G) tall trees with deep roots
   - (H) roses
   - (J) mosses and lichens

5. **A certain area regularly floods at least twice every year. Tell how this might affect the way people live in this area.**

____

____

____

____

6. **Describe two ways natural events in the physical environment might affect the life of a farmer. Be specific.**

____

____

____

____

Name ______________________________ Date ______________

Social Sciences

Geography

14.C.2b

Geographic Factors and Society

DIRECTIONS: Choose the best answer.

1. Which of the following is *not* a reason people sometimes choose to live in mountainous areas?

- (A) protection from neighbors
- (B) frequent landslides
- (C) lots of tree-covered land
- (D) abundant wildlife

2. Over the past few decades, many Middle Eastern countries have quickly gone from very poor to very wealthy. Which resource is most responsible for this economic growth?

- (F) exotic fruits
- (G) oil
- (H) coffee
- (J) camels

3. Ships carry about 80 percent of all international cargo from one country to another. How might this fact affect the economic activities of a country that had no port or access to the ocean?

- (A) The country would have a more difficult time trading with other countries.
- (B) The country would probably be the richest one in the region.
- (C) The country's economic activities would be limited to farms and livestock.
- (D) The country would not be able to receive any supplies.

4. Where do you think the great majority of people on earth live?

- (F) in forests
- (G) in deserts
- (H) in mountainous regions
- (J) along the coasts of oceans and lakes and along river valleys

5. Which of the following places will probably attract the most settlers?

- (A) A region surrounding a very polluted lake.
- (B) A region where the only crop that grows well is rutabagas.
- (C) A region where temperatures reach well below zero most of the time.
- (D) A mild region with fertile land where many crops grow well.

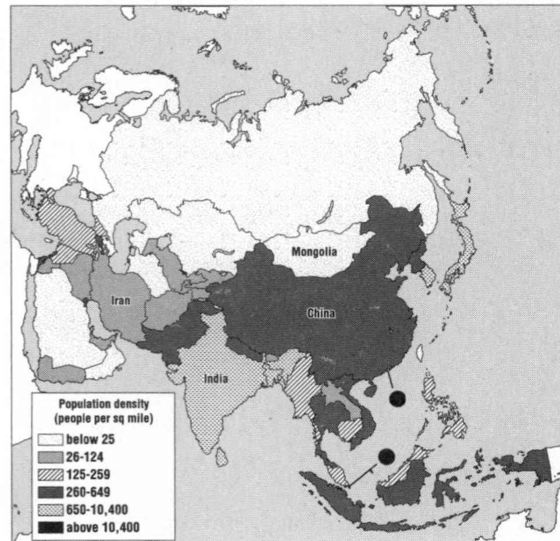

6. Based on the map above, which Asian country is the most crowded?

- (F) India
- (G) Mongolia
- (H) China
- (J) Iran

Name ______________________________ Date ______________

Social Sciences **Geography**

14.C.2c

Effect of Human Activity on the Environment

DIRECTIONS: Choose the best answer.

1. When soil erosion occurs ___________ .

- (A) soil washed into a river or stream can block the sunlight and slow the growth of plants in the river or stream
- (B) farmlands can become less productive over time
- (C) fertile topsoil is lost
- (D) all of the above

2. All of the following are attempts by people to improve the quality of water environments *except* ___________ .

- (F) facilities that treat the water
- (G) widespread use of fertilizers that are filled with harmful chemicals
- (H) laws that prevent people from using wetlands
- (J) restrictions on things that cause pollution

DIRECTIONS: Read the following passage and answer questions 3 and 4.

Human beings living in an area killed all the native timber wolves. The wolves were the natural predators of white-tailed deer. Over time, the deer population grew. The available plant life could not support the increased deer population. As a result, thousands of deer died of starvation.

3. Based on the above passage, which of the following statements do you think is true?

- (A) Human being activity never affects the animal population.
- (B) The loss of one species from an ecosystem may lead to the overpopulation or extinction of other species.
- (C) Human activity usually affects only one species in an environment.
- (D) The deer in this ecosystem would have died out anyway.

4. What is one way human beings in this ecosystem could help reduce the number of deer that die of starvation?

- (F) bring timber wolves back into the ecosystem
- (G) allow controlled hunting of deer
- (H) both F and G
- (J) neither F nor G

Name ______________________________ Date ______________

Social Sciences **Geography**

14.D.2b

Settlement Patterns in the United States and Illinois

DIRECTIONS: Choose the best answer.

1. **Generally, settlement of the United States __________ .**
   - (A) began in the west and moved east
   - (B) began in the east and moved west
   - (C) began in the south and moved north and east
   - (D) began in the north and moved west and south

2. **The Mississippi River accounts for a large part of this state's early settlement.**
   - (F) Montana
   - (G) Ohio
   - (H) Maryland
   - (J) Louisiana

3. **One reason New York City has grown into one of the most important cities in the world is __________ .**
   - (A) its large harbor invites trade and is a welcome arrival point for immigrants
   - (B) the large silver mines that can be found throughout the city
   - (C) the cost of living is much lower there than anywhere else in the world
   - (D) all of the above

4. **A large arrival of settlers to California in the late 1840s was caused by __________ .**
   - (F) the removal of the last Native Americans in the region
   - (G) the realization that California farmland was very fertile
   - (H) the discovery of gold there
   - (J) the legalization of slavery there

5. **The biggest obstacle for pioneers heading into the far west was probably crossing the __________ .**
   - (A) Rocky Mountains
   - (B) Mississippi River
   - (C) Grand Canyon
   - (D) Great Plains

6. **This state has large oil and mineral resources. However, settlers were slow to move here in great numbers because of its isolated location and harsh climate.**
   - (F) Florida
   - (G) Alaska
   - (H) Massachusetts
   - (J) California

7. **This state's central location makes it a main center of transportation. Shipping by train, truck, plane, and ship is an important part of the state's economy. Which state is it?**
   - (A) Maine
   - (B) Hawaii
   - (C) Illinois
   - (D) Oregon

8. **This Illinois city's location on the Great Lakes provides easy shipping routes that go to the east. Which city is it?**
   - (F) Chicago
   - (G) Rockford
   - (H) Springfield
   - (J) East St. Louis

STOP

Name ______________________________ Date ______________

Social Sciences **14** For pages 237–243

Geography

Mini-Test 4

DIRECTIONS: Choose the best answer.

1. **Reindeer, caribous, arctic hares, and snowy owls are commonly seen in which environments?**
   - (A) grasslands
   - (B) tundra
   - (C) desert
   - (D) tropical rain forest

Desert

Average temperature of 25°C
Average annual rainfall of less than 25 cm
Poor soil
Supports little plant life

Tropical Rain Forest

Average temperature of 25°C
Average annual rainfall of more than 300 cm
Poor soil
Supports abundant plant life

2. **According to the information above, what is the biggest difference between a desert and a tropical rain forest?**
   - (F) temperature
   - (G) soil
   - (H) amount of plant life supported
   - (J) amount of annual rainfall

3. **Which of the following human activities is most responsible for changing grasslands into deserts?**
   - (A) planting a wide variety of trees
   - (B) removing plant life from the soil and leaving the soil exposed to the wind
   - (C) irrigating the area extensively
   - (D) too much hunting of native animal species

4. **What usually happens when organisms in an ecosystem must compete with one another for food, living space, and other resources?**
   - (F) The population growth of the species remains the same.
   - (G) The population growth of the species is limited.
   - (H) The population growth of the species increases.
   - (J) Competition has no effect on the population growth of species.

5. **Every year, a rancher lets his livestock graze the native pastureland down to bare ground. Soon after, weeds take over the pasture. Nature continually provides the bare soil with seeds from weeds. How can the rancher best use natural events in the physical environment to solve his problem?**
   - (A) He should kill the weeds with chemicals.
   - (B) He should change how his livestock grazes in the pastures to allow for normal growth of plants. This would crowd out the weeds.
   - (C) He should bring in several species of weed-eating birds and then kill the birds after they have done the job.
   - (D) He should install large fans on his property to blow the seeds from the weeds away.

6. **Deserts cover over 20 percent of the earth's surface and support about _____ of the world's population.**
   - (F) 5 percent
   - (G) 20 percent
   - (H) 50 percent
   - (J) 90 percent

Social Science Standards

Social Systems

Goal 15: Understand social systems, with an emphasis on the United States.

Learning Standard 15A—Compare characteristics of culture as reflected in language, literature, the arts, traditions, and institutions.

15.A.2 Explain ways in which language, stories, folk tales, music, media, and artistic creations serve as expressions of culture. *(See page 246.)*

Learning Standard 15B—Understand the roles and interactions of individuals and groups in society.

15.B.2a Describe interactions of individuals, groups, and institutions in situations drawn from the local community (e.g., local response to state and national reforms). *(See pages 247–248.)*

15.B.2b Describe the ways in which institutions meet the needs of society. *(See pages 247–248.)*

Learning Standard 15C—Understand how social systems form and develop over time.

15.C.2 Describe how changes in production (e.g., hunting and gathering, agricultural, industrial) and population caused changes in social systems. *(See page 249.)*

Name ______________________ Date ______________

Social Sciences

15.A.2

Expressions of Culture

Social Systems

DIRECTIONS: Choose the best answer.

Culture is all the things a society produces, including its arts, beliefs, and traditions. You can tell a lot about the things a society values by looking at the way the society expresses itself in its culture.

1. **Which of the following is an expression of a society's culture?**
   - (A) the movies people watch
   - (B) the clothes people wear
   - (C) the holidays people celebrate
   - (D) all of the above

2. **Christmas is a holiday celebrated by Christians around the world. In the United States, Christmas is widely observed. Schools and most businesses close on Christmas Day. People of other faiths celebrate religious holidays, too. But most schools and businesses in America do not close on those holidays. Based on this fact, which of the following do you think is most likely true?**
   - (F) Most Americans are Christians.
   - (G) Most Americans care little about religion.
   - (H) It is illegal to practice any religion besides Christianity in America.
   - (J) Most Americans are Jewish.

DIRECTIONS: Read the passage and then answer questions 3 and 4.

In Country A, poor people are expected to refer to wealthier people as "My Lord" and "My Lady." There is not much direct contact between the rich and poor. When there is, the rich are usually polite but distant toward the poor.

In Country B, poor people are not allowed to talk to wealthier people at all. The poor and the rich almost never come into contact with each other. They even celebrate completely different holidays. A rich person feels disgraced if he or she happens to touch a poor person.

In Country C, poor people and wealthy people refer to each other as "Sir" and "Ma'am." Rich and poor often attend the same schools, attend many of the same cultural events, and come into fairly frequent contact. The two groups are usually friendly to each other.

3. **Based on the above passage, which society probably places most value on ideas such as equality and fair treatment?**
   - (A) Country A
   - (B) Country B
   - (C) Country C
   - (D) All societies highly value equality and fair treatment.

4. **Based on the above passage, which society probably places most value on ideas such as tradition and keeping in your proper place?**
   - (F) Country A
   - (G) Country B
   - (H) Country C
   - (J) They all highly value such ideas.

5. **In the United States, most professional sporting events begin with the playing of the national anthem. What do you think this fact says about American society? Be as specific as you can.**

____

____

____

____

Name ______________________________ Date ______________

Social Sciences

15.B.2a/15.B.2b

Individuals, Groups, and Institutions in Society

Social Systems

DIRECTIONS: Read the passage. Then, answer the questions.

On September 11, 2001, terrorists hijacked four American airplanes. Two of the planes were crashed into the World Trade Center Towers in New York City. The third plane crashed into the Pentagon in Washington, D.C. The fourth plane crashed in a field in western Pennsylvania. Heroic passengers on this plane are believed to have fought the terrorists and prevented the plane from hitting another target.

New York City firefighters and police officers rushed to the scene of the World Trade Center. They made a huge effort to try to save victims. When the towers collapsed, many firefighters and police were killed. Several thousand people who were at work in the towers were also killed.

American citizens immediately took action. Many rushed to donate blood. Doctors and nurses stood waiting outside of hospital emergency rooms. They were ready to care for the injured. Rescue workers and specially trained dogs spent days searching for survivors. Many businesses donated resources and money. Along with the American Red Cross, volunteers gave food and water to the rescue workers. And U.S. citizens around the country displayed the American flag on their houses, their cars, and their clothing. They wanted to show their support for the United States. The country felt united in the tragedy and was determined to show that such acts could not diminish American strength and pride.

1. What event happened on September 11, 2001, that caused people and institutions in America to come together?

- (A) The Vietnam War ended.
- (B) Terrorists attacked the United States.
- (C) The Gulf War began.
- (D) George W. Bush was elected president.

2. Many charitable organizations helped the victims of the September 11 tragedy. The passage identifies one in particular. Which organization was it?

- (F) the New York City Fire Department
- (G) the New York City Police Department
- (H) the American Red Cross
- (J) the Salvation Army

3. The first people who were on the scene to help at the World Trade Center were ____________.

- (A) firefighters and police
- (B) soldiers
- (C) the president and the mayor of New York City
- (D) doctors and nurses

Name ______________________ Date ______________

4. How did hospitals help meet people's needs on September 11?

- (F) They sent trained dogs to help look for victims.
- (G) They provided food and water to rescue workers.
- (H) They took care of people injured in the attacks.
- (J) They helped put out the fires at the World Trade Center.

5. How did individual Americans help out on September 11?

- (A) They donated blood.
- (B) They helped search for victims.
- (C) They gave food and water to rescue workers.
- (D) All of the above

6. Following the events of September 11, many Americans displayed the flag. What did this accomplish?

- (F) It helped raise money for the victims.
- (G) It helped Americans feel united and strong.
- (H) It prevented the terrorists from striking again.
- (J) Only "real Americans" displayed the flag, so the police knew that anyone who didn't was a terrorist.

7. Which of the institutions mentioned in the passage are run by the government and paid for by tax dollars?

- (A) the New York City Fire Department
- (B) the businesses that made donations
- (C) the American Red Cross
- (D) the hospitals

8. How did the passengers on one of the September 11 planes work together to accomplish something heroic?

____
____
____
____
____
____
____
____

9. Name at least one other group or institution not mentioned in the passage that helped on September 11, 2001. Identify the organization and explain how it helped.

____
____
____
____
____
____
____
____

Name ______________________ Date ______________

Social Sciences

15.C.2

Changes in Social Systems

Social Systems

DIRECTIONS: Read the passage and then answer the questions.

During World War II, most American industries produced supplies to help the war effort. Production of many consumer goods, such as cars and appliances, either stopped or was greatly reduced. After the war ended, production of consumer goods began to rise quickly. Americans were trying to get back to normal life. The economy grew, and there were plenty of jobs.

The good economy caused many changes in post-war America. For one thing, the marriage rate doubled. More children were born during this time than any other period in U.S. history. At first, many new families lived in their parents' house or crammed into small city apartments. But between 1950 and 1960, one quarter of the U.S. population moved out of the cities and into the suburbs. Not everyone benefited from the economic growth, however. The suburbs were largely white and middle class. Prejudice and poverty kept most minorities in the inner cities or rural areas.

The rise of the suburbs led to an increase in building. Roads were also built to help with the increase in traffic. New roads and businesses covered land that used to be used for farming or ranching. Living in the suburbs caused people to depend on their cars for transportation. In the mid-1950s, the federal highway system began linking every part of the nation.

The growth of the suburbs brought many Americans a higher standard of living. However, it also brought problems. Some of the problems included air pollution, cluttered landscapes, the decline of cities, and a sameness to life across the nation.

1. What changes occurred in the U.S. economy after World War II?

(A) The Industrial Revolution began.

(B) Businesses once again began making consumer goods.

(C) Farming and ranching became more widespread.

(D) Most men decided to stay home with the children, and the vast majority of jobs went to women.

2. How did the population change in the United States after World War II?

(F) Large numbers of people left the country to return to their native lands.

(G) Most Americans were elderly, and the number of children decreased.

(H) There were at least four times as many men than women.

(J) Many new families were started and lots of children were born.

3. How was the use of cars affected when Americans began moving to the suburbs?

(A) It decreased a little bit.

(B) It increased a great deal.

(C) It stayed about the same as before the war.

(D) It almost completely died out.

4. Which government program was started at least partly because of the movement of Americans to the suburbs?

(F) public libraries

(G) municipal fire departments

(H) the public school system

(J) the federal highway system

Name ______________________________ Date ______________

Social Sciences

15

For pages 246–249

Mini-Test 5

Social Systems

DIRECTIONS: The old American folk song "John Henry" is about a legendary railroad worker who laid more track than a steam drill. Read the words to the song. Then answer the questions.

When John Henry was a little baby
Sittin' on his daddy's knee,
He picked up a hammer and a little piece of steel.
He said, "This hammer gonna be the death of me,
  Lord, Lord.
This hammer gonna be the death of me."

Well the Captain said to John Henry
"Gonna bring that steam drill 'round.
Gonna bring that steam drill out on the track.
Gonna whop that steel on down Lord, Lord,
Gonna whop that steel on down."

Well, the man that had the steam drill
Thought he was mighty fine.
John Henry drove his fifteen feet.
The steam drill only did nine, Lord, Lord.
The steam drill only did nine.

John Henry hammered on the mountain
And his hammer was striking fire.
Well, he hammered so hard that he broke his poor
  heart,
And he laid down his hammer and he died Lord, Lord.
He laid down his hammer and he died.

1. **Which of the following do you think this song tells us about nineteenth-century American society?**
   - (A) Railroads had become an important part of society.
   - (B) The Industrial Revolution was underway, and people had mixed feelings about it.
   - (C) Railroad work was a hard, dangerous job.
   - (D) All of the above.

2. **What do you think the people who wrote and sang this song thought of themselves?**
   - (F) They felt timid.
   - (G) They saw themselves as being strong and proud.
   - (H) They did not value hard work.
   - (J) They wanted to leave America for a better life elsewhere.

DIRECTIONS: Choose the best answer.

3. **Suppose a local company is dumping raw sewage into a local lake. In an effort to stop this, people and groups can do all of the following except ____________ .**
   - (A) write threatening letters to the company president demanding a change
   - (B) stop buying that company's products
   - (C) hold a peaceful public demonstration against the company
   - (D) put up signs around town stating the facts about the situation

4. **All of the following are institutions that help meet people's needs in a variety of ways. Which one is *not* run by the government?**
   - (F) police departments
   - (G) churches, synagogues, and mosques
   - (H) public schools
   - (J) highway maintenance departments

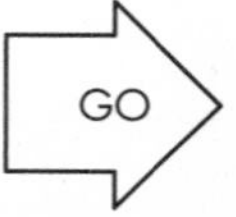

Name ______________________________ Date ______________

5. **Schools benefit American society by ____________ .**

   (A) educating citizens
   (B) teaching people how to work together and get along
   (C) providing free or reduced-cost meals to needy students
   (D) all of the above

DIRECTIONS: Read the passage and then answer questions 6 and 7.

In 1908, the Ford Motor Company sold its Model T automobile for $825. Henry Ford kept looking for ways to save money in the making of the car. By 1916, the price of a Model T had dropped to $345. By 1924, a brand-new Model T Ford cost only $290.

6. **Based on the above passage, it is safe to assume that the number of Americans who owned Model T Fords was greatest in ____________ .**

   (F) 1908
   (G) 1916
   (H) 1924
   (J) cannot tell from the passage

7. **Name one change you think happened in America because of the events described in the passage. Be specific.**

____

____

____

____

____

____

____

____

____

____

____

____

STOP

How Am I Doing?

Mini-Test 1 Page 197 **Number Correct**	**6** answers correct	**Great Job!** Move on to the section test on page 254.
	4–5 answers correct	**You're almost there!** But you still need a little practice. Review the practice pages 191–196 before moving on to the section test on page 254.
	0–3 answers correct	**Oops!** Time to review what you have learned and try again. Review the practice section on pages 191–196. Then retake the test on page 197. Now move on to the section test on page 254.
Mini-Test 2 Page 210 **Number Correct**	**7** answers correct	**Awesome!** Move on to the section test on page 254.
	5–6 answers correct	**You're almost there!** But you still need a little practice. Review the practice pages 199–209 before moving on to the section test on page 254.
	0–4 answers correct	**Oops!** Time to review what you have learned and try again. Review the practice section on pages 199–209. Then retake the test on page 210. Now move on to the section test on page 254.
Mini-Test 3 Page 235 **Number Correct**	**9–10** answers correct	**Great Job!** Move on to the section test on page 254.
	6–8 answers correct	**You're almost there!** But you still need a little practice. Review the practice pages 213–234 before moving on to the section test on page 254.
	0–5 answers correct	**Oops!** Time to review what you have learned and try again. Review the practice section on pages 213–234. Then retake the test on page 235. Now move on to the section test on page 254.

How Am I Doing?

Mini-Test 4 Page 244 **Number Correct**	**5–6** answers correct	**Awesome!** Move on to the section test on page 254.
	3–4 answers correct	**You're almost there!** But you still need a little practice. Review the practice pages 237–243 before moving on to the section test on page 254.
	0–2 answers correct	**Oops!** Time to review what you have learned and try again. Review the practice section on pages 237–243. Then retake the test on page 244. Now move on to the section test on page 254.
Mini-Test 5 Page 250 **Number Correct**	**7** answers correct	**Great Job!** Move on to the section test on page 254.
	5–6 answers correct	**You're almost there!** But you still need a little practice. Review the practice pages 246–249 before moving on to the section test on page 254.
	0–4 answers correct	**Oops!** Time to review what you have learned and try again. Review the practice section on pages 246–249. Then retake the test on page 250. Now move on to the section test on page 254.

Name ______________________________ Date ______________

Final Social Science Test

for pages 191–251

DIRECTIONS: Select the best answer.

1. According to the United States Constitution, how old must you be to become president of the United States?

Ⓐ there is no age requirement
Ⓑ 35
Ⓒ 25
Ⓓ 18

2. The U.S. federal government is responsible for all of the following except __________ .

Ⓕ declaring war
Ⓖ maintaining water treatment plants in each American city
Ⓗ coining and printing money
Ⓙ governing the U.S. capital

3. As a citizen, you have a responsibility to take part in your community. All of the following are good ways to do this, except __________ .

Ⓐ write to the president of a company protesting the treatment of women in the company's commercials
Ⓑ read the newspaper regularly
Ⓒ secretly remove books from the library that think are unpatriotic
Ⓓ vote in every election

4. Which of the following actions is unconstitutional?

Ⓕ owning a hunting rifle
Ⓖ reading a book praising the September 11, 2001, attack on the United States
Ⓗ refusing to serve a customer in a bar because he has had too much to drink
Ⓙ refusing to serve a customer in a restaurant because she is Asian

5. Which of the following is a foreign policy issue for the U.S. government?

Ⓐ China wants to tax all the vehicles it imports from the United States.
Ⓑ The state of Illinois wants to increase the gasoline tax by one cent.
Ⓒ Congress hopes to pass a new law that helps senior citizens in the U.S. get prescription drugs more easily.
Ⓓ You write a letter to your pen pal in Brazil.

6. The United States has this kind of economic system.

Ⓕ socialist economy
Ⓖ developing economy
Ⓗ free market economy
Ⓙ communist economy

7. Janine is a full-time college student who works 15 hours a week at a hamburger restaurant. William is a retired postal worker. Alice was laid off from her job two years ago; she is still not working, and by now she has given up even looking for a job. Brent quit his job last month; he searches the want ads daily and calls every one that looks promising. Which one of these people is unemployed?

Ⓐ Brent
Ⓑ Alice
Ⓒ William
Ⓓ Janine

DIRECTIONS: Read the passage. Then answer the questions.

The most popular snack food in years has hit the stores recently. Everyone wants to try the new Beef-o Chips. These hamburger-flavored potato chips are so popular, the manufacturer is having a hard time

Name ______________________________ Date ______________

keeping up with demand. Grocery stores across the nation have been mobbed by hungry customers looking to buy bags of Beef-os. The local Food Clown store reports that an entire shelf of Beef-os was cleaned out by customers yesterday in about five minutes.

8. When Beef-os first came out a couple of months ago, each bag cost $1.99. Based on the information in the passage, what do you think Beef-os might be selling for now?

- (F) 25¢
- (G) 99¢
- (H) $1.99
- (J) $2.99

9. Explain your answer to question 8.

- (A) Hamburger-flavored potato chips? Yuck! Who would buy those?
- (B) When supply is high and demand is low, prices usually go down.
- (C) The price was $1.99 just a couple of months ago. That's too soon for any price change to occur.
- (D) When supply is low and demand is high, prices usually rise.

Work began on the Erie Canal in 1817 and was completed in 1825. It connected Lake Erie at Buffalo, New York, with the Hudson River at Troy and Albany, a water distance of 363 miles.

DIRECTIONS: Read the words to the old folk song "Erie Canal." Then, answer the questions.

I've got an old mule, her name is Sal
Fifteen miles on the Erie Canal.
She's a good old worker and a good old pal
Fifteen miles on the Erie Canal.

We've pulled some barges in our day
Filled with lumber, coal, and hay
And we know every inch of the way
From Albany to Buffalo.

Low bridge, everybody down!
Low bridge, 'cause we're comin' to a town!
And you'll always know your neighbor.
You'll always know your pal.
If you've ever navigated on the Erie Canal.

10. Which historical event influenced the writing of this song?

- (F) construction of the transcontinental railroad
- (G) founding of Buffalo, New York
- (H) construction of the Erie Canal
- (J) the first trip of Robert Fulton's steamboat, the *Clermont*

11. The Erie Canal __________ .

- (A) was an important transportation route for trade
- (B) helped people move west toward the Great Lakes
- (C) contributed greatly to the growth of the country
- (D) all of the above

12. This state was named after English king George II.

- (F) Florida
- (G) Georgia
- (H) Ohio
- (J) Maryland

13. Which of the following was *not* a cause of the American Revolution?

- (A) people who left England to live in America were self-reliant and had an independent spirit
- (B) England's management of the colonies was poor
- (C) the British Parliament taxed the Americans in a way many colonists considered unfair
- (D) English writer Samuel Johnson published his *Dictionary of the English Language* in 1755

GO

Name ______________________________ Date ______________

14. In 1803, Thomas Jefferson purchased the Louisiana Territory from Napoleon, who was the ruler of _________ .

- (F) Russia
- (G) Germany
- (H) France
- (J) England

DIRECTIONS: Read the passage. Then answer the questions.

In 1850, Congress passed five bills known as the Compromise of 1850. The laws were called a compromise because both northern and southern states gave up some things they wanted. For example, the Compromise of 1850 allowed California to be admitted to the U.S. as a free state. Texas, New Mexico, and Utah could each decide whether they wanted to have slavery. Another part of the Compromise was called the Fugitive Slave Act. This allowed blacks in the North to be taken back to the South to slavery. It also tried to make people stop helping slaves escape.

15. The Compromise of 1850 occurred _________ .

- (A) just before the start of the American Revolution
- (B) just after the end of the American Revolution
- (C) a few years before the Civil War broke out
- (D) a few years after the Civil War ended

16. Why do you think Congress passed the Compromise of 1850?

- (F) Congress was trying to encourage settlers to move west
- (G) Congress was desperately trying to keep the United States together
- (H) Congress wanted to encourage hostility between northern and southern states
- (J) Congress was trying to make it easier for black Americans to find jobs

17. Many early civilizations were ruled by powerful kings. Such societies are called _________ .

- (A) monarchies
- (B) democracies
- (C) city-states
- (D) republics

18. The term *democracy* came into use during the 5th century B.C. in Greece. What does the word *democracy* mean?

- (F) rule of the wealthy
- (G) to rule alone
- (H) rule by a few
- (J) rule of the people

19. This great plant scientist developed many useful techniques in agriculture. He was especially known for his work with peanuts.

- (A) Alexander Graham Bell
- (B) George Washington Carver
- (C) Eli Whitney
- (D) Thomas Edison

20. The invention of this farm tool about 6,000 years ago helped farmers grow more food. This eventually freed others to do things besides farming and hunting.

- (F) plow
- (G) steam engine
- (H) tractor
- (J) cotton gin

21. The first electronic computer was developed _________ .

- (A) around 500 B.C.
- (B) in the 1800s
- (C) by the 1940s
- (D) about ten years ago

Name ______________________________ Date ______________

22. Which of the following towns did not experience growth because of ranching and the westward expansion of the U.S. in the 19th century?

- (F) Abilene, Kansas
- (G) San Antonio, Texas
- (H) Boston, Massachusetts
- (J) Cheyenne, Wyoming

23. Nineteenth-century settlers often referred to Illinois as the __________ .

- (A) Aloha State
- (B) Grand Canyon State
- (C) Mountain State
- (D) Prairie State

24. One of the first means of transportation used by the first explorers and settlers to Illinois was __________ .

- (F) the Mississippi River system
- (G) O'Hare Airport in Chicago
- (H) the Interstate Highway system
- (J) the transcontinental railroad

25. People in early hunting and gathering societies used rivers __________ .

- (A) for fishing
- (B) for cleaning
- (C) for carrying away garbage
- (D) all of the above

Desert
Average temperature of 25°C
Average annual rainfall of less than 25 cm
Poor soil
Supports little plant life

Tropical Rain Forest
Average temperature of 25°C
Average annual rainfall of more than 300 cm
Poor soil
Supports abundant plant life

26. According to the preceding table, what is the biggest weather difference between a desert and a tropical rain forest?

- (F) temperature
- (G) soil
- (H) amount of plant life supported
- (J) precipitation

27. The tundra lies close to the North Pole. It is an extremely cold, dry region sometimes called a cold desert. The soil is not very fertile. Only the top portion of the soil thaws during the short, cold summer. Based on these facts, which of the following statements is *most likely* to be true?

- (A) tall evergreen trees with deep roots thrive in the tundra
- (B) the tundra is too cold and dry to support any plant or animal life
- (C) tundra plants are adapted to drought and cold and tend to consist of mosses, grasses, and small shrubs
- (D) the tundra is the most biologically diverse place in the world

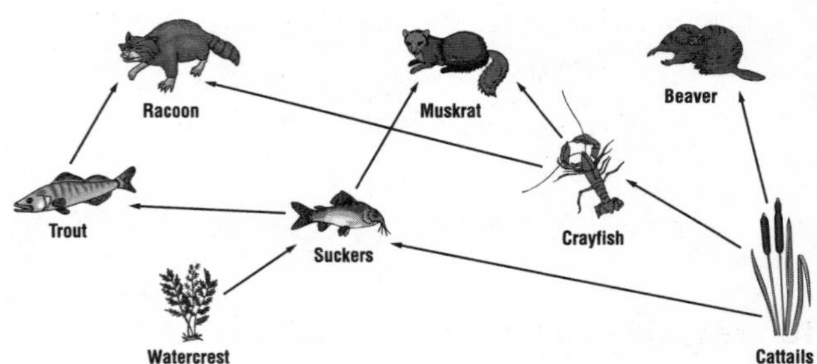

28. Which populations shown in the above food web would likely decrease if the crayfish were removed from the ecosystem?

- (F) beaver
- (G) cattails
- (H) muskrat and raccoon
- (J) trout and raccoon

STOP

Name ______________________________ Date ______________

Final Social Science Test

Answer Sheet

1 (A) (B) (C) (D)
2 (F) (G) (H) (J)
3 (A) (B) (C) (D)
4 (F) (G) (H) (J)
5 (A) (B) (C) (D)
6 (F) (G) (H) (J)
7 (A) (B) (C) (D)
8 (F) (G) (H) (J)
9 (A) (B) (C) (D)
10 (F) (G) (H) (J)

11 (A) (B) (C) (D)
12 (F) (G) (H) (J)
13 (A) (B) (C) (D)
14 (F) (G) (H) (J)
15 (A) (B) (C) (D)
16 (F) (G) (H) (J)
17 (A) (B) (C) (D)
18 (F) (G) (H) (J)
19 (A) (B) (C) (D)
20 (F) (G) (H) (J)

21 (A) (B) (C) (D)
22 (F) (G) (H) (J)
23 (A) (B) (C) (D)
24 (F) (G) (H) (J)
25 (A) (B) (C) (D)
26 (F) (G) (H) (J)
27 (A) (B) (C) (D)
28 (F) (G) (H) (J)

Answer Key

Page 8
1. B
2. H
3. A
4. H
5. A
6. F
7. B

Pages 9–10
1. B
2. H
3. B
4. G
5. C
6. F
7. D
8. H
9. pre; Sample sentence: We saw a preview of this movie at the theater.
10. un; Sample sentence: The class was unhappy when the field trip was cancelled.
11. be; Sample sentence: We should never belittle someone because he or she is different than us.
12. co; Sample sentence: My mom's coworkers had a birthday party for her.
13. dis; Sample sentence: She had a great distrust of strangers.
14. re; Sample sentence: We will replay the game when the rain stops.

Page 11
1. C
2. F
3. C
4. G
5. D
6. F
7. C
8. F
9. A
10. F

Page 12
1. A
2. H
3. B
4. F
5. C
6. H
7. D
8. G

Page 13
1. B
2. F
3. A
4. G
5. B
6. F
7. B
8. F

Page 14
1. D
2. G
3. D
4. F
5. C
6. J
7. D

Page 15 Mini-Test 1
1. B
2. F
3. B
4. G
5. B
6. J
7. B
8. F
9. C

Page 17
1. D
2. G
3. C
4. Sample answers: join, help, fun, joy, sticker, pizza party

Page 18
1. B
2. G
3. A
4. H
5. B

Page 19
1. D
2. F
3. B
4. a. The sun causes water to evaporate from the earth.
   b. Clouds form when the water in the air cools.
   c. Fog is a low cloud.

Page 20
1. A
2. J
3. In this version, Goldilocks is taken away to the police station.

Page 21
1. D
2. H
3. A
4. Answers will vary. Students should briefly describe assignments where they learned more than they expected to learn and what they learned.

Page 22
1. A
2. H

Page 23
1. B
2. J
3. T, F, T, F

Page 24
1. regular ice
2. dry ice
3. regular ice
4. dry ice
5. dry ice
6. dry ice

Page 25
1. B
2. F

Page 26
1. B
2. Answers will vary.

Page 27
1. D
2. F
3. H
4. A
5. G
6. B
7. C
8. E

Page 28 Mini-Test 2
1. D
2. F
3. C
4. H
5. B

Page 30
1. Answers will vary. Students should make predictions about how the Great Lakes were formed.
2. Sample answer: The Great Lakes were formed by melting glaciers and rain.
3. B
4. J

Page 31

1. Students should mention the origin and importance of the telegraph.
2. Students should cite details from the reading selection, such as Morse's inspiration on the ship and the stages of development of his invention (1835, 1844, and 1849).
3. Answers will vary. Summaries should briefly convey the point of the selection.

Page 32

1. Yes. The passage states that *hydro* refers to water, so *hydropower* refers to a power that comes from water.
2. A
3. J
4. A

Page 33

1. fiction
2. a problem
3. the mother
4. *Mom to the Rescue*

Page 34

1. The people of Rabaul had an escape plan. They knew the volcano had erupted before and prepared for the next time.
2. Scientists told them to leave when they noticed earthquakes.
3. The eruption in Pompeii happened 2,000 years ago when the people did not have the technology to detect volcanic eruption that is available today.

Page 35

1. true
2. true
3. false
4. true
5. false
6. false

Page 36

1. A
2. G
3. B
4. J
5. A

Page 37

1. stick things together; gelatin; sticky juices; plants; insects; glue; many special
2. hide; bone; fish
3. B

Pages 38–39

1. Answers may include: shows Minnie, farmer, and garden; farmer destroying Minnie's home.
2. Answers should mention fear or surprise as shown in Minnie's eye.
3. Answers may include the extensive tunnel needed to escape; fear and frantic digging to escape; helps with picturing what moles look like.
4. Answers will vary.

Page 40

1. Samantha. Today is her birthday.
2. Samantha's mother. She refers to Samantha's "father and me."
3. Samantha's sibling (brother or sister unknown). The passage refers to Mom and Dad.
4. A

Page 41

Fahrenheit—invented by Gabriel Fahrenheit; water freezes at 32°F; normal body temperature is 98.6°F; water boils at 212°F.

Celsius—invented by Anders Celsius; water freezes at 0°C; normal body temperature is 37°C; water boils at 100°C.

Page 42 Mini-Test 3

1. C
2. F
3. C
4. J

Pages 44–45

1. Both stories deal with telling the truth.
2. Students may suggest that Phil is the better friend since he could not lie to his friends.
3. Answers will vary but may suggest that lies are usually found out.
4. Answers will vary but may suggest that honesty is the best policy.

Page 46

1. why the sun and the moon appear in the sky
2. why porcupines have four claws on each foot
3. One Who Walks All Over the Sky and Walking About Early; Porcupine and Beaver
4. They both cared about and wanted to change their environment.

Pages 47–48

Bits's life

Bits's street: Alten Road

Bits's tree: maple tree

Bits's home: nest in the tree

Bits's problem

The new guest: red-haired woman

The new guest's pet: cat

The new guest's bad habit: let her cat out every day to hunt;

Bits was hungry because she could not get to the ground to dig up food.

Bits was thirsty because she could not get to the stream for water.

Bits was scared because she saw the cat chasing other animals.

Bits had to be careful of: cats, cars and trucks, owls;

Bits's solution
Way in which the problem was solved: Guest left at the end of the summer
Time of year the problem was solved: autumn

Page 49
1. a dog
2. No. He is dirty and hungry.
3. Yes. He is wearing an old collar with an identification tag.
4. He was hungry.
5. She does not like Ralph. She sprays him with the hose and swats him with a broom.

Pages 50–51
1. Tim
2. Sara
3. Abdul
4. Valerie
5. Abdul
6. Valerie
7. Tim
8. Sara
9. Sara
10. Valerie

Page 52
1. B
2. G
3. D
4. H
5. A
6. H
7. B
8. F

Page 53
1. D
2. G
3. Answers will vary.

Page 54
4. pillows
5. children
6. a glass (mirror)
7. Answers will vary.

Page 55
1. Answers will vary. The narrator likes the family tradition, but some students might say that the narrator hints that he or she might like more of his or her own.
2. Maggie hugged her stuffed animal and looked at the narrator.
3. Because it is not like a traditional birthday.
4. Yes, because the narrator seems to enjoy the happiness the tradition brings to others.

Page 56
1. Rhyme scheme of the poem is a, b, a, b, c, c
   a—shore, more
   b—see, free
   c—above, love
2. Answers will vary.

Page 57
1. zooming
2. plink
3. rustling
4. pitter-patter
5. sizzling
6. Answers will vary.

Page 58
1. C
2. F
3. D
4. H

Pages 59–60
1. D
2. G
3. B
4. Students' answers should include supporting facts from the passage.
5. Answers will vary. Students should explain why they agree or disagree with the author's view regarding recumbent cycles.

Pages 61–62
1. Both passages are about the spelling bee.
2. Students should mention that Ben is somewhat nervous but has studied hard and believes he can do well. He is hoping he can win.
3. Students should mention that Ben is proud and/or happy. He mentions he was scared at the beginning of the spelling bee.
4. Ben mentions that Rebecca wins at practices, and she did win the actual spelling bee just like the practices.

Page 63 Mini-Test 4
1. C
2. J
3. A
4. H

Pages 66–69
Final Reading Test
1. B
2. F
3. D
4. F
5. B
6. F
7. B
8. H
9. A
10. J
11. C
12. H
13. A
14. H
15. B
16. H
17. C
18. G
19. B
20. F
21. C
22. G
23. C
24. J
25. C
26. F
27. A
28. G

Page 73
1. A
2. H
3. C
4. H
5. A
6. H
7. B
8. H

Page 74
1. C
2. H
3. C
4. G
5. A
6. F
7. D
8. G

Page 75
1. 327.6
2. 59.44
3. 6.879
4. 4521.307
5. A
6. J
7. B
8. F
9. D

Page 76
1. D
2. F
3. C
4. H
5. D
6. G

Page 77
1. D
2. F
3. D
4. H
5. A
6. F
7. B
8. J

Page 78
1. B
2. G
3. D
4. F
5. A
6. H
7. C
8. G
   3: 21, 27, 30
   4: 20, 24, 36
9. A
   6: 42, 48, 66
   9: 18, 45, 54, 72

Pages 79–80
1. B
2. H
3. B
4. H
5. A
6. H
7. C
8. F
9. A
10. G
11. A
12. H
13. B
14. F
15. B
16. G

Pages 81–82
1. B
2. G
3. C
4. G
5. A
6. J
7. A
8. G
9. A
10. G
11. B
12. F
13. C
14. J
15. B
16. J
17. A
18. H
19. D
20. G

Page 83
1. D
2. F
3. D
4. F
5. C
6. G
7. C
8. J
9. A
10. H

Page 84
1. A
2. H
3. A
4. J
5. D
6. F

Page 85
1. 9
2. 8
3. 11
4. 8
5. 7
6. 3
7. 1
8. 5
9. 3
10. 2
11. .5
12. .6
13. .7
14. .8
15. .4
16. 2.9

Page 86
1. B
2. F
3. C
4. H
5. C
6. F
7. B
8. F

Page 87 Mini-Test 1
1. .71
2. left
3. D
4. J
5. B
6. J
7. C
8. H
9. B
10. H

Page 89
1. 90°
2. 15°
3. 48°
4. 60°
5. 137°
6. 105°
7. 70°
8. 55°
9. 35°

Pages 90–91
1. 21 feet
2. 2 feet
3. 2 yards
4. 52,800 feet
5. 5 feet
6. 10 yards
7. 62 inches
8. 36 inches
9. 40 inches
10. 2,640 feet
11. 2 feet
12. 1 yard
13. 12 feet
14. 1 yard
15. 39 inches
16. 9 quarts
17. 56 pints
18. 20 cups
19. 4.5 quarts
20. 12 teaspoons
21. 6 gallons
22. 80 fluid ounces
23. 32 fluid ounces
24. 32 tablespoons
25. 32 oz.
26. 10 lbs.
27. 240 oz.
28. 8 t.
29. 160 oz.
30. 2.5 t.
31. 12,000 lbs.
32. 320 oz.
33. 4 lbs.

Page 92
1. 340 mm
2. yes
3. 300 cm
4. no
5. 5,000 m
6. 10 km
7. 1,000 cm × 1,200 cm

Pages 93–94
1. 5
2. 6
3. 6
4. 5
5. 14
6. 9
7. D
8. H
9. A
10. H
11. B
12. J

Pages 95–96
1. D
2. G
3. C
4. F
5. D
6. A
7. E
8. F

9. D
10. C
11. B
12. L
13. kL
14. mL
15. L
16. mL
17. kL
18. g
19. g
20. kg
21. kg
22. g
23. kg

Page 97

1. 90°
2. 180°
3. 360°
4. 270°
5. 180°
6. 180°
7. 180°
8. 270°
9. 270°
10. 180°
11. 90°
12. 90°
13. 360°
14. 90°
15. 180°
16. 270°
17. 90°
18. 90°
19. 270°
20. 360°

Pages 98–99

1. 5 cubes, 5 cubic units
2. 9 cubes. 9 cubic units
3. 10 cubes, 10 cubic units
4. 8 cubes, 8 cubic units
5. 8 cubes. 8 cubic units
6. 12 cubes, 12 cubic units
7. height = 4, length = 3, width = 1, 12 cubic units
8. height = 2, length = 4, width = 4, 32 cubic units
9. height = 3, length = 3, width = 2, 18 cubic units
10. height = 3, length = 1, width = 2, 6 cubic units
11. height = 2, length = 5, width = 1, 10 cubic units

Page 100

1. Students should draw a square with 2-inch sides.
2. Students should draw an isosceles triangle with two sides of 3 inches and one side of 2 inches.
3. Students should draw a pentagon with sides totaling 19 centimeters, example: 3 sides of 3 inches and 2 sides of 5 inches.
4. Students should draw a rectangle with length of 2 inches and width of 1 inch.

Page 101 Mini-Test 2

1. A
2. J
3. B
4. G
5. C
6. J
7. C
8. H

Page 103

1. 7, 9; +2
2. 60, 40, 30; −10
3. 29, 36, 43; +7
4. 27, 24, 21, 18; −3
5. 70, 55, 40, 25; −15
6. 37, 28, 19, 10; −9
7. 41, 49, 57, 65; +8
8. 90, 72, 66, 60; −6
9. 77, 55, 33, 22; −11
10. 48, 60, 72, 84; +12
11. 50, 57, 64
12. 54, 48, 42

Page 104

1. 21; Rule: Add the two previous numbers to get the next number
2. 32; Rule: Add by increasing consecutive integers (each successive number is +1, +2, +3, etc.)
3. 62; Rule: Subtract by integers increasing by threes (−3, −6, −9, etc.)
4. 17; Rule: Alternate adding and subtracting by increasing integers (+1, −2, +3, −4, etc.)
5. 45; Rule: Add the number to itself and subtract 1.
6. 44; Rule: Add by integers increasing by fours (4, 8, 12, etc.)
7. 89; Subtract by increasing consecutive integers (−1, −2, −3, etc.)
8. 71; Rule: Add by increasing even integers (+2, +4, +6, etc.)
9. 51; Subtract 3, add 2, repeat
10. 78; Add 5, subtract 8, repeat

Page 105

1. variable: *n*
   (or any other letter sentence:
   $3 + n = 9$
   solution: $n = 6$
2. variable: *p*
   (or any other letter sentence:
   $4 + p = 13$
   solution: $p = 9$
3. variable: *b*
   (or any other letter sentence:
   $b \times 314 =$ \$612,300
   solution: $b =$ \$1,950
4. variable: *k*
   (or any other letter sentence:
   $7 + 5 = k$
   solution: $k = 2$

Page 106

1. D
2. F
3. C

Page 107

1. 80, 72, 64, 56, 48, 40, 32, 24
2. 9, 22, 35, 48, 61, 74, 87, 100
3. 16, 17, 19, 22, 26, 31, 37, 44
4. 123, 122, 119, 114, 107, 98, 87, 74
5. 53, 62, 59, 68, 65, 74, 71, 80
6. 23, 25, 29, 35, 43, 53, 65, 79
7. 74, 62, 51, 41, 32, 24, 17, 11

Page 108

1. IN: 16
   OUT: 9, 24, 42
   Rule: IN − 13 = OUT
2. IN: 25, 42
   OUT: 90, 46
   Rule: IN + 9 = OUT

3. IN: 50
OUT: 35, 17, 30
Rule: IN ÷ 2 = OUT
4. IN: 11, 27, 6
OUT: 45, 126
Rule: IN × 3 = OUT

Page 109
1. 0, 3, 6, 9, 12, 15
2. 3, 9, 15, 21, 27, 33
3. 10, 11, 13, 15, 18, 20
4. 4, 12, 24, 32, 40, 52
5. 8, 11, 14, 17, 20, 23

Page 110
1. C
2. G
3. D
4. H

Pages 111–112
1.

Shape	Number of Tiles
1st	1
2nd	3
3rd	6
4th	10
5th	15
6th	21
7th	28
8th	36

2. The pattern grows by successive integers: +2, +3, +4, +5, +6, etc.
3. 55
4.

Number of Tables	1	2	3	4	5	6	7	8
Number of Guests	4	6	8	10	12	14	16	18

5. The number of guests increases by two for each table added.
6. 22
7.

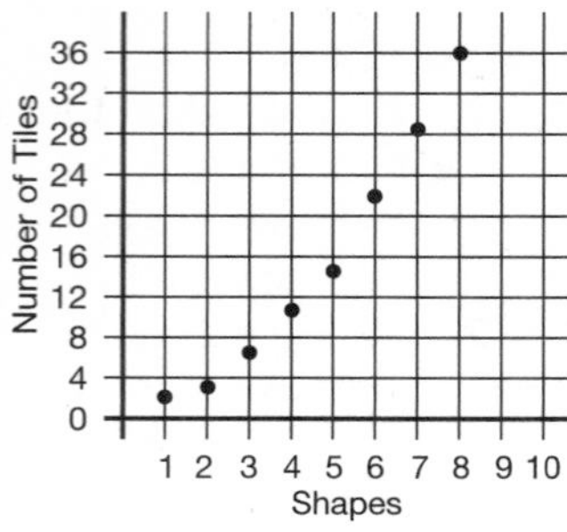

8.

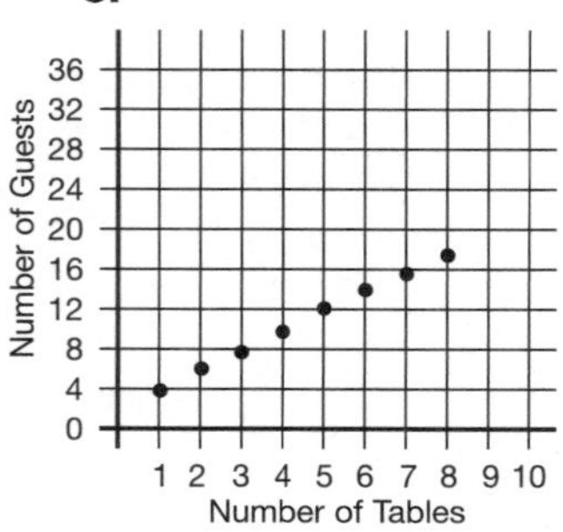

9. Pattern B has higher values in the beginning. Pattern A has higher values at the end.
10. Pattern A begins growing gradually, but then gets steeper. Pattern B grows by the same amount each time.

Page 113
1. C
2. J
3. B
4. F
5. D
6. J
7. B
8. F

Page 114
1. C
2. F
3. D
4. G
5. C
6. F
7. D
8. H

Page 115 Mini-Test 3
1. C
2. G
3. C
4. F
5. C
6. G
7. B

Page 117
1. D
2. C
3. E
4. A
5. B

Page 118
1. B
2. H
3. D
4. J
5. A
6. J
7. C
8. G
9. A
10. J

Page 119
1. B
2. F
3. C
4. J
5. A
6. J
7. C
8. F

Page 120
1. regular
2. regular
3. irregular
4. irregular
5. regular
6. irregular
7. irregular
8. Students should draw an equilateral triangle.
9. Students should draw a square.
10. Students should draw a pentagon with unequal sides.

Pages 121–122
1. boat
2. picnic basket
3. acorn
4. frog
5. butterfly
6. fish
7. worm
8. lily pad
9. flower
10. bird
11. leaf
12. rock
13–16. Check students' placements of items on graph.
17. Students' graphs should resemble evergreen trees.
18. C
19. Students' graphs should resemble the letter P.
20. F

Page 123
1. Graphs should show coordinates that satisfy the equation $y = 3x + 1$. Example: (0, 1) (1, 4) (2, 7) (3, 10)
2. Graphs should show coordinates that satisfy the equation $y = 2x - 1$. Example: (1, 1) (2, 3) (3, 5) (4, 7)

3. Graphs should show coordinates that satisfy the equation $y = x + 1$. Example: (1, 2) (2, 3) (2, 4) (4, 5)
4. Graphs should show coordinates that satisfy the equation $y = 2x$. Example: (1, 2) (2, 4) (3, 6) (4, 8)

Page 124

1. nonpolygon
2. nonpolygon
3. polygon
4. polygon
5. polygon
6. nonpolygon
7. polygon
8. polygon
9. nonpolygon
10. nonpolygon

Page 125

1. radius, radius
2. diameter, diameter
3. chord, radius
4. chord, chord
5. chord, diameter
6. radius, radius

Page 126

1. yes
2. yes
3. yes
4. yes
5. no
6. no
7. yes
8. yes
9. yes
10. no
11. yes
12. no

Pages 127–128

1. Students should draw circles with radiuses of 3/4 inch.
2. Students should draw circles with radiuses of 3 1/2 inches.
3. Students should draw circles with diameters of 2 inches.
4. Students should draw circles with diameters of 1 1/4 inches.

Pages 129–130

1. similar
2. congruent
3. neither
4. similar
5. congruent
6. neither

7–8. Students should draw shapes to match in a size either larger or smaller than the one shown.

9. B
10. J
11. C
12. G
13. D

Page 131

1. prism
2. neither
3. pyramid
4. pyramid
5. prism
6. neither
7. prism
8. pyramid
9. prism

Page 132 Mini-Test 4

1. A
2. H
3. B
4. G
5. C
6. G
7. C
8. H
9. D
10. F

Page 134

1.

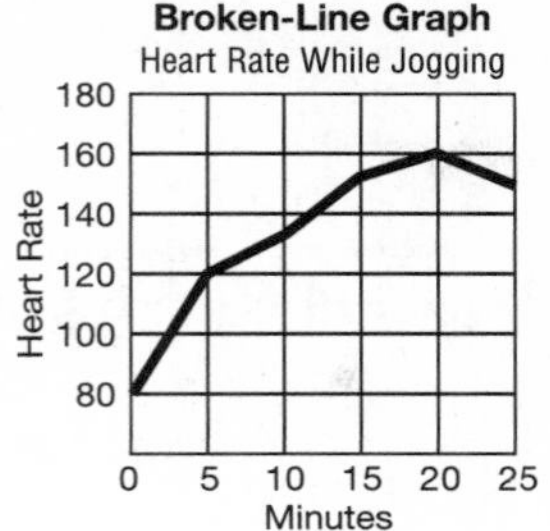

2.

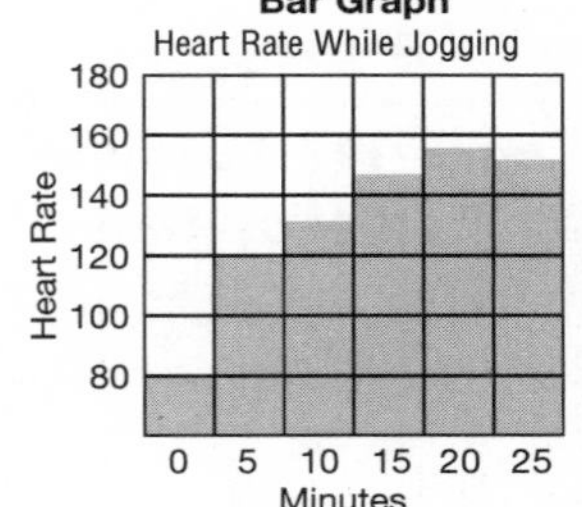

3. 20 minutes
4. from 0 to 5 minutes
5. from 10 to 15 minutes and from 15 to 20 minutes
6. from 20 to 25 minutes

Page 135

1. D
2. G
3. D

Pages 136–137

1. D
2. G
3. C
4. F
5. B
6. F
7. C
8. J
9. C
10. H
11. C
12. G
13. C
14. G
15. D
16. G
17. C

Page 138

1.

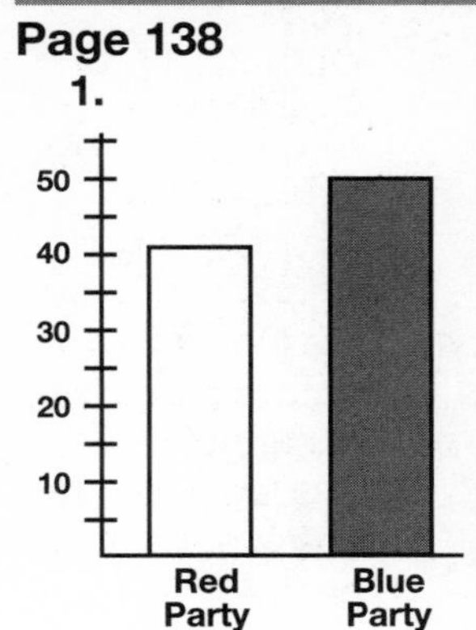

2.

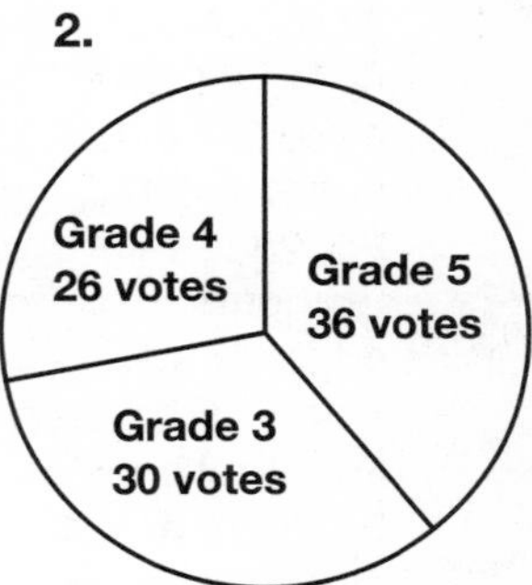

3. The bar graph shows total votes for the red party and for the blue party; it does not break down the votes by grade. The circle graph shows the number of votes per grade; it does not show the party for which the votes were cast.

Page 139

1. 37
2. other board games
3. chess
4. larger
5. other board games
6. chess
7. other board games and checkers

Page 140

1. Answers will vary. Students should use graphs of their choice. Check that axes are labeled and data is recorded accurately. Students should break out data by choice of fruit and may choose to also break out data by gender, although this is not requested.
2. Answers will vary. Students may suggest asking neighbors, watching purchases at the local grocery store, or obtaining data from the grocery store management.

Page 141

1. B
2. J
3. A
4. F
5. C
6. J

Page 142

1. unlikely
2. unlikely
3. impossible
4. likely
5. likely
6. likely
7. likely
8. impossible
9. impossible
10. unlikely
11. certain
12. certain
13. impossible
14. impossible

Page 143

1. 6 out of 15
2. 4 out of 13
3. 5 out of 15
4. 4 out of 15
5. 1 out of 3

Page 144 Mini-Test 5

1. C
2. G
3. D
4. J
5. D
6. G
7. B

Pages 147–151 Final Mathematics Test

1. A
2. F
3. C
4. F
5. B
6. H
7. B
8. F
9. C
10. F
11. D
12. H
13. D
14. G
15. A
16. F
17. C
18. H
19. A
20. G
21. D
22. G
23. D
24. G
25. A
26. G
27. D
28. F
29. B
30. F
31. A
32. F
33. B
34. H
35. A
36. H
37. B
38. G
39. C

Page 155

1. Can people tell the difference between cold tap water and cold bottled water?
2. C
3. Ryan needs to analyze the data he collected, then draw conclusions from the data. He should decide if the conclusions support his original hypothesis.
4. Answers will vary. Students may suggest that Ryan present his findings in graph form along with his written report.

Page 156

1. D
2. G
3. D
4. F

Page 158

1. B
2. G
3. A
4. F

Page 159

1. B
2. H
3. Based on the distance it flies compared with the other two planes, Plane 2 seems to have the most significant design problem. That problem seems to be that the wings are slanted up.
4. Answers may vary. One possible answer would be to slant the wings down or make them level, to match either Plane 1 or Plane 3.
5. Answers may vary. One possible answer would be to fly the redesigned

Page 157

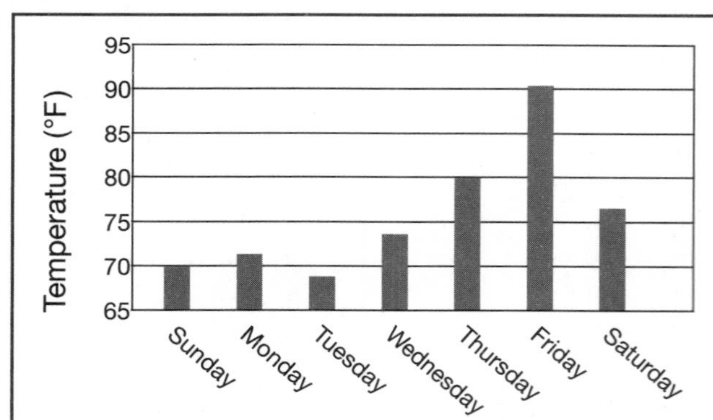

plane, record the distance of its flights, and compare those distances to the original distances.

Page 160 Mini-Test 1

1. C
2. F
3.

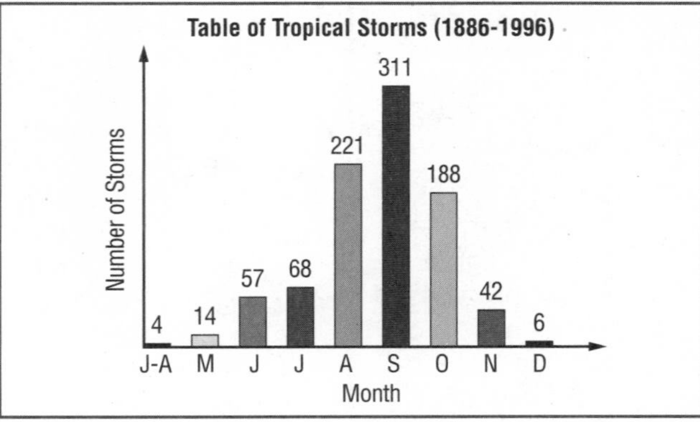

4. The design problem is that the table has only three legs. Possible solutions include adding a fourth leg at the corner where there currently is no leg, or moving one of the legs to the center of the back part of the table to create a three-legged table.

Page 162

1. 2, 4, 1, 3
2. 3, 1, 2
3. 1, 2, 3
4. 2, 4, 1, 3
5. 3, 2, 1
6. C
7. F

Page 163

1. L
2. I
3. I
4. I
5. L
6. I
7. L
8. I
9. I
10. L
11. L
12. I
13. I
14. L
15. Answers will vary. For learned characteristics, students may describe any skills, hobbies, or other unique behaviors that they exhibit. For inherited characteristics, students may describe such traits as hair color, eye color, or height.

Page 164

1. habitat
2. community
3. niche
4. ecosystem
5. producer
6. consumer
7. decomposer
8. B
9. J

Page 165

1. b
2. f
3. e
4. l
5. g
6. a
7. d
8. j
9. h
10. i
11. k
12. c

Page 166

1. C
2. H
3. B
4. F
5. A
6. H
7. C
8. F

Page 167

1. B
2. F
3. B
4. H
5. B
6. F
7. B

Page 168

1. P
2. V
3. C
4. P
5. C
6. V
7. P
8. C
9. V
10. P

Page 169

1. A
2. F
3. C
4. H
5. B
6. G

Pages 170–171

1. B
2. F
3. A
4. G
5. D
6. G
7. B
8. F
9. D
10. F
11. D
12. G
13. A
14. F
15. B
16. J
17. A
18. F

Page 172

1. A
2. G
3. A
4. J
5. B
6. G

Pages 173–174

1. Mercury
2. Venus
3. Earth
4. Mars
5. Jupiter
6. Saturn
7. Uranus
8. Neptune
9. Pluto
10. C
11. G
12. D
13. H

Page 175

1. B
2. C
3. E
4. A
5. D

Page 176 Mini-Test 2

1. B
2. H
3. B
4. F
5. C
6. G
7. C
8. H

Page 178

1. B
2. H
3. Answers may vary. Possible answer: Lauren made accurate, detailed records of the results of her experiment. However, she should have either used new flash-lights for both experiments, or used the same old flashlights for both experiments. This would have given here a more clear idea of how long the batteries last under specific conditions.
4. B

Page 179

1. C
2. J
3. A
4. F
5. Answers will vary. Possible answer: A scientist may communicate finding to other scientists via a computer e-mail message.
6. Answers will vary. Possible answer: Heart monitors have allowed doctors to keep better track of their patients' health.

Page 180

1. B
2. A
3. E
4. D
5. C
6. D
7. B
8. F
9. E
10. D
11. A
12. Answers will vary. One possible answer: Computers have allowed more work to be done at a faster rate than would otherwise have been possible. Computers allow family members to stay in closer touch with one another.
13. Answers will vary. One possible answer: Excessive television viewing has resulted in a more sedentary population, damaging the overall health of the population.

Page 181

1. C
2. J
3. A
4. G
5. B
6. G
7. D
8. J

Page 182 Mini-Test 3

1. D
2. Answers will vary. One answer is that the day of the second experiment is cooler than the day of the first experiment, so the temperature is not likely to rise to the same level as the day 1 experiment in the same amount of time. Nevertheless, yellow is a light color like white, and orange is a darker color like black; the darker, orange box seems more likely to be warmer than the lighter, yellow box, based on the results of the day 1 experiment.
3. J
4. D
5. H
6. D
7. H

Pages 184–187 Final Science Test

1. B
2. H
3. B
4. F
5. D
6. G
7. C
8. H
9. A
10. J
11. A
12. H
13. C
14. G
15. A
16. J
17. C
18. J
19. D
20. F
21. B
22. F
23. B
24. F
25. B
26. J
27. D
28. J
29. C
30. G
31. C

Page 191

1. B
2. G
3. C
4. H
5. C
6. J
7. C
8. F

Page 192

1. D
2. G
3. C
4. G
5. C
6. J
7. D
8. H

Page 193

1. C
2. J
3. Answers will vary. One possible answer: Voters have a responsibility to understand the issues and know where the candidates stand on them before voting.
4. Answers will vary. One possible answer: It benefits the accused by ensuring that he or she receives a fair trial.
5. Students' responses will vary. They are to rank the rights shown from most to least important to them personally, then explain their rankings.

Page 194
1. B
2. F
3. C
4. J
5. B

Page 195
1. D
2. G
3. A
4. G
5. D
6. H

Page 196
1. I
2. C
3. C
4. I
5. C
6. C
7. C
8. G

Page 197 Mini-Test 1
1. C
2. F
3. B
4. H
5. B
6. F

Page 199
1. B
2. H
3. B
4. J
5. C
6. F

Page 200
1. H
2. M
3. H
4. L
5. L
6. H
7. M
8. L
9. H
10. E+
11. E
12. E+
13. E−
14. E−
15. E+
16. E
17. E−
18. E+
19. Income is closely tied to the level of education attained.

Page 201
1. B
2. F
3. C
4. G
5. C
6. J

Page 202
1. C
2. J
3. C
4. F
5. B

Page 203
1. C
2. Producers would be more likely to produce more thing-a-ma-bobs at the highest price because they would make a higher profit, which is why all companies are in business.
3. F
4. B
5. F
6. D
7. Answers will vary. Most students will conclude that people wanted to purchase the generators because they needed another source for their electricity. They were willing to pay a higher price since their normal source of electricity was unavailable.

Page 204
1. C
2. J
3. A
4. J

Page 205
1. B
2. H
3. A
4. G
5. A
6. G
7. A

Page 206
1. C
2. G
3. B
4. J

Page 207
1. C
2. J
3. A
4. F
5. C
6. J

Page 208
1. B
2. F
3. B
4. D
5. B
6. D
7. B
8. The Speedy Bicycle Company probably builds more bicycles in a typical week. Specialization and division of labor usually increase productivity of workers.

Page 209
1. B
2. J
3. B
4. J
5. B
6. N
7. S
8. L
9. N
10. L
11. L
12. S

Page 210 Mini-Test 2
1. C
2. F
3. B
4. J
5. B
6. J
7. C

Page 213
1. D
2. B
3. F
4. A
5. E
6. C

Page 214
1. B
2. H
3. B
4. F

Page 215
1. C
2. G
3. A
4. G
5. D
6. J
7. C

Page 216
1. A
2. G
3. D
4. H

Page 217
1. D
2. H
3. B
4. F
5. C

Page 218
1. D
2. G
3. C
4. G
5. A
6. J
7. A

Page 219
1. A
2. G
3. B
4. H
5. C

Page 220
1. C
2. J
3. A
4. H

Page 221
1. C
2. G
3. S−
4. S+
5. S−
6. S+
7. S+

Page 222
1. C
2. F
3. B
4. H
5. C
6. Answers will vary. Possible answer: These plantations could not be operated without slave labor. Thus, the demand for slaves increased with the demand for cotton.

Page 223
1. D
2. G
3. C
4. J

Page 224
1. B
2. H
3. A
4. H
5. D

Page 225
1. A
2. H
3. D
4. H
5. B

Page 226
1. C
2. F
3. C
4. J
5. B

Page 227
1. B
2. F
3. A
4. G
5. A
6. H

Page 228
1. C
2. G
3. A
4. J
5. C
6. H

Page 229
1. C
2. G
3. D
4. G

Page 230
1. D
2. H
3. A
4. G
5. D
6. H

Page 231
1. A
2. H
3. C
4. H
5. B
6. J

Page 232
1. C
2. J
3. D
4. F
5. A
6. G
7. C

Page 233
1. C
2. F
3. B
4. J

Page 234
1. C
2. E
3. A
4. F
5. B
6. D
7. G
8. Answers will vary. Students should explain how they think the electric lightbulb has impacted the environment.

Page 235 Mini-Test 3
1. C
2. F
3. B
4. H
5. B
6. F
7. B
8. G
9. D

Page 237
1. D
2. G
3. A
4. H
5. D

Page 238
1. B
2. J
3. A
4. H
5. C
6. G

Page 239
1. B
2. F
3. D
4. F
5. C
6. H

Page 240
1. D
2. F
3. C
4. F
5. Answers will vary. One possible answer: People build their homes on high stilts to avoid the regularly occurring floodwaters.
6. Answers will vary. One possible answer: (1) Excessive heat and (2) inadequate rainfall could put a farmer's crop in jeopardy.

Page 241
1. B
2. G
3. A
4. J
5. D
6. F

Page 242

1. D
2. G
3. B
4. H

Page 243

1. B
2. J
3. A
4. H
5. A
6. G
7. C
8. F

Page 244 Mini-Test 4

1. B
2. J
3. B
4. G
5. B
6. F

Page 246

1. D
2. F
3. C
4. G
5. Answers will vary. One possible answer: American society highly values expressions of patriotism and love of country.

Pages 247–248

1. B
2. H
3. A
4. H
5. D
6. G
7. A
8. They fought the hijackers and prevented the plane from crashing into another building, probably saving hundreds of lives.
9. Answers will vary. One possible answer: Schools helped explain the situation to America's children and gave them a place to talk about what was going on.

Page 249

1. B
2. J
3. B
4. J

Pages 250–251 Mini-Test 5

1. D
2. G
3. A
4. G
5. D
6. H
7. Answers will vary. One possible answer: More people began driving cars, requiring more and better roads.

Pages 254–257 Final Social Sciences Test

1. B
2. G
3. C
4. J
5. A
6. H
7. A
8. J
9. D
10. H
11. D
12. G
13. D
14. H
15. C
16. G
17. A
18. J
19. B
20. F
21. C
22. H
23. D
24. F
25. D
26. J
27. C
28. H

Notes